Whitley Stokes

The Saltair na rann

a collection of early Middle Irish poems. Vol. 1, Part 3

Whitley Stokes

The Saltair na rann
a collection of early Middle Irish poems. Vol. 1, Part 3

ISBN/EAN: 9783744735766

Printed in Europe, USA, Canada, Australia, Japan

Cover: Foto ©Thomas Meinert / pixelio.de

More available books at **www.hansebooks.com**

Anecdota Oxoniensia

TEXTS, DOCUMENTS, AND EXTRACTS

CHIEFLY FROM

MANUSCRIPTS IN THE BODLEIAN

AND OTHER

OXFORD LIBRARIES

MEDIAEVAL AND MODERN SERIES. VOL. I—PART III

SALTAIR NA RANN

EDITED BY

WHITLEY STOKES, LL.D.

Oxford
AT THE CLARENDON PRESS

1883

THE

SALTAIR NA RANN

A COLLECTION OF EARLY MIDDLE IRISH POEMS

EDITED FROM

MS. RAWL. B. 502, IN THE BODLEIAN LIBRARY

BY

WHITLEY STOKES, LL. D.

HONORARY FELLOW OF JESUS COLLEGE

Oxford

AT THE CLARENDON PRESS

1883

𝔏𝔬𝔫𝔡𝔬𝔫

HENRY FROWDE

OXFORD UNIVERSITY PRESS WAREHOUSE

7 PATERNOSTER ROW

PREFACE.

THE *Saltair na Rann*, 'Psalter of the Staves or Quatrains,' a collection of 162 Early-Middle-Irish poems now for the first time printed, is contained in its entirety only in the Bodleian MS. Rawl. B. 502, ff. 19-40. But there is a copy of one of the poems (No. X) in the Lebar Brecc, a MS. of the fifteenth century; and corrupt and modernised copies of poems IV, V, and VI are to be found in a MS. also belonging to the Royal Irish Academy, marked 23. G. 25, written by one O'Longan about seventy years ago. The Lebar Brecc version of No. X will be found at p. 111ᵇ of the lithographic facsimile of that MS., Dublin, 1876.

The *Saltair*, like the Félire Oengusso and other pseudonymous matter, is attributed to Oengus the Culdee, who flourished in the beginning of the ninth century; and his name—*is me Oengus cele Dé*, 'I am Oengus the Culdee'—actually occurs in line 8009. But that this attribution is erroneous follows, first, from the numerous Middle-Irish forms which the poem contains[1], and which cannot possibly be due to the transcriber, and, secondly, from its mention, in l. 2342, of an event —the murrain which began A.D. 985—and in ll. 2349-2365 of certain contemporary kings, as well as of Dub-dá-lethe, one of S. Patrick's successors in the see of Armagh, who died A.D. 1061.

Our MS., Rawl. B. 502, is a large quarto, now containing 83 leaves of vellum in a hand of the twelfth century, and 20 leaves of paper. The vellum portion has been so fully described by the late Dr. Todd (*Proceedings of the Royal Irish Academy*, vol. 5, pp. 164-168) and by Mr. Macray (*Catal. Codd. MSS. Bodl.*, Part V., fasc. 1, cols. 719-722) as to render further description unnecessary. Only this opportunity may be taken to note that the 'Short Tract on Irish Grammar' stated to occur at fo. 63ᵇ is really one of the so-called Brehon law treatises—*Coic*

[1] e.g. natrimúir 399, 421, scérdair 443, na slóig 709, betit 853, cestait 953, istsléib 4109, etc., etc.

b

conara fugill, 'five paths of judgment,' of which there is (according to Dr. O'Donovan) a fuller copy in a MS. in the library of Trinity College, Dublin, marked II. 3. 18—and that the Latin passage at fo. 53 b. seems to run thus: Hii omnes sancti (*sic*) inuoco in auxilium meum per intercessionem sanctæ Mariæ et sanctarum et (sanctor)um, quarum et quorum Deus nomina nominauit, et quos praesciuit et praedistinavit conformes fieri imaginis Filii sui in uitam æternam in Christo Jesu Amen. The poems now printed begin at fo. 19 a. 1 and end at fo. 40. b. 2. They are written in double columns, with 50 lines in each.

According to the scribe's note following line 7788 the poems now printed fall into four divisions, (1) the Psalter. (2) the poem on repentance, (3) the poem on confession, and (4) the ten poems on the Resurrection. That note means: 'Thus far the body of the Psalter of the Quatrains, to wit, the thrice fifty poems (*duana*). Two after, (one) for confession, and (the other) for repentance; and ten to set forth the Resurrection; so that there are twelve and thrice fifty poems altogether.' The thrice fifty poems—equal in number to the psalms, and hence 'the Psalter'—deal for the most part with incidents from the Old Testament. But the first poem contains a kind of description of the universe; poems XI (on the penance of Adam and Eve) and XII (on the death of Adam) are founded on the *Vita Adae et Euae,* two texts of which have been published by W. Meyer (München, 1879); and poems XLII-L relate to the life of Christ. Poem CLI expresses repentance for transgression and prays for forgiveness. No. CLII is an expression of ignorance of God and his various works. Nos. CLIII to CLIX describe the events on each day of the week before the last Judgment. Sense here is so completely sacrificed to metrical requirements that these seven poems are, to a large extent, unintelligible to me. CLX deals with the seven resurrections—namely, (1) that of the apostles, (2) of the prophets, (3) of the confessors, (4) of the martyrs, (5) of the saints, (6) of the virgins, penitents, and baptized infants, and (7) of the rest of the human race. Poem CLXI treats of the coming of the demons out of hell to earth, the fall of the idols, etc. The last poem, CLXII, describes the triumph of the angels over their foes, the rewards of the righteous, the punishments of the wicked.

It may be well to give a *précis* of the three most important of the poems, namely, I, XI, and XII.

I.[1] The creation of the world (line 3), the sun (5), heaven (13), earth (15), light and darkness (17, 18), day and night (19, 20), the earth separated from the primal material (29, 30), surrounded by the firmament (34), the world like an apple (36), the mists, the current of the cold watery air (44), the four chief winds, the eight sub-winds (45–52), the colours of the winds (53–80), the distance from the earth to the firmament (97–101), the seven planets (101–104), the distance from the earth to the moon (105–112), the radiant heaven, that from moon to sun (113–116), the windless, ethereal heaven, the distance between the firmament and the sun (121), the motionless Olympus or third heaven (125–128), the distance from the firmament to heaven (133–136), from earth to the depths of hell (141), the five zones, the firmament round the earth like its shell round an egg (165–169), the seventy-two windows in the firmament (181, 182), with a shutter on each (188), the seventh heaven revolving like a wheel (199), with the seven planets from the creation (204), the signs of the zodiac (205–220), the time—30 days, 10½ hours—that the sun is in each, the day of the month on which it enters each, the month in which it is in each sign (233–256), the division of the firmament into twelve parts, the five things which every intelligent man should know—namely, the day of the solar month, the age of the moon, the height of the tide, the day of the week, saints' festivals.

XI. The Penance of Adam and Eve. For a week after the expulsion Adam was without fire, house, drink, food, or clothing (1483–1486). He laments to Eve their lost blessings (1491–1530), and admits his fault (1531–1534). Eve asks Adam to kill her, so that God may pity him the more (1535–1546). Adam refuses to destroy his own flesh and blood (1547–1560). Then, at Eve's request, Adam goes to seek for food and finds nought but herbs (1561–1572), 'the food of the lawless beasts.' He proposes to Eve to do penance, to adore the Lord in silence, Eve in the Tigris for thirty days, Adam in the Jordan for forty and seven, a flagstone under their feet, the water up to their necks, Eve's hair dishevelled and her eyes directed to heaven in silent prayer for forgiveness (1573–1628). Adam prays the Jordan 'to fast with him on God' (*co troisced lais for Dia*) with all its many beasts, that pardon

---

[1] A Middle-Irish prose abstract of part of this poem will be found in the first volume of the Laws, pp. 26–30.

may be granted to him. The stream ceases: gathers together every
living creature that was in its midst; and they all supplicate the angelic
host to join with them in beseeching God to forgive Adam (1629-1652).
Forgiveness is granted to Adam and to all his seed save the unrighteous
(1653-1660). When the Devil hears this, 'like a swan, in the shape of a
white angel,' he goes to Eve as she stands in the Tigris and gets her
to leave her penance, saying that he had been sent by God. They then
go to Adam, who at once recognises the Devil and reveals the deceit
to Eve (1661-1716). Eve falls half-dead on the ground, and reproaches
Lucifer (1717-1756). Lucifer defends himself, repeating at length the
story of his expulsion from heaven for refusing to worship Adam (1757-
1872). He concludes by threatening vengeance to Adam and his de-
scendants (1873-1880). Adam then leaves the river and Lucifer departs
(1884). Adam and Eve then live alone for a year on grass, without
proper food, fire, house, music, or raiment; drinking water from their
palms and eating the green herbs in the shadow of trees and in caverns
(1885-1896). Eve brings forth a beautiful boy, who at once proceeds
to cut grass for his father, and whom his father called Cain (1897-1910).
God at last pities Adam and sends Michael to him with various seeds,
and Michael teaches him husbandry and the use of animals (1913-1932).
Seven years afterwards Eve brings forth Abel (1933). In a vision Eve
sees Cain drinking the blood of Abel. Adam therefore builds a house
for each of the brothers (1941-1956). Gabriel announces the murder
of Abel and foretells the birth of Seth (1957-1968). Adam's seventy
sons and seventy daughters are born to him after the transgression
(1969). The signs set in Cain's forehead (1997-2000). Cain's death
in the Valley of Jehoshaphat, which is thenceforward barren (2005).

XII. Adam's death. Adam, being 930 years old and feeling his
death at hand, tells Eve of his approaching end (2021-2032). Eve
regrets that she does not die first (2033-2037). Adam comforts her
by saying she will die in nine months, and tells her how to act after
his death (2040-2076). Michael comes at Eve's entreaty to cleanse
Adam's soul and take it to heaven (2077-2152). God comes to receive
Adam's soul, which remains in the third heaven, named Ficconicia
(2153-2208), till the Resurrection. Adam's body is anointed with the
Oil of Mercy and buried in Hebron (2217-2228), where it remained

till the Deluge. His head was then swept to Jerusalem, and remained in the gateway till Christ's cross was planted therein (2229-2240). Enos, Noah, and other patriarchs are then mentioned (2241-2292). The numbers of years from Adam to the Deluge, from the Deluge to Abraham, from Adam to the birth of Christ (2293-2336), the number of years to the murrain, the names of some of the leading princes reigning about that time in Ireland and in Scotland, those of Eadgar on one side of the English Channel and Illothair on the other, an allusion to the ravages caused by the Danes from Denmark (2337-2380): the rest till the day of doom nobody could declare except the high King of the sun, whose life never ends (2381-2388).

The tradition mentioned in lines 7529, 7530, that Christ was born from the crown of the Virgin's head, is worth noting [1]; and the description of some of the signs at the Crucifixion (7761-7772) may be quoted as a specimen of the style of the poem (I omit two chevilles), and as illustrating Sophus Bugge's theories about the Baldr-saga :—

> Darkness sprang over every plain :
> Earth's dead arose :
> Dear God's elements were afraid
> When the veil of the temple was rent.
> Every creature wailed—
> Heaven and earth trembled :
> The sea proceeded to go over (its) bounds :
> Hearts of black rocks split.
> The King who suffered in (his) fair clay,
> A cross for sake of Adam's children,
> Thereafter took a prey (of redeemed souls),
> So that he overcame Hell.

The metre in which the bulk of the *Saltair* is composed is *deibide*, each line of the quatrain consisting of seven syllables, the second and

---

[1] So according to the A.S. *Adrian and Ritheus* (Kemble, *Salomon and Saturnus*, p. 204) Christ was born of his Mother, 'þurh þæt swéðre breóst,' *through her right breast*. So the Bodhisattva was born from Mâyâ's right side (Kern, *Der Buddhismus*, 30, n.). See, too, other strange births, Liebrecht, *Volkskunde*, 490; and note the punishment of certain sinners, *Visio Tnugdali*, ed. Wagner, 1882, p. 28 : 'Pariebant, dico, non solum femine, set et viri, non tantum per ipsa membra, que natura constituit tali officio convenientia, verum per brachia simul et per pectora, exibantque erumpentes per cuncta membra.'

fourth ending with a word exceeding in the number of its syllables the words respectively ending the first and third; the first and second lines rhyme together, as do the third and fourth. Alliteration is frequent, and a word in the middle of one line often rhymes with a word in the beginning or middle of the following line (e.g. *rúinib, dúilib,* lines 9, 10, *sorcha, dorcha,* 17, 18). Poem CLII is in a different metre, *rannaigecht mór,* each line ending in a monosyllable, and only the second and fourth lines rhyming. In CLIII-CLXII the first and third lines of each quatrain regularly end in rhyming trisyllables, the second and fourth in rhyming dissyllables. Internal rhymes are frequent, e.g. *fogur, domnuch,* 8021, 8023, *luaichthi, cruaidi,* 8037, 8039. The first, second and third words in the first line of a quatrain sometimes rhyme respectively with the first, second and last words of the third line; see e.g. 8125-8127, 8137-8139.

The text has been printed with the utmost care. It is right to say that in the MS. several of the marks of length are so faded that they can be discerned only by the keenest eyes and in the most favourable light. I may, therefore, have undesignedly omitted some of these marks. Contractions have been extended, and the extensions represented by italics. The text has also been punctuated, proper names spelt with initial capitals, apostrophes have been used where vowels have been omitted, and hyphens introduced to separate the transported *t* and *n* from words beginning with vowels.

In conclusion, though several of the words are explained in the Index, it contains so many new vocables as to the meanings of which I am either doubtful or quite in the dark, that I have called it an Index Verborum rather than a Glossarial Index. It will, it is hoped, be useful to future Irish lexicographers.

W. S.

SALTAIR NA RANN.

P saltar narann inso sis dorigni Oengus Celi-De.

[Rawlinson, B. 502. fo. 19 a. col. 1—fo. 40 b. col. 2.]

I.

[fo. 19 a. 1.]

M orfse rí nime nair,
cenhuabur, cenimmarbaig,
dorósat domun dualach,
morí bithbeo, bithbuadach.

5 Ri osduilib thargea gréin,
rí ósfudumnaib aicgéin,
ri tess, tuaid, tíar ocus tair,
fris níderntar immargail.

9 Ri coruinib robai, fail,
riandúilib, rian-aimseraib,
rí bithbeo beus, blaith adenn,
ri centossach, cenforcenn.

13 Ri dorigne nem noithech,
nihúaibrech, ni[i]mchloithech,
ocus talam, tolaib tlacht,
comtren, comíossaid, comnart.

17 Ri dorigne sorcha saer
ocus dorcha con-anaeb[1] :
indaranai islaithe[2] lan,
araile isadaig imlan.

21 Ri rodelb tétadbul De
dochetadbur nandule,
. . . . . s frisamla suthach
inmass amra écruthach.

25 Ri rodelb eisse cachnduil

rosderb cengesse coemruin,
eter mín isgarb condath,
eter marb ocus beothach.

29 Ri rothepi, bladmar, brass,
asinchetadbar admas[3],
talam tromm toracht, delm chert,
dian'fonn fothacht fotlethet.

33 Ri rochruthaig, níscuac cinte[4],
hicuairt nafirmiminte,
domun delbda derbda druing,
mar ubull febda fircruind.

37 Ri rodelb dluma iartain
hura coderb imthalmain,
rith roseim osbith, buaid ngle,
indaeor uair uscide.

41 Ri c(ria)thras usce n-an, n-úar
foriathmass nan-al n-ollmuad,
iarsrebaib cosesraib sruth
iarmesraib comesrugud.

45 Ri roordaig ochí ngaetha
torgaib cenlocht lanaeba,
cethri prímgaetha cotngaib,
cethri fogaetha feochrai[5].

49 Cethri fogaetha aile,
rádit auctair ergnaide,
bidhi an-arim [fír]chert
dogaethaib dagaeth deec.

[IV. 3.]

53 Ri rodelb datha nangaeth
rosderb frisratha slannaeb,
iarclechtaib rith roratha (?),
combrechtaib cachilldatha.
57 INgel, incorcarda glan,
inglass, induaine allmar,
inbuidi, inderg, derb dána,
nisgaib fergg frisodála.
61 INdub, indliath, indalad,
intemen, inchiar chálad,
indodar, doirchi datha,
nidat soirchi sogabtha.
65 Ri rosordaig oscachmaig
na ocht fogaetha feochrai¹,
rodelb cenditha, dín saeth,
cricha nacethri primgaeth.
69 Anair incorcra glanbda,
andess ingel gle, amra,
atuaid indub gailbech, grach,
aniar² indodur engach.
73 INderg, inbuidi 'male,
eter gil³ ocus corcrai,
indúani, inglass, croda (?)⁴ lir,
eter huidir isglegil.
77 INdliath, inchiar, grainne anguir,
eter huidir iscirduib,
intemen, indalad tair,
eter duib ocus corcair.
81 Coir rocoraiged acruth,
doronad an-orddugud,
fogaessaib glessib cenchlith
iarsessib, iarsuidigthib.
85 Na da gaeth dec, tolaib tress,
tair ocus tiar, tuaid istess,
rii roscuibdig cotagaib,
roscuibrig fo sechi nglessaib⁵.

[fo. 19 a. 2.]
89 Ri dosnarbair iarsessaib
imthalmain con-ilglessaib,
cach digaeth dib imglés ngle
isoengles foraib huile.
93 Ri dosrat iarnglessaib clecht,
iarmbessaib centarimthecht,
indarahuair, blaith iarmblai,
induair aile ainbthechae.
97 Ri tadban tomus donleirg
othalmain cofirmimint,
fris domidet, met glanna,
fritiget natalmanna.
101 Rosuidig secht rinn[e] reim
ofirmimint cotalmain,
Satuirn, Ioib, Mercuir, Mars,
Sol, Uenir, Luna lánmas.
105 Ri rorimi, rigda inbla,
otha talmain coesca,
semile fichet archet
fordamidet 'naglanmét.
109 IS hé sain int-aear huar
linib halal friimluad,
dianidainm triallach, derb tra,
annem niabach n-airerda.
113 INdrae ohescgu cogrein
ri rorím congle glanleir,
dacet mile, mor insmacht,
latri cethair cethrachal.
117 ISse sin int-ethier huais
cengaeth, cenaear n-angluais,
dianidainm, cen balba mbla,
innem n-amra n-etherda.
121 Trichutrumma, intsain doleir,
eter firmimint isgrein,
morí rindbalec, roffr sein,

¹ MS. feochraig.　² MS. anair.　³ MS. gel.　⁴ MS. garoda or gardda, but
c is written over g, and there is a dot under the first a.　⁵ Sic. Read nglassaib?

dorindnacht dorimirib.
125 IS hisin indOlimp huag,
cenchumscugud, cenimluad,
iarsliucht saer nasruthe sen,
dianidainm intresnoebnem.
129 Damile déc, torainn ṅgle,
archoiccétaib déc mile,
cain rith rindrethait insain
ofirmimint cotalmain.
133 Met naré, ruathar cint,
othalmain cofirmimint,
isse inmet sain, srethaib srath,
ofirmimint coriched.
137 Cethrimili fichet sain
artrichait cet domilib
oshunn coriched, reim n-oll,
cenmotha firmamentom.
141 A met na ree sein uile [1]
othalmain corigsuide,
issed fil othalmain tinn
sís cofudomnaib Iffirn.
145 Rí cachthuir thuathaig, dein, deirg,
rofuathaig fein firmiment,
feib baderb laiss oscach maig
rosdelb donmaiss ecruthaig.
149 Ri nan-uile n-adbar n-án,
arm-buili bladmar bithmár,
inglóruill cocessair chain
dosrorainn icoic[c]ressaib.
153 INcuiced criss guires chness
morí ruithes triasirthes,
frisasad sluagda saigthe [2]
dahuarda imdamesraigthe.
157 Huarda andess isuarda atuaid,
indamesraigthe, ismórbuaid,
incriss tessaigthe [3], isderb de,

eter nada mesraigthe.
161 Rí targcai cech ruirig reil
rosuidig smachtai fouagre[i]r,
rodagni cenchétlud ṅgle
dochetchruth nafirmiminte.
165 Amal bis abloesc immog
acht noslui línib hilchor,
fial nafirmiminti imbith
tria bithu forabithrith.
169 'Macuaird focheird atoimsi,
iarsreith suairc fri sirsoillsi,
isannsu infomus 'moa mbeir,
ní triit tarsnu toimsideir.
173 Rorannad iarn-intliucht fail,
feib rodelgnaisset auctair,
dasebratta fochis chain,
dasé phairt 'nan-irchomair.
177 Huide mís dogrein cachphairt,
iarseis nan-ugtar n-ardaitt,
forith hinathur [4] (?), [gluair] ṅgle,
cech mbliadain dosstimchellae.
181 Hisindfirmimint cogle
sesca dáse senistre,
dothaitni fridia 'malle
cachphairti se senistre.
185 Ata iartúini indrig reil
rodelb duine : : : huagreir,
fodluthad, cendolma ṅdein,
comla forcach senisteir.
[fo. 19 b. 1.]
189 Trénbrat demin, torom n-án,
marbad gemen coem comlán,
tuinech torachta rosrig
imthalmain contib immib.
193 IM thrínimi ata centair
trinimi impe, hit himsláin,

---

[1] MS. uili.   [2] MS. saigthi.   [3] MS. tessaigthi.
[4] MS. riathur, with a dot under and a mark of aspiration over the first *r*, and a stroke over the *i*.

insechtmad nem, isse sein
rochertad eternimib.

197 Ni sossad suairce slóig a[i]ñgel
    acht iscuairt chóir coemdaingen,
    ama/bis rothmol forluth
    triabithu forbithimputh.

201 INdfirnnimint, ilar ṁbla,
    isnasechtrind airegda,
    ata *for*oenrith, gluair ñgle,
    otha inn-uair rocruthaigthe.

205 Ri rorann ruandath osleirg
    nifualrad fann firmimeint,
    srethaib samlaib, slemnaib slecht,
    indibrannaib derbdai déc.

209 Ri osca*ch*airm, osca*ch*dinn,
    dorat aínm forcachn-oenrinn,
    nimennair iarñdligud dlecht
    donadibrennaib deec.

213 Fuath ca*ch*renna, ruathur ñgle,
    itimchuairt firmiminte,
    feib rosderbait delgnaid [   ]
    ishuandelbaib ainmnigt*er*.

217 Aquair, Pisc, Ariet, Tauir [1] treb,
    Geimin choir *ocus* Cancer,
    Leo, Uirgo, Libru, Scoirp scrus,
    Saigitair, Capricorn*us*.

221 Ri corúnaib roscoraig
    innanñdlumaib dermoraib,
    sreith nasliab, osca*ch*blai,
    frisreith [2] grían *ocus* escai.

225 Tricha lathi, lórda [3] luad,
    ladech n-úara *ocus* lethuar,
    cot*r*íall trechess osca*ch*dind
    rethess grían inca*ch*oenrind.

229 IN grían suairc, iarn-urd riagla,
    forcuairt cacha oenbliadna,

hi quindecim ka/de, cain dind,
issann téit incachn-oenrind.

233 Grían in-Aquair, hed centáir,
    doróined im-mis Enáir,
    ocus hiPisc [   ] cogle
    dorimther im-mis Febrae.

237 Grían in-Ariet, aurdairce dí,
    dothadbat im-mis Martfí,
    ocus hiTauir grían diareir
    dothaitni im-mís Apréíl.

241 Grían hiñGemin im-mis Máii
    isdemin, ni imarchláí,
    nochochiuin guires ca*ch*treib
    im-mis Iúin grían iCanceir.

245 IM-mís Iuil ingrían il-Leo,
    issann ferass alangleo,
    teit grían adenu*s* fríatuisc
    inUirginum [4] in-Auguist.

249 Dothaitni grían fhiadcachdruñg
    iSeptimb*er* inLibrum,
    grían nodafoilce nochosceil
    iScoirp im-mis Ochtimb*er*.

253 IN Sagitarium grían dosfeitn
    osca*ch*rían inNouinbeir,
    inDecimb*er*, ischian clú,
    bidgrian inCapricornú.

257 Athe sein indaserind
    dosrosat Fiadu forfinn,
    osca*ch*rían rethaii fonṁbith
    riu reithes grían alanrith.

261 A coic ca*ch*lae d'físs cenbrath
    dlegair docachintliuchtach,
    docachoen, cengláma gné,
    bis fograda ecailse.

265 Laa mis grne, ésca aes,
    rith mara cen immarbáes,

---

[1] MS. piscu ta uir.   [2] MS. fris reith.   [3] *lór* is written as a correction over the *luar* of *luarda*.
    [4] *um* is written as a correction (I) of *em*.

laa sechtmaine, feili noeb n-uag,
iarcertglaine con-imluad.
269 Ri rosrethaig, sróenaib slamm,
dorethaib roenaib retlann,
feib nosairbrig osrannaib
rosanmnig dian-anmannaib.
273 Cid caem lenn inleth fail frinn
firmiminti nan-ilrind,
inleth aili, lith cengeis,
nocon-eitchiu ciachemme[i]s.
277 Ri rogni clichis cenmeirg
iarnafithis firmimeint,
comfocus tadbain adreich
imthalmain docachoenleith.
281 Ri rodelb firmimint fir
conarennaib cendimbrig,
immontalmain, cengoi ngle,
imsoi ontrath coaraile.
285 Ri dorigní muirlinn mair
osanfirmimint imslain,
inmuirlinn aili isi inmuir,
fo[r]dasniada imthalmain.
[fo. 19 b. 2.]
289 Ri dorairngert cachfáith
coimdiu cumtaig cachcoemgraid,
dorosait grein crotha glain,
forosna nem imthalmain.
293 Ri dorigni esca n-án
ocus indfairrgge imslán,
foriaguil dosrona inri,
condatcora, comchuibdi.
297 Sessed rann domuin cechdú
hissi meit fil in-escu,
ocus isingréin coglan
sé commet dec intalman.
301 Ri dorigne ilar mil

fondfairrce ndermair ndirim,
nithadbann nech acht mori
an-anmann nach an-airmi.
305 Ri dorigni sreba sluag
donahénaib friimluad,
doaltaib isnaslebib,
dograigib formagreidih.
309 Hilerda nan-anman n-án
is nan-ildelbda ndermár,
nifail hierf rimess sin
acht mad inrí donoebnim.
313 Ri dorigne aéar n-uar,
ocus tene reil rorúad,
ocus talam bladmar, brass,
ocus sruth raglan rethess.
317 Ri rosil talmain iartain
dolubaib, dofidbadaib :
lan indomun diambolud,
con-immad an-iltorud.
321 Ri conic huacht ocus tess,
mori firen frim'firless,
ishe rosuidig cachseis,
rí centuirim, cenaisnéis.
325 INrí reil narun corath
doarfaid dún cachn-ingnad,
diathuicsin treothu, din ngle,
is trialin amirbaile.
329 Ri rogni cachnduil folcith,
aicseid ocus nemaicseid,
acht inri rodelba sain
nifail nach rí fortalmain.
333 Nifail dodainib daingnib,
doaínglib na harchaínglib,
nech thucas triadindchur de,
na fail d'ingnud¹ lam'rigse,
Morísc ri nime náir².

---

¹ MS. dingnaud, but with a dot under *an*.   ² This and similar lines, being mere
repetitions of the first line of each poem, do not count in the numbering.

II.

337 Ri dorigni riched reil
conachrichaib diacomrdir,
treb thogach, duanach, daṅgen,
dosluag amra árc[h]aṅgel.

341 Richeḋ conilhur adroṅg,
saer, sithech, nadimchumung,
cathir dronoll cocetrath,
met dondomonn adechmad.

345 Failet ann trimuir cenmeth,
duirimthimchellat¹ riched,
mur doglain huaine, gnim cain,
mur dior, mur dichorcair.

349 Mur n-uaine cenchess im-mach,
mur n-óir fricness nacathrach,
im-medon frigelgloir cain
mur ṅdermor dichorcairglain.

353 Fail ann, cotrichim trethan,
cathir chrichid, chomlethan,
fail inti, frisd solus,
set sir cethriprimdorus.

357 Met cachdoruis dib foleith
donacethriprimdoirsib,
toeb fritoeb, dini iartomus,
mili darcachn-oendorus.

361 Fail crois d'ór incachdorus
frisella slog sirsolus,
ri rosdelba centalgga,
hite remra roárdda.

365 En dodergor forcachcrois
oschind lerglor nach anfois,
incachcrois frihernól cuir
gemm dermor doleic logmuir.

369 Archaṅgel cechlai, luad ṅdil,
conasluag orís richid,

coclasschetal, coceol glé,
timchell cacha oenchrose.

373 Fail ann faithchi cechdoruis
cain frilaichmi derbthomuis,
samlaim[se] cech dib fofeib
fritalmain conamuireib.

377 Cuaird cachafaithchi foleith,
conagrencbaib airgdidib,
conabrugaib foblath bil,
conalubaib ligaidib.

381 Ced adbal lib, lathar ṅgle,
met nafaithchi fairsiṅge,
mur d'argut, cengnim n-aithbi,
rogniḋ imcachoenfaith(chi).

385 Airfortoich namur im-maig²
immodun docachoenleith,
[fo. 20 a. 1.]
cosostaib slanaib sidib
diarmidi dohilmilib.

389 Ocht n-airfortaig ann frisreith
cocomraicet 'moncathraig :
nimtha samail nasét sruith
donmét fail cachairfortuig.

393 Cachairfortach lan lubaib,
conangrencbaib credhumaib,
mur dochriad chaim rochalcaḋ
cotren imcach n-airfortach.

397 Damur de[e]c, toraind ṅglé,
'nan-airfortach, 'nafaithchi,
cenmthat natrimúir im-maig²
failet im[on] primchathraig.

401 Cethracha dorus hitreib
richiḋ conarigsuidcib,
atri cacha faithchi feith,
isatri cachairfortaich.

405 Cethridoruis airri im-mach

---

¹ MS. duir imthimchellat. ² MS. immuig.

nan-irfortach n-immechtrach,
frisintetblai, tolaib smacht,
frisincetna [a]thchomarce.

409 Comla d'argut, cain ardreich,
cachdoruis dondfaithchisin,
comlada creda corath
fridoirsi nan-irfortach.

413 Nafrithmuir ondun im-mach
innan-huili n-airfortach,
samlaithir fribladbail mbla
otha thalmain cohesca.

417 Mur nafaitchi, feib dasli,
rosdelbtha dofindruini,
an-airde, adbul foneib,
otha thalmain coglangrein.

421 Natrimuir, met an-athfaig,
timchellait inprimcathraig,
tadbain an-airde cenmeirg
othalmain cofirmimeint.

425 Suidigud namur im-maig
immondun, immoncathraig,
rathrian cachmúir, monor ñgle,
reil radiall secharaile[1].

429 Ri rosfossaig cotangeib
nassossaid 'monprimchathraig,
deimni ataichmi ondun im-mach
'nafaithchi, 'nan-irfortach.

433 Sluaig sil Adaim, aidble baind,
innandalaib frianderbraind,
gle iarñdligud dib rosoich
sechinud cech oensossaid.

437 Bid cachsluag di[i]b foleith
'nan-airfortach, 'nafaitchib,
lánaib doligaib fofeib
dosidaib, dosonmigeib.

441 Noeb isnúibhuaga corath

fobraenbuada, iarmbraenchath :
scérdair frisinslog im-maig,
bertair isinmorchathraig.

445 Cathir De conasoillsi,
cidat mora aprimdoirsi,
nitheit inti óthalmain treib
acht mad oentrìar dodoeneib.

449 Duni conái dligid Dé,
duine óg iarfirinne,
congnim adma nadchlithe
duine amra athirge.

453 Congérdair cobáid im-maig[2]
nanaeb isinprimchathraig,
febdae fo lib, lith rochlos,
cach dib daraprimdoros.

457 Nadoirsi chaindelbdai, glain,
lainderdai dondlíc logmair,
con-ollbladaib, segtait slóig,
conacomladaib dergoir.

461 Tri athchomairc cechdoruis,
cain glanthogairt toebtomuis,
fricachclothalt, erim ñgúr,
athchomarc[3] for cachoenmúr.

465 Aurdrochait nandorus n-og
cain set solus dodergór,
atat fonéim, nassad ñgle,
airddiu cachceim araile.

469 O cheim docheim, erim ñgur,
isreid dreimm isinprimdun,
cainsluag sidi, set rosaig,
mór mili cét dochétaib.

473 Hicuaird nam-mur, mor n-athbach,
im-medon naprimchathrach,
lebinn glainidi glórdai,
drochte dronai dergórdai.

477 Filet ann brugi bláthi

---

[1] MS. secharaili.   [2] MS. immuig.   [3] MS. atchonnarc.

bithura cach bithráthi,
colorthib cachthoraid dil,
*co*mambolthaib milidib.

481 Fail ann centoirsi didnad,
fail soilsi cenáirdibad,
ceoil gluara, caini, gr*i*nni,
buana, baidi, blaithbinni.

485 Fail ann ni sásas ce*ch* slóg
hirichiud rigda romór,
[fo. 20 a. 2.]
fogur na*ǹ*gr*a*d, nacéol *ǹ*gle,
bolud namblath *ṁ*boltnaigthe[1].

489 Fail mór dosostaib, saer slán,
fail mór class cobsaid comnar,
fail ann mor slúag, seol snassi,
fail mor ceol ce*ch*oenclassi.

493 Failet ann linni lethna,
ailli aninni anoebtrethna,
gleorda immocanat classi,
suarca, segdai, somblassi.

497 Failet ann srotha se*ǹ*gga
docheniul cach coemlenna,
fr*i*sasad sloig, sir sotlaib,
fail ann mór dofindtopr*a*ib.

501 Failet ann lecga lordai,
failet foraid forordai,
for*b*rig naslog dosrogaib,
fail ann mór do rigsrothaib.

505 Fail ann mór *ṁ*bfle *ṁ*broga,
mór tiri fr*ṁ*thoga,
mor sét sétach, slán saine,
mor cet cctach clármaige.

509 Mor ceol caimnaig cenbine
fail iroenmaig rindnime,
mor seol suilig, mor sreth séis,
nadróig tuirim noaisneis.

513 Fail ann iarset, srethaib smacht,

cet acethair cethrachat,
fiadgnuis indrig cotagaib
iar n-árcm afochraicaib.

517 O thosuch domuin cobrad
clann Adaim, cidhe acomrad,
ni choemsaitis, digr*a*is seis,
ce*ch* oen fochraic dib d'aisnes.

521 Cenmothat sain cotaigaib
fail innim dofochraicaib,
lir bannai fleochaid, fuám tr*i*cc,
no slamma snechta snigit.

525 Sossad slan morig rathmar
fil forlar napr*i*mchathr*a*ch :
ismor cet mili 'mobeir
hitimchuaird afosscemeil.

529 Dior derg rogn*i*d huile[2]
dorig richid rig*s*uide :
ri corúnaib dofo*r*gaib
osnamúraib erordaib.

533 Sossaid Aiǹgel[3] cosoillsib
nessaim donapr*i*mdoirsib,
Archaǹgeil conan-airbrib
isnessam donaebaiǹglib.

537 Uirtutes, nerl osca*ch*maig,
isnessam doArchaǹglib,
Potestates, deoda ilus,
isnessam Uirtutibus.

541 Principat*us*, blaith aseis,
isnessam Potestatés,
Dominationes, droǹg demein,
fodiuplaib indfosscemeil.

545 Amra inslog roscing uili
forscemul indrigsuidi[4] :
nóeb inrori roscoǹgaib
Troni conamórdroǹgaib.

549 Sluaig Iiruphin rosfossaig
itimchuairt indrigsossaid,

---

[1] MS. *ṁ*botlnaigthi.   [2] MS. huili.   [3] MS. naiǹgel.   [4] MS. -suide.

tuas sech ce*ch*oen fondrig reil
sernait slog sáer Saraphin.

553 Noiṅgr*a*d nime, noebda am*b*al,
imrig nan-uili n-adbar,
cendimbúaid fr*i*briga blat,
cen imhuail, cenimmf*or*mat[1].

557 Lainib lánaib forig recht,
isshé an-arim fírchert,
dase *scsc*at, sluag fofcib,
ce*ch*oengr*a*id donagr*a*daib.

561 Arim ce*ch*sluaig, lith cenmeth,
nifail nech rodasfessad,
achl marofit*i*r inrí
dodosrosat donemphní.

565 Ri huasal uasdaib uili,
ri richid con-imdruine,
ri febda firian fossud,
rí rigf*i*al[2] 'narigsossud.

569 Ri rohóc, ri sen icein,
ri rodelb nem imglangrein,
ri nan-huile noeb corath,
ri caim, ri cain, ri cruthach.

573 Ri dorigni nemthech necht
doainglib centarimthecht,
tir nanóeb, namac ṅbethad,
clar find, fota, forlethan.

577 Rosrethaig sosad, sid saer,
fossad forethaib rig roen,
cuaird cháin, glanna, c*ri*chid, gle,
doaes amra athirge.

581 Morí immarthus osintslóg
san*c/us* Dominus[3] Sabaoth,
diacain uasdind, f*or*seol screc,
ceol *cethri* sanct find *fich*et.

585 Ri roordaig inclais chert
na *cethri* sancht find fichet,

[fo. 20 b. 1.]

cáin canait canth*us* dontslo*g*
sanc*t*us D*eu*s Sabaoth.

589 Ri fossud fial, febda, find,
sid sossud, selbda, soenmind,
lasfail trct nan-úan, nuall ṅgle,
'món-Úan n-úag nemlochtaigthe.

593 Ri reil rohorddaig inn-Úan
iarsintsleib f*or*aimluad,
cethrimili mac 'naṅdiaid,
cethorcha ocus cét glanriad.

597 Crichid class, congloraib cruth,
donahógaib ceneilniud,
canait ceol ṅgluair immalle
indiaid indUain etrochtai.

601 Comchoema, comluatha, gluair,
iarsintsleib indiaid indUain,
scríbtha 'nangnuisib corath
an-ainm isainm indAthar.

605 IN ri rohordaig inguth
donanemdaib fr*i*tinphiud,
lethan, londg*ur*, lathar ṅgle,
am*al* tondg*ur* n-iluisce.

609 No am*al* guth crot carait nuall,
canait cenna*ch*locht lórmuad,
linib lerthol uasce*ch*raind,
no am*al* nuall dermór toraind.

613 Ri bili bethad foablath
slige fr*is*rethad soergrád,
abarr, abroenrad ce*ch*leith
roleth darroemag richid.

617 Forsasaid indénlaith án,
*con*gaib glerath cheol comlan,
cenaurchra, corogud rath,
dothorud *no* duilerad.

621 Alaind indenlaith cotṅgæib,

---

ce*ch*en glermaith cet n-etteib,[1]
canait cenbet, cogleor gle,
cet ceol ca*ch*a oenheitte.

625 Ri rogni mór n-adba n-an,
mór ṅgnim cadla, cóir, comlan,
lam'rig rogmár osce*ch*maig
fil ce*ch* ollgrad cenesbaid.

629 Fail leis *secht* nimi, nert n-uag,
cengeis, cenbine findluad,
imthalmain [2], tolaib tine,
con-anmaimm ce*ch*oennime.

633 Aear, ethiar osca*ch*druṅg,
Olimpus, firmamentum,
nem n-us*ce*, nem n-aṅgel n-uag,
nem hifail Fiadu findmuad.

637 Fil leis ilar n-amra ṅdroṅg,
fil mor n-adba cenimroll,
fail lais *nói* ùgr*a*id, cossar chaid,
fail lais sosad ce*ch*oengr*a*id.

641 Fail indechmad, gr*a*d *con*gaib,
censechnad [3] slan sil Adaim,
dóini foadoi tr*i*amnai trel,
cotaoi Fiada findgel.

645 Fail ann sid, fail suba slán,
cenguba, cenathchosan,
*fri*srethu sluaig, segda thuir,
fail bethu buan bithsuthain.

649 A fail domaith lárṅDia dil,
dianoebaib innanoemtr*e*ib,
nifail iarsetad naseis
nech conní acetmad d'aisneis.

653 Coimdiu conn ce*ch*gr*a*da gluair,
targ[ ] droṅg betha bithbuain,
romsaera iarṅdul acr*i* cath,
inri dorone inriched.

Ri dorigni riched reil.

III.

657 R i dorosat nanoiṅgr*a*d
nimi *fri*eumtach coemnár,
foglanblad achrotha glain,
*fri*aadrad, *fri*aairmitin.

661 Trigr*a*d doib, torainn glan,
asnessu dochum talman,
Ang*e*li *fri*sretha seis,
Archang*e*li, Uirtutes.

665 Pol*e*states, oebind bla,
ithe tr*i*gr*a*id medoncha,
Principatus, bag centreis,
ocus Dominationés.

669 Trigr*a*id hisuachtarchom dib
ifrecnarcus indardr*i*g,
Troni *fri*rigṡuide r*é*il,
Hiruphin is Saraphein.

673 IN dechmad gr*a*d, canar lib,
censechnad slan síl Adaim,
uasbith cenguas*acht* icr*i*
dodosruasat monaebr*i*.

677 Ri rochoimsig nagr*a*da
cotoimsib cech degdána,
linib lianmag angnim cain,
*fri*an-iarair, *fri*an-airmitin.

681 Secht ṅgr*a*d ann, airegda ingnim,
*fri*asainṡemla indardr*i*g,
dogr*e*ss doib, cenchithu cruth,
tr*i*abithu coaairñtiud.

[fo. 20 b. 2.]

685 Dagr*a*d dib, derbdu dalaib,
fritorroma síl Adaim,
fricech[c]angin ṅgnatlımair ṅglain,
Aṅgil *ocus* Archaṅgeil.

689 Aṅgeil gléglana, gnim cert,

---

[1] *e* written over the *a* of 'nettaib.'   [2] MS. imthalmaind.   [3] MS. censechrad.

doreir Dé fritechtairecht,
indArchaiṅgil cenchaire,
ithé nauasaltechtaire.

693 Uirtutes, nerta cechthan,
fridenam nafirt findglan,
Potestates, delbda atlacht,
atfebda frifollomnacht.

697 Principat*us*, blathi gne,
frfa1hi naṅgnim cinte,
Dom*i*nationes, nóebda cruth,
sluag soerda fr*i*smachtugud.

701 Troni, dichraidiu combrig,
fiadri[g]suidiu indardrig,
hilar shircanait ceol ṅgleir
Hiruphin is[S]araphein.

705 Crichid cenchrinhed inchlass
fochanat riched rindmass,
cliar gel formaig rind roalt
nacethrisen find fichet.

709 Nosfreccr*a*t naslóig slana
doib conhettgat hilgr*a*da,
conidhed canthus inslog
sanctus Deus Sabaóth.

713 Ri rofoilsig dam, deilm¹ n-an,
ni dothoimsib nan-hilgr*a*d,
diasostaib saidbrib sluagdaib,
dian-airbrib, dian-ilbuadaib.

717 Dodeccr*a*i osbetha bann
srethaib ilretha rétlann,
caine mar góo gréne,
connaibe fochomglére.

721 Diafebsai aidchi huimle,
diacennsai, diangnathchuibdi,
diacainduthracht² cenchaire,
diandeeircc, diatrocaire³.

725 Diaslaine⁴, slicht cendochta,

dian-áne, dian-etrochta,
diacruth gle, coemda, glanna,
dlaṅgne noebda n-adamra.

729 Diasidaib, srethaib seolaib,
diaṅgnimaib, diaṅglanche[o]laib,
diamodaib amraib aildib,
dian-aitdib, dian-ilarmib.

733 Arim nan-aṅgel innim,
doreir arFiadat findgil,
friaidbsigud, derb ṅdana,
iarfailsigud⁵ spirtalda.

737 Nihed an-airim, amorf,
lin acuire fochoemli,
acht madlin intsluaig atr*a*ig
icoemthecht cacharchaiṅgi(l).

741 A hoen, adó, atrf trel,
ado friu conidcuicfer,
dacuiciur, iarṅgairib gle,
isshi indarim deichde.

745 Dadeich derba, torainn tr*i*cc,
tiagait hisincertfichit,
oc*us* tr*i*deich, tr*i*allait blait⁶,
iss*ed* tiagait hitrichait.

749 IArsintr*i*chait, taidbret bí,
doaidbet imut arf,
cethrideich, iarslanaib smacht,
isi indárim cethrachat.

753 Coicdeich iarsreith sliucht fónait,
is*ed* tiagait icoicait,
sedeich, cengairim, cenacht,
issed indárim sescat.

757 Secht ṅdeich hisechtmog*a* sl*a*n,
ocht ṅdeich *ochtmoga* ollmar,
nodeich innochait iarset,
oc*us* deich ṅdeich inglanchet.

761 Deichcet inmili, mod mór,

¹ Or *delm*, if the dot under *i* is a punctum delens.   ² MS. ·chain·.   ³ MS. dia*n*trocaire.
⁴ MS. ·slaine.   ⁵ *iar* is written as a correction over *fri*.   ⁶ *l* is written over *r*.

c 2

ocus deichmili inlegeón,
deichlegeon dogres cachdia,
issed tiagait hicuinla.

765 Deichcunia, coleir ciagléis,
issed tiagait inmarés,
deichmares, miad milib bla,
techtas coderb caterua.

769 Decim caterua rochlús
tíagait in-exercitús,
deich[n]exercitús, teanm tra,
tiagait coderb inturba.

773 Deichturba derb nandroṅg nden,
issed tiagait in-agtnrn,
deich n-aigmen aṅgel gráid ṅgil
icoemthecht cacharchaṅgil.

777 Fail secht n-archaṅgliu innim
laruiri richid rindgil,
lacachn-archaṅgel foleith
sechtdeich agmen doaṅglib.

781 IShésin innomad grad,
dorónad fornim noebnár,
aṅgel ṅgleglan cenmennar
icoemthechtaib archaṅgel.
[fo. 21 a. 1.]

785 Na ocht grad cenmothá sin,
dostósat Dia coderbden,
acht mori ráṅgle fornim
nifail roairme an-árim.

789 Tuirmem fríagairm fiadrig reclit
ainm na cethri fer find fichet,
droṅg duassach d'arbrib aṅgel
nan-uasal, nan-archaṅgel.

793 Gabriel, Michél, maith an-greim,
Raphiel, Panachel oebind,
Babichél, Raguel roclos,
Mirachel, Rumel rigdos.

797 Fafigial, Sumsagial slán,

Sarmichiel, Sarachel saergráil,
Ur[i]el, Hermichel maith mass,
Sarachel, Darachel bladbras.

801 Lihigiel, Darachél cenchol,
Segiel, laSariel sairdron,
Lonachel, Arachél[1] tan,
Stichiel, Gallichiel gleglan.

805 Guidem doíb, derb dín cenmeth,
arinrig rodelb riched,
'mobethu cenchithu, cruth cain,
trrábithu 'nambithoentaid.

809 Cibhe gabas cuit nói ṅgrad
etir iarmerge is tiugnar,
rodihbia nem, nassad ṅdaṅgen,
imbithoentaid archaṅgel.

813 Datrian insein, sluaig roclos,
robai innim rian-imarbos,
atrían huili, fotheidm thinn,
dochuatar dochum n-Iffirn.

817 Atethach, aChoimdiu cain,
dom'forcraid, dom'hessbadaib,
tabair dam dilgud hifus
dom'ainblib, dom'aneolaus.

821 Ciarobai doanble aríd
airmi aidbli nan-ilgrád,
anroradius, sonad sír,
isdomolad mororíg.

825 Cianobeth cét ieṅgad ṅdron
frisirlabra cenairchron,
níaisneidfind trmbithsír
cétmad adamra m'ardríg.

829 A[r]druiri búan betha brice
doruirmi cachsluag sainglic,
arcli, arnduasach, arn-abb,
inrí huasal doruasat.

      Ri dorósat nanoe[ṅ]grád.

---

[1] MS. darachél.

IV.

833   M oRſ rigda oscachthur
      roraide friLuciphur :
    ' biait ſót, ſeib dochangen ṅgel,
    airbri imdai archaṅgel.

837 ' Tabair uait airmitiu iarsreith
    doAdom, dom'chomdelbaid,
    na *uói* ṅgrad coibli gleir glain
    biait ſoimti frꞵ'airitein.'

841 ' Airmitiu d'Adam, nichél,
    arimsiniu, nithibér,
    ar badairniul fiadcachthur
    dianamthairbiur fonsósur.'

845 Roraidi frꞵs rſ narind,
    aFiadu firen firfind,
    ' nocotbia airmitiu glan,
    úarnatabrai reir d'Adam.'

849 Roraidi Lucifur leir
    aithesc ṅdiumosach ṅdrochceil :
    ' bamri reil oscach caiṅgin,
    fomgniſet indilaiṅgil.

853 ' Betit indaṅgeil fomtraig,
    dogén ſéin mochomtocbáil,
    biam tigerna oseechdruṅg,
    nibia rſ aile huasum.'

857 Lucifur colin agraid
    rot[r]ascair achomthocbail,
    rotairinn adiummus tind,
    dorimmart dochum n-Iffirn.

861 Mili bliadan, mod ṅglanna,
    adfiadat nascribenna,
    ochruthad aṅgel, gnim cert,
    conostarraid tarimthecht.

865 Ruiri narind réltai máil
    targai dind domuin drechmair :
    niseng abrig oscach bla :
    ferr cach rig morſ rígda.

      Mori rigda oscach thur.

V.

869   R i dorigni carcair cain
      doLucifur, diademnaib,
    tſr ṅdorcha ṅdub[ach] ṅdér ṅdrenn,
    ger, diani[d]comainm Iffern.

873 Cathir grainne, glérib cath,
    censlane, serb, sirechtach,
    aigthech, uamnach, ilar ṁbrath,
    gaibthech, guamnach, golpartach.

877 Buidni biasta, buiriud pian,
    ruibni riastrai frianriad,
    bádud, plagud, breud, bruth,
    tragud, largud, leod, loscud.

      [fo. 21 a. 2.]

881 IMonṁbeist ṁbuirr, blóraid benn,
    ostuind truim, tolaib ilchend :
    duilgib drichnes fricachsluag,
    coruibnib riches roruad.

885 Coic cel cenn fridiartain tinn,
    coic cel fiaccail cechoenchind,
    cel lam, cel bass, indel ṅglaiss,
    cel n-ingen forcachoenbaiss.

889 Ilar thor ṅdoel, duba druiṅg,
    ilar cruma cael clenchruind,
    ilar cuan ṅgér, ciasta, cerb,
    ilar ṁbiasta ṁbuan, ṁbelderg.

893 Ilar loscond lan dogail,
    foralar icimsergain,
    fricach imchuaird nacathrach,
    ilar nathrach n-imathlam.

897 Ilar ṁbrothlach nambled ṁberg,
    nambiasta n-ochrach n-airderg,
    ilar ṅdelb ṅdomblas aṅgal,
    ilar lonnbras leoman.

901 Ilar lasrach lonn cechleth,
    ilar casrach ṅgarbthened,
    ilar ṅdlúm ṅdlomtha tuarcat,
    ilar ṅdorcha ṅdubluachat.

905 Fail mór domuirib¹ moamúr,
hIffirn cotuilib tromthúr,
fríplagud nasluag siabar,
fría[m]badud, fria[m]bithphianad.

909 Muir ńdublemen, temel truag,
muir ńdaiged tened tromruad,
muir ḿbren, muir tren, deńgge dath,
muir nél, muir neme natrach.

913 INmuir serb suiges insluag,
mor ńdelb drubas fothromnual,
incach ńaird fobrón ffantach,
gol mairg ocus mórhiachtad.

917 Hĺttu, huacht ocus tess
crintu, chúac, grandaib garbchess,
sluag luath landub foralar,
cońglamrud, con-athchossan.

921 Gáir gér gríbi, hĺr isĺerg,
fothair díni ńdér ńherderg,
friańgrella cenchoibli ńgle,
sroigli tenna, teinntide.

925 Acethair cethorchat cet
nisechmalat foroenshét,
failet fridamnad Diabuil,
in-Iffurn dohilphĺanaib.

929 Cianobeth cet mili fer,
conatengthaib iarnaideib,
oenphian dib, cobrath ḿbrudin,
nichoemstais doderbthurim.

933 Madnofail d'hilphianaib ann,
in-Iffurn huathmar imgann,
lia natluibi formaigaib,
no duili for fidbadaib.

937 Fail ann rig nadrigda bes,
gríbda, gann, cetaib ilglés,
duairc, doer, dressachtach adrech
cloen, cessachtach, cossaitech.

941 Crimnach, gruamnach, gnath ic-
brath,
hirach, uarach, airbirech,
ciar, cernalach, caras cath,
dian, drenngalach, diumussach.

945 Engach, huaichlech, ilar crech,
tedmnach, tuaimnech², disceinmnech,
grístaig, cracstuib, granne agne,
discir, doescair, dergnaide.

949 Ri dorat tromdigail tind,
forsluag n-anhettail n-Iffirn,
truaga, tána frigortai,
buana, bana, bithbochtai.

953 Anduili³ cestait intslúaig,
icrácsluch⁴ Iffirn adruaid,
ciarombet cét tengad dein,
niaisneidfind frím'aimsir.

957 Adba n-Iffirn, ilar phian,
mairg bĺs fócrithfeidm comchian,
glenn golmar, gann, gráne ali,
morĺ rogmar dorigni.
    Ri dorigni carcair cain.

VI.

961 Ri dorigni Pardus ḿblaith,
  cuairt⁵ crichid, cobsaid, com-
snáid,
caintĺr toirhech, digrais foss,
dodainib rian-immarbos.

965 Rĺ robennach bruig reid ḿblaith,
Pardus frísuirded sáergraid,
iarcinniud cachthuir thogaig,
con-immud cechĺltoraid.

969 Col-láinib loraib lubaib,
comagib, comorbrugaib,

---

coscathaib scoth *for*cachmaig,
conamblathaib bolordaib.

973 Cocadius cainol roclos,
con-ainius, con-aebinneos,
*con*abruig barrglas, bladmar,
feidb tadbas babithsamrad.

977 Bethrach, broena*ch*, broga*ch*, bras,
tir tethra*ch*, toga*ch*, tonnglas,
[fo. 21 b. 1.]
saer saech[t]airtbír, suthach srath,
caem, cain, cetharchair ¹, cruthach.

981 Clar cóir, cobsaid, cumtaig dind,
fal frítóir *for*said *for*find,
isdín caich, is mur *n*broigthech,
bithblaith, bithur, bithtoirthech.

985 Sossad slan, sutha*ch*, sid sáer,
fal fossud, fulach, ffrnoeb,
sreba sencha, selbcha sreith,
cenérchra, cenimhesbaid.

989 Mag maith, moinech, milib mind,
doinech, daith, dinib derb dind,
cosrethaib saidbrib seolaib,
airbrib aidblib, ilchéolaib.

993 Rí roordaig innadail,
topur indhordain forláin,
astecat glaini crotha,
cethrisreba sirsrotha.

997 Sruth d'fín, sruth d'ola², dal dil,
sruth loga lemnacht langil,
*s*ruth maith mela, monar ńglan ',
frisasad nanoebanman.

1001 Ainm foleith cech*s*rotha slain,
cenchleith frí*c*lotha coemdail,
Fisson, Geon, cain cenlen,
Tibris ocus Eufratén.

1005 Fisson sair sires areim,
Tibris siar siles slanéim,

Eufraten combuaid fodes,
Geon fothuaid⁴ dian dirges.

1009 INdola sáir, iarslicht slán,
infin siar srethaib sirdal,
inmil fodess, dig*r*ais buaid,
inlemnacht sflas sairthuaid.

1013 IMsoat, dosoat iarsain,
doréir indrig donoebnim,
cenmeth, cenditha, cenchais,
ce*ch*leth fochricha Pardais.

1017 Rfi foides enlaith n-en ńdil,
cenlen darróendes richid,
*co*canat ceola cenchais,
beoda fobiliu Pardais.

1021 Docain coglerdaith cengreis,
indenlaid caim cenaithmeis,
set sáire frír*i*agla raith,
cliara caine cet ceolmaith.

1025 Cet dochetaib en iallaib,
cét n-itte, c*et* ceol cliaraib,
mor cet ceol calad cencleith,
gleor canar dorig richid.

1029 Rí rodelb Pardos foali,
ishe arn-armdos airgdidi,
dorat mur mor n-inime thenn,
díor immaimthimchell.

1033 Ri betha barrglais boirchich,
ri Pardais con-iltoirthib,
rodelb lanamain iartain,
donahuilib anmannaib.

1037 Ri doruasat Adam n-án,
fochruth cengúasacht coemnar,
*con*grad, cenamlós rochlos,
hiPardos rian-immarbos.

1041 Bai Adam tritra*th* centess,
imbadud fograd glanches,
*for*talmain tinn centreorud,

---

¹ MS. cetharchain.   ² MS. dfola.   ³ *a* written over *oc*.   ⁴ MS. futhaid.

cenanmain, ceninbeogud.

1045 Bai corp Adaim tribtrathaib,
cenanmain fricerbfathaib,
friindrad centrist, delm ngle,
icfigrad Crist d'esserge.

1049 ISsintresló iarnagein,
rodelbad anim Adaim,
iartoebthogud friadin ndocht,
cenoentogud friafirchorp.

1053 Coroainmniged iarsain
onacethri rétglannaib,
Archon, Dissis, rotdelb Dia,
Anatole, Missi[mb]ria¹.

1057 Noimís lána, lathar ndil,
orohet Adam anmain,
iarsliucht sruithi senchad slán,
corodelbad abanscal.

1061 Dianid comainm Eua án,
crichid, chorcorda, coemnar,
dil, delbda², toga³ rainni,
fotha febda fírclainne.

1065 Iarsain asraracht Adom
assaṡuan cenimgabud,
confacca inmnái, mín adath,
segda, suaichnid, sochrutach.

1069 Amal rodeccai aggnuis
dosroega sechcach nderbduis,
dorarngert dí, eraim ngle,
combad ṡaiṅṡerc sochaide.

1073 'IS orot rirfes cencleith
cach amathair 'saathair :
ondiu triabithu, buaid nein,
biaid cechoen uainn⁴ dit'ogréir.'

1077 Ardruiri indroith, rigda ail,
gargruide fricroich coemnair,
[fo. 21 b. 2.]
rofigli 'nacrí roclos,
inrí dorigní Phardos.

Rí dorigni Pardos mblaith.

VII.

1081 Ri rorade aithesc nglan
friEua ocus friAdam,
toírthi Parduis, bag cengeis,
iartimnu De domeldais.

1085 'Aratoimlid frisid sáin
toirthi Parduis, bolad náir,
ile, uile, aurdaig rann,
isdiles duib acht oenchrann.

1089 'Cofessabair bith fosmacht
centruaigi, centochomrac,
censnim, censacthar frisreith,
cenaes, cenolcc, cenanim.

1093 'Cenchrine, cengalar cruaid,
imbithbethaid combithbuaid,
farndul conem, nassad ngle,
in-aes togach trichtaige.'

1097 Mili bliadan, buadach gair,
ocus se huara dohuaraib,
cengoe, cengabud, roclos,
robai Adum hiPardus.

1101 Dia artooir, derbait mail,
rodelb cech cooir comlain :
nitli tlaithcumtaig arcest
inrí roraid inn-athesc.

Rí rorade athesc nglan.

---

¹ Corruptions of Ἄρκτος, Δύσις (ήλίου), Ἀνατολή, Μεσημβρία. Compare MS. Harl. 3362. fol. 7,
cited by Kemble, Salomon and Saturnus, p. 194 :
Anathole dedit A, Disis D, contulit Arctos,
Et Mesembrios M ; collige, fiet ADAM.

² MS. delba.   ³ Written as a correction over forgu.   ⁴ MS. uain.

VIII.

1105 Baſormtech Diabul desin
    friAdam conachlannaib,
am-bith sunn cenlocht, luad ṅgle,
'nacurp n-uág dochum nime.

1109 Nahuili anmanna icrí
dodosrosat monóebrí[1]:
friPardus imuich cenchad
isAdom nosordaiged.

1113 INdúair theigtis ascecherích
sluaig *secht* nime 'monardríg,
ca*ch*anmanna corptha cain
doticed dochum n-Adaim.

1117 Cach díb assa airm corath
ſoagairm *ocus* fríaadrad,
doAdaum, balainn [in]mod,
dothictis diaairfitiud.

1121 Rosmachtastar Dia donim
forsnahuilib anmannaib,
atichtu asce*ch*leith cengreis,
combitis ard[r]eich Parduis.

1125 IArsain imsaitis ſordeis
censil n-úabair nahaincceiss,
cach dib díaadbai coglan
iarṁbennachad doAdam.

1129 Baſeochair féig, fichtib ell,
inbeist imamnas, imchenn,
ciachruth ſogebaid ſonim
conair d'admilliud [Adim.]

1133 Lucifer, lin cest ṅglanna,
luid im-mesc nan-anmanna,
'sintsluag friPardus im-maich[2],
conid ann ſuair innathraig.

1137 'Nirbdimmain dobith im-maich[3],'
arDiabul frisinnathraig,

'arthuaichle tricce, delm ṅgle,
ardoglicce, arth'amainse.

1141 'Bamor inguassacht 'sincol
Adam huassot d'ordnigod:
ossar nanduli[4] methlad,
nibadchin duini amandrad.

1145 'Orat noisichu frícath,
toisechu rothuistiged,
atgliccu assaimdil ce*ch*cruth,
nachat[t]airbir ſondossor.

1149 'Gaib mochom*ir*le cenchess,
denamm cotach iscarddes,
coiste ſadein frim'cheil ṅglain,
'ass náteig dochum n-Adaim.

1153 'Tabair dam inad it'churp
iarmodliged, iarm'intliucht,
condechsam fogr*is* iarṁb]a
arndís adochom n-Euá.

1157 'Aura[i]llem fuirri 'malle
torud incrainn aurgairthi,
cor*h*heralasi coglan
iarum inṁbiad forAdam.

1161 'Acht condechsat andís 'malé
as dartimna atigernai,
nisbia grad laDia iſ*us*,
ticſait cenblath oPhardus.'

1165 'Cialuag nomtha fiadca*ch*thur,'
arinnathir friDiabul,
'arſailti duit im'ch*i*rp chain
cenna[ch]locht dom'chomaittreib?

1169 'Arthreoir duit iar[s]et sain
d'admilliud Euá isAdaim,
ardul lat iarfír frigreis,
ciphe gním frisan-eirreis?'

1173 'Caluag ismo dob*er* duit
feib ata meit armorhuilcc,

[1] MS. monóembrí.   [2] MS. immuich.   [3] MS. immuich.   [4] *i* written as a correction over *a*.

D   [IV. 3.]

[fo. 22 a. 1.]

arn-óentu iarnbes, iarnbruth,
bid dogres arn-anmnigud.'

1177 O sofuair adbai donbrath
rosamlai indelb nanatrach, deilb
isfóil dodeochaid frifoss
iarcoir Parduis dondoros.

1181 Rogart indnathir im-maig :
'indamchluini, aben Adaim ?
deni, aEua chrotha cain,
sechcách cena m'acallaim.'

1185 'Nimhuain fríacallaim ncich,'
arEua frisinnathraig :
'itu icfrithalim im-mach
nan-anmanna n-indligtech.'

1189 'Massathú indEua roclos
coclú frifeba hiPardos,
ben Adaim alainn nadchres,
furri alim molanles.'

1193 [' INtan nadbi Adam hifos
isme chometas Phardos,
cenchess,'amil blaith banna,
dognim less nan-anm[ann]a.'

1197 'Ciaheret teit Adam uait,
cialejth focheird achainchuaird,
tan nadbi frihuáir ifos
frithalmi intsluaig iPardos ?

1201 'Fofacaib lim, lith nglanna,
frithalim nan-anmanna,
[intan teit foglanblad cenmeth
fadein d'adrad inChomded.

1205 'Ail dam ní d'athchomarc huait¹,'
arindnathir chóel comsuairc²,
'uair isglandil dochial chain,
aEuá, aandeir Adaim !'

1209 'Cibhed imraidi dorad
nichomcraidfe, arnfi mindnár,

¹ Written as a correction over fort.
² Written as a correction over chatot.

isderb nibadoirchi ifus
sloinnfi duit iarndiutius.'

1213 'Abbair frim, aEua án,
feib donrala fricomrad,
lasinflaith iarmbretha ifos
inmaith fornbetha iPardos ? '

1217 'Condechsam cenlocht iargreith
innarcorp dochum richid,
nichuingem flaith bismo ifus
nanfil domaith iPardus.

1221 'Cech fia [　] feib roclos
dosrossat Dia hiPardos,
acht oenchrann uili cencleith,
ata dídu forriaguil.

1225 'Hé dodilsig dún Dia dil,
amil banna bánamail,
Pardus fridonad adruing
acht madtorad indoencraind.

1229 'Lecid incrannsa coglan',
rofuacart damsa is d'Adam,
'torud craind gairb darmogair
bethi mairb diandessabair.'

1233 'Ciabethi commeit fornbla,
túsu isAdam, aEua,
ni forgliccu, a choem glanna,
inda oen nan-ánmanna.

1237 'Cia beith slog mór foib im-mach,
istróg niforn-intliuchtach :
amal cech n-anmanna mbor[b]
[s]amlaid ataid fríoenord.

1241 'Nocorrubai forlaith lain
acht mad maith aoenurán,
uair natarfaid duib ni d'ulcc,
ismessaiti forn-intliucht.

1245 'IS mor forn-essbaid imgaes,
ata Dia icfortogáes,
tan is d'oencraunn maidis uile

nadleic duib ni dothormailt.

1249 'Aire arrancas incr*a*nn ṅgúr
ishei̇re nachalecar dúb,
deochair et[er] maith isolcc
conaraib accaib d'intliucht.

1253 'Nabdat dolam, eirg doncr*a*unn
diaḟromad immóenubull,
dechair et*er* olcc ismaith
rotbia codocht ondardílaith.'

1257 'Cidmaith t'intliucht, erim ṅgle,
cid lán raith dochomarle,
dul cosincr*a*nn nilamur
arbith arnahérbalur.

1261 'Tair, anathir, fein doncr*a*unn,
ocus tuc de oenubull,
acht cotora int-ubull dam
rannſat etrom isAdam.

1265 'Roſessammar ſiadca*ch*druṅg
acht condessamarſi̇n̄-ubull,
doscel cenhír, erim ṅgle,
dus inſír mar atbeire.'

1269 'A Eua solus cengeis,
hoſlaic róm dor*us* Parduis,
cenlen acht coros innunn,
dob*er* donchraunn inn-ubull.'

1273 'Ciaoslac rot teis innonn
donchraunn ciab*er*a uboll,
[ſo. 22 a. 2.]
nibia ſuirech ſort hiſ*us*
dothairisem hiPardus.'

1277 'Acht dob*er* inn-ubull duit
dodeochair maith *ocus* uilcc,
cennach[loch]t doreg im-mach
manimthair cacht na cumrech.'

1281 Rooslaic Eua ſoclith
indor*us* riasinnathraig :
cennachceith luid, nirbúṁall,

forarith cosinn-oencr*a*nn.

1285 Doſuc Eua inn-ubull n-úag
dondabaill, bascel n-imthrúag,
doſu*a*id Eua aleth, nirbuglan,
rolcic inleth n-aill d'Adam.

1289 Ri rothraith droṅg Iſi̇rn [_]
rosglaíd ſocrithſeidm comtruag,
rogail cedsaithrach tr*i*chath
inſail ſaebrach baſormtech.
Ba formtech Diabul diſein.

IX.

1293 O shunn dua[i]d Eua ſoleith
leth indubuill aurchotig,
roclaemclai cl*i*, lethanṡmacht,
dorochair di acoemtḣacht.

1297 Eua ſr*i*tindrad cenlocht,
baiṅgnad abith imnocht,
rosgab cr*u*th gréic, cenchruth ṅglan,
coroleic guth ſorAdam.

1301 Fogairm Eua, ſeib rodlecht,
dodechaid cenſrithṗidecht,
Adam ſein cenaè, cenlocht,
conſacca aṁnai lomnocht.

1305 'Noconalaind maratai,'
arsé, arAdam, ſriadagmnai,
'cid aṛdoṭralaid hicacht?
cia rotſáraig' 'motnoebthlacht?'

1309 'Nochonep*er* rit inſein,
amothigerna, aAdaim,
coragba huaim, cenhuath ṅgle,
coluath leth indubuillse.'

1313 O rogab Adam cenclith
leth indubuill aurchotig,
roſacaib athlacht ceṁhycht
corabe ſesin lomnucht.

1317 'T̯i̯² rotbrathaig, aben baith,

¹ MS. rotſaraid.

² *Sic.* Read Ci?

D 2

rotrathaig narbsat fírgaeth?
donrat frisnim saethraich sějs, ?
rotbaithig, rombaethigeis.'

1321 'Nathir iarfír, feib roclos,
gaid dím atichtu iPardos,
iartichtain dí sunn tuc de
ubull doncraunn aurgairthe.

1325 'Atrubairt rim iarsein sunn :
'aben, geib uaim inn-ubull,
madail duit cofesser olcc,
ar[na]bad essel t'intliocht.'

1329 'A Eua, afiss madail duit,
dechair maith¹ ocus morhuilcc,
geib inn-ubull[sa] caem, ṅglan,
raind etrut ocus Adam.'

1333 'Rogabussa huad innsain
ubull cosinsrithorgain,
huair násetar ciarét olcc
cofacca mobith lomnocht.

1337 'IMthegind siar ocus sair,
forfemdinn athimargain,
niblaith, bahiṅgnad rith rois,
rofaid fofídrad Pardois.

1341 'Nathir rongáel, garb agraph,
donrat frisaeth tríaaslach,
dochéin rochind agnim cain,
abreic ronmill, aAdaim.'

1345 'A Euá, conhilur glonn,
nimanfacamar th'uboll,
isreil fornn fcib atam nocht
condrancamar fríamorolcc.

1349 'Ata ni ismessu de tra :
scarthain cuirp ocus anma,
corp lobtha hitalmain tind,
isanmain dochum n-Iffirn.'

1353 Huair dorochair dib atlacht

roslín truaigi istocomrac,
duaire leo dochraid acuirp gil,
cenfial ṅglan dian-imditin.

1357 Réil dochach dib daih achuirp
oforfacaibthi glenuicht :
arscath aféile, fuam ṅgle,
tucsat duílli naficlie².

1361 Nifrith fríligthorba ṅdul
acht indficomna ahoenur,
fid fann iPardus corath
nach crann forsm-beth duilirath.

1365 Cocuala Adam hitrial
aṅgel coarad fríGabrial :
'seintír lat cocoir cornn ṅgle,
coroa agloir fo secht nime.

1369 'Heirgid huili coṅgraid glain
hicomdail fríarṅDulemain,
combúaid frignfm daṅgen ṅdil,
slúaig aṅgel do secht nimib.
[fo. 22 b. 1.]

1373 'Tinolaid forsluagad slan,
níbahuathad forcomdal,
condechsaid cogle rochlos
hicoemthecht Dé doPhardos.'

1377 IArsain doluid inrí rúad
doPhardus conamorsluag,
remi codaṅgen cenchol
class aiṅgel icocétol.

1381 Dessid hiruphin iarfir
bahe rigsuide indardrig,
im-medón Phard[uis] corath,
inbale hífail crann bethad.

1385 Rosernad cech sluag iarsreith
cechgrad gluar conaairbreib,
ocus dessid morí reil
fodessin forhiruphein.

---

¹ There is a horizontal stroke over *h*.

' Written as a correction over *palme.*

1389 Dellid[1] ind[í]idbad forlar
Parduis frifidrad fonnram,
rostairbir adduiri den
arairmitiu aDuleman.

1391 'INcualabarsi coglan
ingním dorigni Adam,
adula, cenidna nglan,
darm'thimna, darm'forcetal?

1397 Dodechaid cach dib forleth
iscáth inchrainn forteched,
coñ-erbairt guth Dé donim:
'nimaith romba, aAdaim!'

1401 Roraid Adam, erim n-úag,
friDia aaithesc n-erthrúag:
'marosárugus dosmacht
moben forom roaslacht.'

1405 Atbert Dia d'Adam coglan:
'dochin huair nachatamar,
dogénat doclanna iartain
dogres acin d'imresain.

1409 'Diambad athirge dognéth
Adam con-immud achnéd,
dodilgfitis do coglé
achinta doridise.

1413 Forforcongart fein fofeib
inflaith feig foraaiñgleib:
'curid Adam cengnim nglan
aPhardus dochum talman.'

1417 Lotar indaiñgil iarsain
dodlomad Eua isAdaim,
dograig domma frigorta,
lobraig lonna lomnochta.

1421 Gaid Adam doibrárforclu
'anaid frim, anocbaiñgliu,
comblassind riandul im-mach
ni dothorud crainn bethad.'

1425 'Anfamit frit, moñuar bal,'

arsluag añgel friAdam:
'istruag linni fiadcachthu
an-dorinni Luciphur.'

1429 'INdamchluine, aDe dil,
arth'añglib, arth'archañglib?
indeonaigi dam triarath
ni dothorud craind bethad?'

1433 'Ni blasñ torad inchraind
bethad fralolad mordruing,
hed beit 'mole fogris grinn
an-dís dochorp ist'anim.

1437 Rosbade atol triafroiss,
rosplage bal immarbois,
roslín ciabair'granne cath
iarum oshunn doduad.

O shunn duaid Eua foleith.

X.

1441 Ri rorádi, eraim nglan,
friEua ocus friAdam:
'dochuabair huaim darmorecht,
nípta ni dom'deolaidecht.

1445 'Eirgcid imbethaid ribáethraig,
seirgthig, snimaig, sirsaethraig;
toirsech, tróg, cenfiala fos,
forbia log farn-imarbos.

1449 'Forclanna, formeic, formna,
fogniat duib cachoenlaa,
noc[h]osta maith, monar ñden,
conosti allus forhécen.

1453 'IMmad n-oñg[g]alar fortá,
scarad cuirp ocusanma,
snim ocursaethar cechthan,
áes ocus crfni chrithlam.

1457 'Frithalid[2] aslach[3] Diabuil
cechlaithi cechoenbliadain,
nachforfuca lais diathig,

---

[1] MS. Dellig.   [2] d written over m.   [3] ch written over ig.

dochum n-Iffirn adhuathmair.

1461 ' Forṅgnimrada diamatglain
iarm'thimnaib, iarm'forcetlaib,
doberthar nem, noithech cruth,
dochach iarnachainairliud.'

1465 Ri richid ráṅmair, nisuail,
ri betha bládmair bithbuain,
nitlaith aglegraim cechtan,
ri roraid, éraim n-erglan.

Ri reraide, éraim ṅglan.

XI.

[fo. 22 b. 2.]

1469 R i doridnacht talam tlacht
doAdaum iarnatharmithecht,
nirbo dimdach dóDía dein
manbad airc[h]ra dinaimsir.

1473 Bái Adam sechtmain ífos
iarnathathchor aPardos,
fritoirsi centein, centech,
cendig, cenbiad, cenheted.

1477 Húair rombatar imbochtai
dochúatar in-huachtgortai ;
mor doimaithbeur' incachthan
bái eter Eua isAdam.

1481 ' A Eua chóir crotha cain,
artróig tra dot'impartain,
fuarfr, ronlad aPardos
triat'mignim, triat'immarbos.

1485 ' ISmor forfácsam domaith
orochradsam arn-ardflaith,
Pardus ronbai fogairm glain,
conahuilib airmitnaib.

1489 ' Oetiu, failti dún roclos,
slainte, aine, oebinneos,
bruigi balthai, glannai cruth,

---

lubai amrai, airfitiud.

1493 ' Sassad saeri, sid slan sain,
nassad noibi d'anmannaib,
aithbi derrit, hilar ndú,
cobrai menic friaiṅgliu.

1497 ' Bithbethu iarmbes forDé deis
dogrés imbrugaib Pardais,
ir-robatar fogne chain,
duile De 'coarn-airmitein.

1501 ' Nahuili anmann fonim
dosrossat moDia derbdil,
forgreim oscachdinn condath
issind nodosordaiged².

1505 ' Ninloiscfed tene, delm ṅgle,
ocus ninbaldfed (usce),
nafaebur fédim, met gal,
nateidm, nacredeṅgalar (?)

1509 ' Nibai dodúilib De dil
duil nothissed friarmenmain,
innim natalmain diarcur,
acht int-aṅgbaid³ Lucifur.

1513 ' Cid Lucifur, linib sess,
nichoemnacair arn-amless,
cein bamar forecht, reim ṅgle,
iartimnu, farforngaire.

1517 ' Húair rosáraigsem Dia dil
dorat dún nahuilisin,
oscachdinn cachduil 'malé
atat frinn⁴ hicotarsnai.

1521 ' NiDia robolochtach rind,
aEua chorcra caemfind,
issinn rosáraig inflaith,
ciarontáraig diabithmaith.'

1525 Roráid Euá, arbai hicacht,
hitruage iartarimthecht :
'aAdaim amrai oscachmaig,
cid nacha[m]marbai im'chintaib ?

---

¹ MS. -feur. ² MS. nosodhord(aig e(d). ³ MS. intangbaig. ⁴ MS. frim.

1529 'ISme dochoid darsinsmacht,
isme doroni intarmthecht :
coir duit momarbad dishain,
amothigerna, aAdaim!

1533 'Acht cotorghrórsa, delm cert,
im'chinaid, im'tharimthecht,
mote dogentar cogle
frit odoDia trocaire.'

1537 'IS lor rochráidsem indrig,'
arsé, arAdam, cendimbrig,
'aben, niden fingail fort,
ciabeo ingortai, ciamtoebnocht.

1541 'Nihimmer molaim, luad neim,
form'fuil nach form'feoil fodein,
cidmor dolocht, linaib gal,
isdom'chorp forcoemnacar.

1545 'Nocochoir duin asnachmud.
atherruch dia athsargud,
nadernai infirflaith, aben,
arndibad, arlándilgen[n].

1549 'Nádechsam huaid huidi cian
lademnu ifudomnaib pian,
nacharndilsi, Dia dochur,
dorisi doLucifur.

1553 'Nifail maith foarndalaib,'
arsi, arEua, 'aAdaim,
cenetach dun, centech te,
cenbiad atbelam gorte.

1557 'Ronbáe biad, ronbai tlacht,
céin bamar centarimthecht,
iartarmthecht dún isiarndial
nicharfail tlacht no dagbiad.

1561 'A fir, cuiri cuaird cenmeth
iarsét suairc forcachnoenleth,
dús infogebtha frifcis
dobiud dún ní domelmais.'

1565 Rola Adam cuaird coléir

hifocus, in-etercéin,
nifuair ni dobiud badglan
fodiud acht lubai intalman.
[fo. 23 a. 1.]

1569 Lubai intalman, glas andath,
biad nan-anman n-indligtech,
nidadtlaithi dun frifcis
iarnhbiadaib blaithib Parduis.

1573 'A Euá denam cogle
pennait buan isatheirge,
corglanmais fiadrig narecht
ni diarcintaib, diartarmtecht.'

1577 'Dena mothinchosc dishain,
amothigernai, aAdaim,
húair nachfetar fiad cachrainn
cinnas dognither pennaind.

1581 'Dena mothinchosc coléir
iarth'intliucht, iardoglanchéil,
nadern féin forcraid nachthur,
naraib form essbaid d'oenmud.

1585 'Adram incoimdid 'mole
hitoe, cenchomlabrae[1],
eirggsiu isruth Tigir trén,
isragsa isruth n-Iordanén.

1589 'Trila trichat, torainn ndil,
dobith duitsiu isruth Tigir,
mésse in-Iordanén fosmacht
secht la caine cethrachat.

1593 'Beir let licc clochi cobsaid
fot'suidi, fot'choemchossaib,
corucsa limm licc n-aili
fochumma, fochosmaile.

1597 'Coraig incloich isintsruth,
dena fuirri fothrucud,
batuicse amalbiae comblait
coriae int-usce dobragait.

1601 'Thofolt scailti cechcruth cenmeth

[1] MS. hicomlabrae.

iarsinsruth forcachn-oénleth,
bi hitost frisnim sneid sain,
dorosc féig frisna nemdaib.

1605 ' Suidig dodalaim cechthrath
fríruirig nimc noe ngrad,
guid iarfirdul ciabé hitoss
imdilgud dot'immarbos.

1609 ' Nidarglain d'acallaim Dé
iartarmthecht, iarn-inglaine,
arnidat gleóir glethig gle
anhbéoil cthcich elnide.

1613 ' Aitchem nahuili duli
rodelb Dia triaglanrúni,
corguidet lenn rig narecht
imdilgud diartarimthecht.

1617 ' Deni inchruthsain domod maith,
ocus attaig infirslaith :
cororcoemchinni cogle,
nitgluase, nitchumscaige.'

1621 Secht la cethrachat cenlén
d'Adaum isruth Iordanén,
trila trichat d'Euai dil
hisruammaib srotha Tigir.

1625 Aingeil De cachlá donim
oDia dothorromu Adaim,
diaforcetal feib roddet
cocenn nóí laa ndeec.

1629 Rogaid Adam hitgi thren ,
iarum forsruth n-Iordanén,
cotroisced lais forDia ndil
conahuilib hilmilaib.

1633 Tarrasair insruth 'nathoss
diaremim, diaanforos,
inrigsruth diarith roan,
cotarddad dilgud d'Adam.

1637 IArsin targlammair insruth
cechmsl beo bái 'nacrisluch,

lín acuiri cruth rosgab
combatar huili imAdam.

1641 Rogadatar dilflinaib,
Adam, sruth is ilmflai', *Cilmilaib*
truag rofersat annual n-án
frisluag n-úag na nóí noebgrad.

1645 Corguiditis leo cenchlith   *Ogr. co ro gestis*
nahuili grada aCoimdid,
cotardad Dia dilgud nglan
cennach ndibdud doAdam.

1649 Gadatar Dia cotasgeib
nanoi[n]grad#i co[n]an-airbreib,
imdilgud d'Adaum hifus
diagábud, diaimmarbus.

1653 Dorigni Dia aragradaib
slandilgud cinad Adaim,
con-aittreib thalman cechthan
connem nallglan noebúasal.   *i. mór, adbal, uasal.*

1657 Ocus rodilig iarsain
diachlannaib, diachinedaib,
acht inthé natibri cert,   *o. is. Kil. pons tí.*
téis darreir nDe in-anrecht.

1661 Marrochuala Demun dub
dilgud dothabairt d'Adaum,
' ragsa iarfebai coglé
dochum n-Euae dorise.

1665 'Congstuc astsruth trathlás,   *Ogr. conda tuc i,i*
conasrucur rith forbás,   *q uasp Zlsi',*
corobadur ni diamud   *developed -s i*
'moacrabud dochumscugud.'   *Jr. conhastus.*
[fo. 23 a. 2.]

1669 Doluid Lucifer luath laind,
infáil feochair firthuachaill,
mar hela ir-richt angil gil,
coEua dosruth Tigir.

1673 Roraid ria int-angel rosmert
darlia, badiaairchisecht :

_____

¹ MS. hilmilaib.

'aEua fial crotha gil,
iscfan atái isruth Tigir.

1677 'A ben, ciarbogle dochruth,
rochoemcláis gné 'singarbsruth,
cenhach mbríg mbládbrais rofeis
rotmarbais[1], rotmudaigeis.

1681 'A ben, tair ardoDía ass,
nabi ní sia istsruth amnas :
dorí ruad romfáid forfecht,
uad tánac dot'iáirchissecht.'

1685 IArsain tic Euá asintsruth,
bai fortir cotirmugud,
dosfánic nél iarsétsain
cotarmairt héc cenanmain.

1689 Nihaithgen Eua cogle
Lucifer linib hilgne,
donbanscail febdai bá hirc[2],
báe amenmai icumtabairt.

1693 'A Eua, cid arnotgeib?
ismor dogni d'imrateib :
cucut glethánac donim
laforngairi De derbdil.

1697 'Tiagum ass dochum n-Adaim,
aben, nábi ichildalaib,
gadamar huili Dia ndil
imdilgud duib forcintaib.'

1701 IArsain dochuatar cotrén
corice sruth n-Iordanén,
coAdam, huastreba tor,
Eua án is Lucifor.

1705 Marrodeir(c)é Adam astsruth
forEua, for Lucifur,
rongab crith, balan dogail,
rol-lin grain gnuisi Diabuil.

1709 'Monuar, aEuá fechtai,
rotmera dothuicthechtai,

fer thánic iat forfecht foss,
ishé rotmert hiPardos.

1713 'A Eua truag, centucht údil,
cid dotfuc osruth Tigir,
cenforhgaire rig rechta,
cenahgel nglan coemthechta?'

1717 Maratchualá Euá insain,
reba adchosain Adaim,
dosfuit forlar, luid is-sás,
isbec nadechaid dianbas.

1721 'A Lucifeir, a Demuin,
cid 'moatai diarlenamuin?
rongailaigeis, cían roclos,
ronbaithaigeis hiPardos.

1725 'O roscarsatar arcuir
nacharlén, a Lucifuir :
triat'chuimleng itám hicacht,
nichuingem dochomaitecht.

1729 'Nisinn rogab domaithius,
nó rotchuir ot'firt'lathius,
nisinn rothimgair fochlid
dochor 'dodindgnaib richid.

1733 'Nisinn rogab nasosta
batar fout, ahanfosta !
nisinn rotscar frit'sluagu,
frit'cheolú, frit'hilbuadu.

1737 'Nisinn dotrat fochairib
ot'brúigib, ot'mormaigib,
condatfil fodeilb Diabuil
triabithu fobithphianaib.

1741 'Nisinn fotragluais donim,
ahanbhuais ! triat'imresain :
nisinn rotscar frit'gnim cain,
nisinn rogab th'airmitin.

1745 'Nisinn rotla ot'soillsib,
fotrochess ot'mórchoimsib,

---

[1] MS. rotmarmais.　　[2] MS. hairc, but with a dot under the *a*.

F.　　[IV. 3.]

dadotſail fodein toimdig
imbithphein, imbithdorchib.

1749 'Dochumthocbail frīrig recht
iarſīr dotrat in-amnert,
foſuarais mor doduilgi
triat'diummus, trīat'anhuimli.

1753 'Cidtái diarſagail hiſus
huáir dorralaid oPhardus,
& ronſlátais 'moarrhbethaid ṅglain,
& donrátais icomrarcain.'

1757 'INcuman lat, a Adaim,
nafuarus d'ulcc foıdagain ?
mochur domaig nirni nair,
m̄bith fothrúaigi digraid.

1761 'INcuman lat, aAdaim,
nafuárus d'ulcc fo[t]dagain ?
mochur acomṅnais aṅgel
in-hIſſern ṅdúr ṅdáirdaṅgen.

1765 'INcuman lat, aAdaim,
nafuarus d'ulcc foddagain ?
mochur fochrithdelm chaire
in-Iſſern cgt ṅgolgaire.
[fo. 23 b. 1.]

1769 'INcuman lat, a Adaim,
nafuarus d'ulcc foddagain ?
mochur aſlaith Fiadat find
itír ſſanḃrat siriſſīrn.

1773 'INcuman lat, aAdaim,
nafuarus d'ulcc trīat'dagain ?
mobith fochiabair cengrud
fodeilb Diabuil, fodóermam.

1777 'INcuman lat, aAdaim,
nafuarus d'ulcc fo[t']dágain ?
niraba conclịith, cenchath,
onló rodattuistigad.

1781 'Trúag [a] Adaim dodigail
trſat' dágain dún diblinaib,
dochursu abrug Pharduis hil,

ismochursa donaebnim.

1785 'Adfíaſa duit cenbréc m̄brais,
orṣam heolach set senchais,
ſ̄ib leir donralad donim,
& missi ocus tússu, a Adaim.

1789 'Diatarat Dia tinſed ṅglan
dochum dochuirp ſtalam,
rodeignad fricachduil tind
inlá rodelbad t'anim. ;

1793 'Diarotchruthaiged coglé
ſochosmailius deilbi Dé,
dian-erbrad fricach ṅduil ṅdil
cotisſad dot'airmitin. ;

1797 'Diarſáid Dia Michel donim
cucut sechcach, áAdaim,
conotruc foglanblad glan
doadrad inDuleman.

1801 'O r'adrais rig naręcht rinn
Fiadait ſīr ſoroll forſind
roidpart Dia cach ṅduil dẹin
tribithu frit'airmitein. ;

1805 'Diarſóed Dia Michél cachdú
con-aṅgliu, con-archangliu,
cotistais cenmerbi mod
doadrad adeilbiseom. ;

1809 'Diarſaid Dia Michel, mod ṅgle,
dochur cuarda secht nime,
cotuc nói noebgraid inraith
in-oendail cosinfirſlaith. ;

1813 'Roraid Michel frīm iarſīr
cotissainn d'adrad indrig,
cenſuirech, cenchoised cath,
combad me toisech tissad.

1817 'IArsain dodecad fodeoid
laforṅgaire maith Michóoil,
cotarrasar ſom'niab glan
hiſiadnaissi inDuleman.

1821 'Rorádi rinn inri rán :

'cluinid alucht nanoingrád!
tabraid uaib airmitiu glan
dom'chomdeilbsi, doAdam.'

1825 'Roraid Michel frisinrig
athesc firen cen dimbríg:
'cóir docachgrad cocruth chain
dochomdelbsu d'airmitain.'

1829 'Radimse friDi[a] asmothas
athesc feochair firamnas:
'nach bé Adam, herim ńgle,
óssar nańdúle n-uile?

1833 'IN córu insinser iarsreith
dodul d'adrad intsósair,
fó insósar, cendalbad ńdil,
ischóir d'adrad intsinsir?

1837 'Roraid trían intsluaig cogle,
etcrańgle isarchańgle,
roforgellsat fiadcachthur,
'isfír forsta Lucifur.'

1841 'IArsain rorade guth Dé:
'cluinte, a Lucifuir coglé!
bidhe intsosar bashuasal
cein beosa 'coadinduasad.'

1845 'Ciathfasat lucht noeńgrad cain
diaairmitnigud Adaim,
niragsa dó, digrais cruth,
huair imsiniu hituistigud.

1849 'Romla fochetoir donim
Día, triat'chinaid, aAdaim,
iarfrithtuidecht damsa amne
fríathimna, fri[a]forńgaire.

1853 'Uair nádernsam cuibdi ńglé
nahuimli fríaforńgaire,
ronfáid lín arsluaig [   ] sińg
cenbuaid indochum n-Iffirn.

1857 'A Adaim, ciabadhe dodúis,

nimmanfacamar dognúis,
triat'chinaid ronlad coglan
donimib dochum talman.

1861 'IArsain tarrasarsu hifos
dararn-essine hiPardos,
basónmech duit ascachcruth
manitissed cumscugud.

1865 'Rothacrus cogér iarsain
tren doratus domenmain,
missi hipfangubaib fogreis,
táesu ińgríanbrugaib Parduis.

g [fo. 23 b. 2.]

1869 'Amrubart brec cofoigli
frit fein, frit'mnai codailbi,
ismaith amrorfus mogus
conabtorlus aPhardus.

1873 'Atberim frit aithesc ńdron,
ancondnfis d'ulc is d'herchol
innim, hitalmain iartain,
isfrit dogen, aAdaim.

1877 'Mannérat cachni 'si[n]biuth
imdochlaind, imdochiniud,
icathaib garbaib cenchleith,
ińgalraib, itedmannaib.'

1881 O rofersat ańgriss ńglain
andíss ocan-imressain,
'dofuargaib Adam astsruth,
rofáid uádaib Lucifur.

1885 Bái Adam iarsain coglé
bliadain forbruig betha[1] ce,
cennech n-aili, foendul feb,
[.a] acht se oenur 'sa óenben.

1889 Centorud tren, delm ńglanna,
acht fér, cuit nan-anmanna,
cenbiad, centenid, centech,
cennós, cencheol, cenhétach.

1893 Ocool usci ṡabois buįlid,
dodig (aię) ṡorsnaglasluibib,
hifoscadaig nacrann ńglan,
inhuamaib tírmaib talman.

1897 Ruc Euá gein, cáin inbṛrt,
ṡochetoir rogab himthecht,
maith atreoir trebair diathreib
icbuain indíeoir diaathair.

1901 Fristoimsidir dath aṡball
soillsidir óen naretlann,
builid, ballda, bláidmar, bras,
badḃ, ṡeochair, ṡramnas.

1905 'ISṃaith robai Dia rind,
a hEua ṡossad, herṡind!
rombái mor domgáes hiṡus
triábáes naċh doṭromarbus.'

1909 Rogart Adam ainm diamac,
Caín[1] garb, cróda, comnart;
ranlin mebul ocus brath,
duine dremun, discailteach.

1913 O roairchis Dia ṡodeoid
doÁdam ichithiụndíeoir,
criċhid imroraid coglan
'ismithid cobair d'Adam.'

1917 Foidis Dia Michel, mod ńglan,
donim dochum natalman,
combṛíg caċhthoraid [　] dil,
is cosṡlaib écsamlaib.

1921 Cotart doÁdam iarsreith
ṡriadṃnad caċhsil sáindleith,
iscor'thinchoisc dó cogle
ordugud natrebaire.

1925 Rosdechraig dó ṡorlicc glain
caċhluib trícc ticc triathalman[2],
'sna huili aidmi corath
batardaiṅgne ṡritrebad.

1929 IS rothaiselb dó iartain

cech mil bgo bái ṡortalmain,
'dena tṛú'ṡognam coglan
andomnad, andegdamnad.'

1933 Secht ṁbliadna iarsain coglé
coruc Euá gein n-aįle,
doAdam, bṛcain íngíal,
mac diarbochomainm Abial.

1937 Togaide De, torum ńgle,
duine ṡirien, ṡirṡuirbthe,
robai iarcomṛam De dil
icṡognam diathuistidib.

1941 'Dotharṡas aslingge dam,'
arsi, arEua friAdam,
'ṡuil Abeil, condruine dein,
doọl huile doChaein.'.

1945 'Tabair domṃnmain insain,
amothigerna, aAdaim,
huamun lam'críde, lam'cheill,
Caín domarbad Abeil.'

1949 'A ben, coḃęrthair insain,
madmaith laDia ńderbdemein,
nibíat in-oentaig ṡriṡes,
biaid caċh díb innathegdais.'

1953 Dorigni Adam dáthech,
tech doceċhtarde ṡorleth,
tech doCháin, cain intrial,
ocus tech aili d'Abíal.

1957 Foidis Día Gabrial ńglan
conderbṡis scéoil cohAdam,
'Caín ciar, garbdai, cenchéil,
atá íctrial marbtha Abéil.

1961 'Acht naṡinnad Eua húad
inscel tṛúṡeba ṡírthrúag,
Caín ibas dig diaṡuil,
uair ismac diles Diabuil.'

1963 'Nacumscaiged tṛú ṡorcial
ciamarbaid Caín Abíal,

---

[1] Here and elsewhere I have placed a diaeresis over the *i* of this name.　　[2] MS. thathalmai n

rombia mac achrotha glain
diamba comainm Seth saindil.'
[fo. 24 a. 1.]

1969 Bretha doAdaum roclos,
cengabud íar[n]¹-immarbus,
sechtmoga mac ladis dein
achertchúmma d'ingenaib.

1973 Ri thuargaib dámac Adaim,
huasnatuathaib dermáraib,
Abél ocus Caïn caïn,
conaclannaib comnartaib.

1977 Ri rothidnacht dodoenib
domun conadegmóinib,
babuidech d'Abial ochein
is badimdach doChaeïn.

1981 Ri dorúasat oscachcruth
nocoderna asídugud,
Caïn cuilech, garg athríal,
iarsin coromarb Abíal.

1985 Dácét mbliadan, mellach miad,
ised roposlán d'Abíal,
nidalb, adfíadar ochéin,
coromarbad oChaéïn.

1989 INrí roraidi iarsin
rocachñ-oen dichlaind Adaim,
aracomaltis areir
conaromarbtais Caeïn.

1993 Ciphé nodmarba fonim
Caïn isincinaidsin,
nigebthar fríagnimrad gal
fair dobrthar sechtdigal.

1997 IArsain dorat mori réil
comartha inchuil forCaeïn,
arnabeth fochlith incol
dobrt cnocc foraheton.

2001 IArsin [ba]marb Cáïn cenrad

fescur inglind Iosofath,
diamben crann crom codocht dron
frisincnocc bái 'nahéton.

2005 Huair dorochair Caïn ann
inglinn Iosophath imgann,
ata fochoibchi chaire
centoirthi, centarbaige.

2009 Ri dorat Seth soer iarcein
d'Adaum inn-inad n-Abeil,
conidhúad silsat iarsain
clanna soera síl Adaim.

2013 Cethracha bliadan, níbalb,
adfíadar cenág n-ergarb,
foseth cengalar, cenchath,
coragaib inSeth síïad.

2017 Arcoimdiu gle corúinib
bae ré rianaprímduilib,
dorimgart corp dochrí chain
inrí doridnacht talmain.

Ri doridnacht² talam tlacht.

XII.

2021 Saegul Adaim, nirbogair,
cenbaegul cofessabair,
tricha dó, derb bai fó feib,
arnoicétaib dobliadnaib.

2025 IArsin tánic galar glan,
feib tic docach, for Adam,
robái fríïeba cachthucht
aben Eua fríaiduchi.

2029 Roñtir Adam adáil,
roráid fríEua findnáir,
' roscarusa rut isrot'chlaind,
isdongalursa atbailim.'

2033 ' Dirsan doDia, toirm nglan,'
arsi, arEua friAdam,

---

¹ Written as a correction over cen.   ² MS. dorignacht.

'nachbisiu friceto¹ ifus,
nachmissi téite arthuus.
1037 'Monuar isdochloemchlod chain,'
arsí, arEua, 'aAdaim !
missi trúag cennert hifus,
tussu dothecht arthuus.'
1041 'A Euá gleir crotha glain,
tabair coleir dot'menmain,
nocobia nacein isgle
sunn ipein darm'éssese.
1045 'ISgarit ciabe cenbrath
re robáe euerarcruthad,
nibia fogras, isgne ngle,
acht nó[i]mís darm'hessese.'
1049 'Abbair frim cenlocht, afir,
cid dogéin fria'chorp coemdil ?
arisderb lat t'éc díshain,
amothigerna, aAdaim !'
1053 'Nachamtaidled cos nalam,
natath duini domhétran,
cotistar oDia donim
d'ordugud mochuirp coemdil.
1057 'Lecid mochorp, cain inmod,
innachacht cenchumscu[gu]d,
derb limm lessaigfid mochrí
insaerdenmaid domrigní.
1061 'Érig, ahEua cogrinn,
ocus heirg itchrosfigill,
foid huait fordeis Dé, aben,
m'anim cogle fornaebnem.
1065 'INdanim dorigni Día dam
hé rostimgair coinglan,
taet euce cohuag diathreib
icoemthecht sluág doangleib.
[fo. 24 a. 2.]
1069 'Aben², nimdana iarfir

immadala moidegtíg,
indferg dorigni, réim ngle,
bann baide ocus trócaire.
1073 'Attaig, Eua, inríg ráin,
coti iarfeba im'chomdáil,
menithí frim'dichial nden
cotí Michial archangel.'
1077 Ataig Eua, insoe forlar,
congul cogoe, codermar,
frite n-uare nodossaig
cotruaigi, conderfadaig.
1081 'Arco-fuin damsa, amoríl'
arsí, arEua cocoemlí.
'incoir iarth'adrad hifus
dún labrad hit'frecnarcus ?
1085 'Meit mochuil, met mophectha,
manimbé set sirhettla,
menitabra dilgud dam
nochomtha labra langlan.'
1089 Fillid aglúni forlar
Eua truag durí chomrád,
'frit arí richid moder
conomthi inmilid Michel.
1093 'Doglanad anma Adaim
diascarad fríadualchaib,
dia imthus, iarndul forcel,
cori arbri archangel.
1097 'Érig, aEua, donlár,
glerib rochlos dochomrád :
rosiacht dind richid doscel,
dotriacht inmilid Michel.
1101 'Dochuaid aanim ochurp
Adaim, haEua coemcucht !
coraig cen grain, cain in dúis,
coda díslaim, achoemgnuis !'
1105 Dodechaid² Euá iartain

¹ e written as a correction over the first t of tete.   ² MS. Aaben.   ³ MS. Dodochaid.

coluath indochum n-Adaim,
cofuair Ádam, met *ngra*da,
centinfissin n̂-anala.
2109 Uair nacuala cocruth chain
guth Adaim diaacallaim,
roscloi aciall cenchoimsi
*fr*icoi cian, frisirthoirsi.
2113 'A Eua, tocaib dorosc
ocus daim dun dothinchosc :
suidig th'imcaisin n̂geir n̂glain
súas coleir donanemdaib.
2117 'A ben, tocaib dognuis n̂glain
dodescin anma Ada[i]m,
feib immurchurthir cogel
et*er*arbri archangel.'
2121 IMsoidi Eua iarsain
dodescain anman Adaim,
*con*facca inn-anmain cóem ciuin
Adaim icoemthecht Michiuil.
2125 INtan bai Eua iartain
icaithni anma Adaim,
*con*facca chuici farsetaib
sluag n-an̂gel *co*classchetlaib.
2129 Confacca Eua riastsluag
saraphin, saer ahimluad [1],
cain intretel dofórgaib
cotrib hettib forórdaib.
2133 Confacca Euá iarsin,
iarsindaeor donoebnim,
*fr*iataitnemchi rosochta
tri heoin gela etrochta.
2137 INtan bái icdeiscin nan-én
Eua féssin cenimlén,
ama*l* ruithni dogrein glain
for*f*emid an-imcasain.
2141 Rochlos inchlas conem nél
nanoebban̂gel im*M*ichél,

rosernsat sreith cosúaire sein
'macuaird immaltoir n-Adaim.
2145 Congabsat claschetal coir
indán̂geil immonaltóir,
roloiscset luib fiadca*ch*drun̂g
dianidainm ornam*en*tum.
2149 Rosined indethach thren
codiriuch triasinn-ahér,
cor'oslaic, cenchoimsi n̂gle,
doirsi nafirmiminte.
2153 Conoebthanic Dia donim
dofrestul anma Adaim,
inrigruiri uascachdu,
condessid 'narigsuidiu.
2157 Luid fiadinrig ran, reim n̂dein,
oenan̂gel án doan̂gleib,
sephain cogr*i*nn çoel n̂glain n̂gil,
bái athoirm dind fo *sech*t nimib,
2161 Foguth inchuirn, cohog án,
doluid slog na *nói* noebgrad :
batar fírdruine acliar glan
fiadrigsuide inDuileman.
2165 Concanat, cainiu rétaib,
fochliaraib, fochlaschétlaib.
isb*en*nachta inca*ch*than
ardrí nan-uile n-adbar.
[fo. 24 b. 1.]
2169 Roslechtatar huili iarlar
sluag n-uag nan-an̂gel noebnár :
rogadatar coDia n̂dil
imdilgud cinad Adaim.
2173 'Dochomdelbaid, amori,
tú doru[a]ssat donephni :
heralmit *f*ort, comul n̂gle,
ardodeirc, ardothrocaire.'
2177 IArsain rofáid inri ruad
saraphin cohoponn uad.

---

[1] MS. ahimluag.

iarleittreib rotoeb naslóg
cosnahettib dodergór.

2181 Coragaib anmain cenches
Ádaim coroda bades,
isruth nasirdruṅg nasnau
indatinum ciriasu.

2185 Cotuc lais anmain ṅgil ṅglain
Ádaim amlaid asruthsain,
orosuidig marthuis tan
f[i]adágnuis inDuleman.

2189 Fodoralaid fein forlár
anim Adaim coc[o]emgrád,
'naligu, fiadinrig ruad,
bái friré teora primhuar.

2193 Cotarat inri iarsain
laim fochenn anma Adaim,
cennachcathim, cáin inscel.
corosathin doMichél.

2197 ' Nibadicheoil, toraind ṅgle,
aMichéoil, friamórgaire,
anim Adaim sunn ifus
rodosamaig hiPardus.

2201 ' Beir inn-anmain ṅgil ṅglain
Adaim áin conaairbrib :
suidig fodiglaim cengreis
isintresrigrainn Parduis.

2205 ' IN tertio carlo,' arDia,
' dianidainm Ficconicia,
bid ann centaidbsin pene
coamsir nahesseirge.'

2209 Nahuili grada cachdú,
eterangliu isarchaiṅgliu,
babind aclasschetal ṅglan
icmolad inDuleman.

2213 Ardilgud d'anmain Adaim
diaphecthaib, diadualchaib,
arabrith cengrisse ṅgress

¹ MS. rocechlaig.

arisse dochum Parduis.

2217 Ola thrócaire duib sunn
isindluib ornamentum,
tabartar imchorp n-Adaim
diaglanad diadualchaib.

2221 Tri hanairt slana, soer sain,
ecortar imchorp n-Adaim,
ocus atnagar coléir
fritaeb adnacuil Abeil.

2225 Corp arsenathar Adaim,
iarn-eladnaib ildánaib,
ochéin fogarbchacht báis brón,
coroadnacht in-Ebrón.

2229 Robai ann fothromthur thenn
cotoracht toungur ṅdilenn,
corp Adaim fodalaib dron
congradaib 'naadnacol.

2233 Trethan dilenn oscachmaig
ismor n-frenn rocechlaid¹,
dothuc doAdaum achenn
coruc coHierusalem.

2237 IArsain tarrasair incenn
indorus Hierusalem :
centrist roclannad iartain
croch Crist icolaind Adaim.

2241 Ianus² arthus trianarath
torogart ainm De Athar,
ocus Noe, nassad ṅdil,
cétnadarinnscan arim.

2245 Nocorogenair fonim,
dochiniud Eua isAdaim,
duine badchoimiu, corp criad,
inda Noe mac Lamiach.

2249 Cethrur gelda, gnimraid gúir,
febdai adfet inscriptuir,
sinium saegul oscachmaig
batar 'sindaimsir toisig.

² i. e. Enos.

2253 Mathusalem, érim úgrinn,
bahe ingradgemm riandilinn,
Noe, Sem slán, balaech liath,
isinmael Melchisediach.

2257 Ochtṁbliadna sescat, niscail,
arnó[i]cetaib dibliadnaib,
cenbaigul raith, rethaib renn,
saegul maith Mathussalem.

2261 Coic cét bliadan iarngaes gle,
issed robae in-aes Noe,
intan breth do clann, cain miad,
Sem, Cham ocus Iafiath.

2265 Tan tanic diliu, delm n-uag,
darsinṁbith, darsinmorsluag,
issed bai in-aes Noe cenchlith
secét caini dobliadnaib.
[fo. 24 b. 2.]

2269 Secht lá cethrachat ar cét
bái Noe 'naairc, ba derbret[1],
iarndilinn, triamna comblait,
bai tri cét bliadan archoicait.

2273 Noifichit secht ṁbliadan bínd
bai Sem mac Noe riandilinn,
ado trifichit cotgaib
iarndilinn arcoiccétaib.

2277 Melchisidech, saigtis slúaig,
anaimthis incachglanbuaid,
iarset cenbaegul cotgaib
sáegul secét dobliadnaib.

2281 Ri rodrósat oscachrainn
dechnebur dóib donchetclaind,
innandalaib, tolaib grinn,
otha Adaum codilinn.

2285 Adam la Seth, srethaib iath,
Ianus, Cainan, Malaliach,
Iareth fial, fichtib rót,

ocus int-amra Enóc.

2289 Mathusalem, serce nasluag,
ocus Lamech, linib luad,
ocus Noe, noithech trell,
rosnái uastonnaib dilenn.

2293 O Adam, herbág arclann,
cotarscur ndermar ndilenn
deichfichit bliadan, buaid ṁbil,
cethri deich ardibmílib.

2297 Otha dilind, troeta sluag,
coAbram n-amra n-adruad
ado sescat, sliucht cenchlith,
dobliadnaib arnóicétib[2].

2301 O Adam coAbram n-án,
congradaib glanmam comlán,
trimili miadbla imchloi nglicc
cethri bliad[na] isnoifichit.

2305 O Abram, cenbaisi becht,
cotanic Moisi ahEgept,
nisechnada forcheill cain,
cethracha archoiccétaib.

2309 O Adam, cenbassi bruig,
coluid Moisi Muir Romuir,
ocht bliadna fochet foli
secht cet isteoramili.

2313 Otha Moise, monor ngle,
coDauid macc n-Iesse,
cenbet, cenbaegul[3] cotgaib,
saegul coic cet dobliadnaib.

2317 Otha Adam, comul ngle,
coDuid mac n-Iesse
cethri bliadna sescat slig
archet archethramilib.

2321 Otha Dauid, cenbaig ṁbroin,
condici brait Babiloin
sesca noiṁbliadna buana

---

[1] Written as a correction over nocobréc.   [2] MS. arnoibcetaib.
[3] After *e* an *i* seems inserted by a later hand.

ocus cóic cét cohuaga.

2325 Otha Adam cosinbrait
Babiloin bai foblathblait,
noirhbliadna cethrachat gní
secht cet cetheoramíli.

2329 Otha inbrait, brechta rainn,
cotuttacht Crist icolaind
coic cét, ciaragla (sic) cachalt,
ocus sé bliadna sescat.

2333 Mad oAdam docachslóg,
congénair mac De dimór
cóic míli iscét, cialla cacht,
ocus sé bliadna nochat.

2337 O gein Crist, cétlach cét mbla,
cohár cetach nacethra
míli fonóibriaguil recht
acht dioenbliadain de[e]c.

2341 O Adam nañglorgrad ñgle
comórár nan-hinnine [1]
se míli, mod ñgíalta ñglicc,
cethribliadna nóifichit.

2345 Tan tanic indígail truag
forhinnilib nan-iltuath,
citnirig rechta, reim ñdein,
robatar 'sindamsirsin ?

2349 IN-amsir Cinaeda cain
meicc Maelcholaim forAlbain,
forherainn cenlethrainn lainn
doChinaed mac Maelcholaim.

2353 Ocus Briain forMumain maiss,
Donncad forLaigniu lanbrais,
isCathal forCruachain chain,
ocus Eochaid forhUltaib.

2357 IS Fergal nan-airech n-ell
forAilech rebrach Rigrenn,
mac Conaing, meic Neill congail,
flaithri sluagach sil Eogain,

¹ Sic. Read indile.

2361 Ocus Dubdaletha lóir
forsretha sil hErimóin,
súi cosaidbri segtai rainn
osmur maigni meic Alprainn.

2365 Othalinus, línib slog,
bamac donOtha hermor,
baforñgairthid uascachmaig
inresin doRómanchaib.
[fo. 25 a. 1.]

2369 Batar dárig, reil asliucht,
fornadathír immuir n-Iucht,
Hlothair² forFrancaib congail
ishEtgair forSaxanaib.

2373 IS Maelcoluim, cetaib ngal,
riambuidnib broga Bretan,
coñgelgart cechcomlainn cain,
degmac Domnaill meic Eogain.

2377 ISsindaimsirsin, cet glonn,
robái loñgas nacúllom,
hicsaigid forcachgním ñgarg
Danair atírib Danmarg.

2381 Ohsain cobráth, brígach beirt,
nidamsnímach etercheirt,
nifail innim nach hicrí
tuccas sain acht monaebri.

2385 Ardri grene, gle roclos,
ishé dorigne Phardos,
isferr cachrig, rigda achruth,
nifail crich forasaegul.
Saegul Adaim nirbugair.

XIII.

2389 Ri roráidi frisil Seth
comet añgnim cocomtren,
cenoentaid immuich nataig
friclainn Cain miscadaig.

2393 Cendula darséis nosmacht

² MS. Blothair.

dartimna indrig dorosat,
foriagail roithenaig réil
cenchardes friclaind Caeïn.
2397 Cenimcloemclod/maine mass,
cenluige, cenlanamnas,
cenchuibdi clethi *no* cuil,
'céin bethi *fordruing*¹ domuin.'
2401 Roaintadaigsetar iarcein
sil Seth *ocus* clann Caeïn,
corothuismiset iartain
trenfir *ocus* trenchoraid.
2405 Clann Chaïn *ocus* sil Seth
roóentaigset cocomthren,
condeochatar dar*cach*smacht
d'adrad idal isarracht.
2409 Romiscnigsetar Dia ndron
achlanna cenimmardol,
corochinn iarnaṅgnimaib
atabairt fothromdigail.
2413 INri corath ríge droṅg
*frisnagaib cath *no* comlonn,
cain conoibi, blaith alii,
ferr *cach* ríg rí roradi.
Ri roraidi frisil Seth.

XIV.

2417 Ri roraide athesc n-an
friNoc‿nassad n-imlán:
'sil Seth dochótar darm'reir
hiclemnas clain[n]i Caeïn.
·421 'Rochummaiseset ciabtarglain
friclaind Cáïn miscadaig:
romsaraigset asca*ch*cruth:
dursan dam atuistigud.
2425 'Huair dochuatar darmosmacht
coclaind [Caïn] cet n-arracht,
dardreich ndomuin, tromsruth tenn

dolecub tonng*ur* ndilenn.
2429 'Dilegfat claind Adaim huaig
cobrugib betha balcbuain,
dos*bér* uili imbas imbath
otha *tur*cbail cofuined.
2433 'Acht Noe ocht*ur* diathreib
nilécim doclaind Adaim,
imbethaid doshin nahóc
acht infer amra Enóc.'
2437 Mori dorosat ca*ch*treib
robae ré rianaaiṅgleib,
atrohet ca*ch*ri cengr*a*in cest,
inri roraid inn-athesc.
  Ri roraidi athesc n-an.

XV.

2441 'Cluin, a Noe noithig, cenlen,
  doticfa diliu trom, trén :
'dentar lat, fr*i*srethad slóg,
het[h]ar dírecra, dimór.
2445 'Adluthath tarbach iartain
dobii isdobitomain,
dofid Lebain, línib clár,
trethaebledach trén, dermar.
2449 'Coica cubat, nignim gr*a*ch,
isintaibled ichtarach,
cethorcha 'sinmedon mud
isintricha 'sinduachtaruch.
2453 'Cethrib sostaib, slicht 'sindairce,
odrumlurgain codrum[s]lait,
sesrachaib sreth soer tr*i*ablait
conespadaib oenchubait.
2457 'Comet centoirsi, centór,
atoimsi cenimfordol,
afot, alethet, luad ṅgle,
eter isle *ocus* ardde.
2461 'Coica cubat, gnim cenbáes,

¹ Sic. leg. druim?
F 2

innalethet centogaes:
    [fo. 25 a. 2.]
tri chél cubat, comul ṅglan,
hed bad[1] fot adrum*lurgan.

2465 'Tricha coir cubat cenchleith
innahairde icomsreith,
frisruam sniges donim noeb
ador*us* assafirthoeb.

2469 'Senistir fritoimsi dein,
frisoilsi, friimcaissin,
innahairdde armosmacht
cenforcraid *acht* oenchubat.

2473 'Hilar n-adba n-amra n-úag
caingnim glanbda fr*i*aimluad,
srethaib sretta fr*i*sid sain
lin leptha dolanamnaib.'

2477 Ri rothimgair imca*ch* ṁbuaid,
romisenig fingail fo[r]rúaid:
nitlaith rotuaslaig delm de,
roraid 'nachluasaib 'cluinte.'
    'Cluin, aNóe noith*ig* cenlen.'

XVI.

2481 R i roraidi fr*i*Noe nar:
    'heirg isinn-ethar n-inislan,
tu isdothrimeic namma,
ocus forcethri cáintmna.'

2485 P*i*rcoba, cainiu ca*ch*fiach,
setig Noe meicc Lamhiach,
mna natr*i*mac, monar ṅgle,
Olla, Oliua, Oliuane.

2489 Sessiur doclainn, cain amfad,
batar icNoe ma*c* Lamfach,
trimeicc mathi, milib lá,
ocus teora ingena.

2493 Sem saer asinser[2], sliucht ṅgle,

                     [1] MS. bae.

innaclainni cruthaige :
genatar fritindrem tlacht
ingen et*er*ca*ch* n-oenmacc.

2497 Olla ben Sem, soer fr*i*aháil,
Oliua ben Chaim choemnáir,
Oliuana, baigthi treith,
asósser ben Iafeith.

2501 Ri dorimmart, nisluag suail,
inaire Noe f[o]roenhuáir,
dineoch rothecht muir istir,
lanamain ca*ch*oenmil.

2505 Innán-adbaib, tiag cenail,
ba sluag mór dolanamnaib,
conalóintib, lathar ṅgle,
isdiambiadaib techtaide.

2509 O rolínad indarc huag
robái indigal forimluad:
adfiadar sir, forum ṅgle,
babriathar rig roraide.
      Ri roraidi fr*i*Noe nar.

XVII.

2513 R i tharlaic sruthlind snamaig
    dodilgenn clainni Adaim,
acht oenchethrur fer namma,
ocus acethri óenmna.

2517 Ocus Enoc crabuid guir,
amal adfiad inscr*i*ptuir,
aoenur othuinn dothuinn,
am*al* ca*ch*n-ethait etruim.

2521 Snegdatar sruamma donim,
romebdatar tr*i*athalmain,
fortuili doib, tola ṅgle,
cethracha lá ocus aidche.

2525 Airdde nadilenn olar,
feib adfet scribenn cóemnar,

                     [2] MS. asinsfer.

cuicprimchubai[t] dec cencleith
rosiacht suas osnaslebih.

2529 INtan conscerthar cachñdúil,
amal adfet inscriptúir,
ishe airet sain rosaig
lassar lái brátha brethaig.

2533 Donech robai imbethaid bi
dorosat Dia hicoemchrí,
dosrat indiliu fothracht
acht inrothecht indoenbarcc.

2537 Ri nimi nair, nassad ñglé,
rí conic traig istuile,
ártuassi cachmbrig, cachmbrait,
huaisle cachri ri tarlaic.
    Ri tharlaic sruthlinn snamaig.

XVIII.

2541 Ri sáer rodosás cogle
    Noe lin amuintire,
cethracha archet lathi lenn,
diambai fothonnaib dílenn.

2545 IArsain rogab techt forcúl
indiliu troeta tremúr,
rorathaig Noe nañgabud
indíairge doimthragud.

2549 Fóidid Noe thechtaire uad,
infiach fechtaide fonnluath,
dus infagba sliab no srath
no iath forsatarrasad.

2553 O fuair fiach abiad fodéin
immaig forcarraic, forsleib,
forachulu cosceol gle
nithanic doridise.
    [fo. 25 b. 1.]

2557 Huanduair thall Noe acheill de
dondfiuc[h] dub delaidi,
conacart fein, febda bainn,

    ¹ MS. tirmim.

iarsain cuca incolaim.

2561 Ri cengrain, cengrís, cengríss,
nimíall bith innahcisleis,
nicli choel, iscoem ali,
inri saer rodosassai.
    Ri sáer rodosas cogle.

XIX.

2565 Foidis Noe incolum ñglan
    uad forinlinnmuir n-allmár,
dus infagbad, hérimm ñgrínn,
talmain trein tarbaig tírimm ¹.

2569 Focheird incolum, cuairt ñgle,
iartimnu, iarforñgaire,
cotoracht inn-aircc cenbrath
nífuair ait forstarrasad.

2573 Roreraig ² Noe uad alaim
arcenn incolaim coemnáir,
cotuc cucai amuig, mod ñgle,
combai im-medon nahaircce.

2577 Combái Noe sechtmain iarsain
centaidbsin, cenimcasin,
dibith buan acht fairggi fraig
dithuaith nótir no talmain.

2581 ISsindochtmad lathi lainn
fó[i]did Noe uad incolaim,
dús infagbad diachuaird chain
taidbsiu dothir natalmain.

2585 IArtrath nona, noithi máil,
tic incolum 'nachomdáil,
dochum Noe, nassad ñdil,
iscroeb dophailm 'nabelaib.

2589 Maritcomnairc Noe fodeoid
inphailm ingulbaun indeoin,
roderb lais, lith cennachcol,
dochuaid diliu dondomon.

2593 Roattlaig buidi dondríg

    ² MS. Rirorig.

robáid inmbith conabrig,
arasoerad, srethaib sell,
dothonngur dermor dilenn.

1597 Huair nachtoracht tren infiach
cofis scél domac Lamiach,
ishé fath incholuim gle
iarsain rofaidi Noe.
    Fo[i]dis Noe incolum nglan.

XX.

1601 Tarrasair, batromm, indarcc,
    amalbis long forfoentracht,
    foglere roslessaig Dia
    forslessaib slebi Armenia.

1605 Ri roforcongart cogle
    forNoe lucht nahairce
    athuidecht immach coglan
    asindaire dochum talman.

1609 IArtuidecht doib asindairce
    ri roraid friu foroenaitt:
    'nabarsflaid frisid sain,
    linaid inbuili talmain.'

1613 INDecimbir kalainn, cáin benn,
    luid Noe fortonnaib dilenn,
    iquint kalainn Mai iarndia
    doluid forsleib Armenia.

1617 Adropart Noe, nuall cencleith,
    edpart uag uad donComdid,
    frilegad cachdruing dorhell
    iaruernam dothuinn dilenn.

1621 IN rí roradi iarsain
    friNoe conachaemclannaib:
    'toirthi indomuin docechleith
    tairrcaid, tomlid, tinolaid.

1625 'Nibartorbae, érim n-uag,
    diliu thromm troeta trensluag,
    hicein atchethi uaseachmaig

intuaig nimi n-illdathaig.'

1629 Mori niclethach cenchrad
rofallnai inn-ethar ndermar,
orian dorian, foraig thaig,
cosinsliab forstarrasair.
    Tarrasair, batrom, indaircc.

XXI.

1633 Ri rotidnacht bith mbuidech,
    otha turcbail cofuined,
    mainib maccraid, mo cachfiach,
    dotrib maccaib meic Lamiach.

1637 Ri rodelb dreich domuin duinn,
    roselb sreith sobáil saerdrúing,
    rohuc cendith, fochucht chert,
    acrich iarfut, iarlethet.

1641 Crich talman cechcruth imracht,
    brig bladmar, bruthmar, breccbárc,
    orian Deprofane anair
    síar [co] colomnaib Herccail.

1645 A lethet, atuaid fades
    diafethet buáid nadimchres,
    oRiphi rigtcrib imra
    codithreib nan-Etheopda.

1649 Mori, nachdoimm diachlannaib,
    raroinn itribrigrannaib,
    [fo. 25 b. 2.]
    roainmnig ingleochu[fa]ird glicc
    Assia, Eoraip issAffricc.

1653 Ri dorat Eoraip nan-iath
    dochlainn[1] amra Iafiath,
    cotuasciurt n-Assia triablait,
    cosrethaib srotha Eofrait.

1657 Ri rothidnacht dochlainn Chaim
    inn-Affraic n-uasail n-imslain,
    cosin Romuir, ruathur cert,

---

[1] MS. clainm.

eter Assia *ocus* hEgept.

2661 Saerchlann Sem diatarat Dia
primrann airegda Assia,
osruth n-Eofrait, nimtha sain,
cocricha airthir domuin.

2665 Coicmeic de[e]e, digrais scel,
robatar laIafeth,
asecht fichet laSem slan,
iscuiciur laCam coemnar.

2669 Ciabeit fribrig mbladmair mbrais
indríg óstalmain telglais,
ferr cachrig rindbalcc nareth
ri doridnacht [1] bith mbuidech.

Ri doridnacht bith mbuidech.

XXII.

2673 Sluáig sil Adaim, aidbli druing,
condanaib domuin dessduind,
rodomnad, ostrebaib dal,
dofognam Demuin codermar.

2677 Ondairiur astorgaib grían
cofuiniud, forgal firian,
rodamnad, fodigail dacht,
d'adrad hidal isarracht.

2681 Onduair atbath Noe nar
coaimsir n-aurdairc ú-Abram,
nifrith dib oenfer foleith
nohetraiged inCoimdeid.

2685 Rodiullsat an-Dia ndil,
roliunsat infirchretim,
tair *ocus* tiar, tess is tuaid,
rodasgab cess conglanbuaid.

2689 Arcathbarr cenduithi dath,
isbrathlaing brúithi bidbad,
nidúi doi indrongaib artuath,
arsúi soi slonnaib arethsluag.

Sluag sil Adaim, aidbli druing.

XXIII.

2693 Rogenair fer maith combuaid
fonél cachnaith Nemruaid,
focan scel cachdruing dualaig,
robotrén foriltuathaib.

2697 Nemruad sein, *mac* Ceo, *mic* Caim,
tuargaib agleo comorgrdin,
gnim tuir othalmain cenmeth,
corissed lais inriched.

2701 Ropomilid, milib gal,
ropfoglainntid, ropfelsam,
ecnaid ermaith cachdana,
ropóhergnaid ilgrada.

2705 Lais cetnaairnecht insain
arthús dochlannaib Adaim,
athomus coglé conglain
indre eternein istalmain.

2709 Doroemaidir, bith combuaid,
anair, siar, fodes, fothuaid,
tirib, tuathaib, tolaib sreth,
mflib, stadib, linib leth.

2713 Senchaidi sil Adaim ain
targclamtha lais in-oendail,
scela dochein leo roclos,
feib réil rolathi aPardos.

2717 Feib rothimgair Caïn cíar
cetnafingail forAbíal,
feib rodiglad, scél doléir,
forsil Seth, forclaind Caeïn.

2721 Acht Noe aochtur fobrón,
'nahethur luchtmar lermór,
clann Caïn, sil Seth nasen,
dorigni indiliu andilgen.

2725 Frithalem rig nimi nél,
flaith cachafini firthrén,
nitharda fornn, delm triagail,

---

[1] MS. dorignacht.

digail seirb seirgthig samlaid.

2729 'Gabaid mochomairle nglain,'
arNebrúad friclainn Adaim,
' forbeir fornem, nassad ngrinn,
ocus nobsaerfa ardilinn.'

2733 Maithgein mairre mo cachmiad,
cathgeib congaire gorfad,
ingrian gluair goires cachngair,
cenmair tuaith diarogenair.
        Rogenair fer maith combuaid.

XXIV.

2737 Rochomarleicsetar iarsain
      airig sil uaibrig Adaim :
' ropadferr dun, tola gle,
techt 'narcorp dochum nime.

2741 ' Turebam tor ndermor olár,
denam friDia comthocbal,
gniad cach huan immasech,
beram conoibi nemthech.
      [fo. 26 a. 1.]

2745 ' Acht rissam nemthech ndaingen
in-oentaid nanoebangel,
nirtora diliu, tren all,
isdemin nachhepelam.'

2749 Forcongair Nemrúad forcach,
conglonnaib gelgrúad coemrád,
athuidmi, frigaile ngair,
frimuinbi maigi Sennair.

2753 Sennar mac Sem, srothaib iath,
hua doNoe mac Lamiach,
sechtmad mac fichet Seim slain,
oroainmniged mag Sennair.

2757 Dorinolsatar intsluaig
dognim tuir noithig Nemruaid,
túargabad, batren indail,

coriacht súas osnanélaib.

2761 INri nadrelic doib sain
rostairmesc tria hilberlaib,
conatucad nech cogle
cid notharged diaraile.

2765 Ri dorat oenberla doib
riacumtauch intuir Nemróid,
roemnastar doib triagart
comtar ado sechtmogat.

2769 Ri dorigni scail intsluaig,
hé rothairmesc tor Nemruáid,
dochuaid glaini ahergnai
dochoemthecht achomberlai.

2773 Ri rodechraig claind Adaim
archéill[1], archruth, argradaib,
nihairim claen, cain insmacht,
dachenel saer sechtmogat.

2777 IArcomarlib Nemruaid nair
cosonardib nasaerdáil,
cenlen istrén rodamert
inscel rochomarleicset.
        Rochomarleicsetar iarsain.

XXV.

2781 Ri rochar Abel nan-iath,
      Seth, Noe, Melchisediach,
Enoc ocus Loth, lith lan,
ocus int-amra Abram.

2785 Rí doraiga Abram n-án
arfirinni aoenuran,
sechsluag sil Adaim nangal
batar icadrad idal.

2789 Rothairnger d'Abram cechmbuaid
arathuidecht omorthuaid,
aradula leis fodess,
rambiad tir bithdiless.

2793 Ri rothidnacht do tír Caim

_____
[1] MS. archeil.

ocus clárbruigi Cannáin,
comba *f*orba dó iartain
diaclannaib, diachenélaib.

2797 Ri lasindeochaid fodess
condnanacair[1] ambithles,
luid lais Loth, linib lathar,
fodes, ma*c* aderbrathar.

2801 Ri ránic doglinn Mamrai
dothegdais Abraim amrai
fodeilb trír, digr*a*is insmacht,
diatormailt inn-oegidacht.

2805 Ri asbe*rt f*riSarrai slan
noberad ma*c* doAbram,
*f*orb*e*rtais achlann iartain
comtis leir fiadgenemain.

2809 Ri rosaer Loth conachlaind
diasai inmnái icoirthi salaind,
diatard digail, deilm n-amra,
*f*orcathracha Sodomda.

2813 Ri rodail d'Abrám[2] ce*ch*toir,
doma*c* Thaire me*i*c Nachóir,
romsaera *f*orcrochad p*f*an,
ri reil rorochar Abial.

    Ri rochar Abial nan-iath.

XXVI.

2817 Ri dorat d'Abram insin
     frisilad, fri*s*frtuistin[3],
isairdirc, *f*obetha barc,
ma*c* diarbochomainm Isac.

2821 Ri dorat d'Isaac, babuaid,
ocus doingin Bathuail,
uaidib genatar, lith lor,
Issau ocus Iacob.

2825 ISsau slechtach, slicht imracht,
roboserccach laIssác,

isIacob, con-idnaib ail,
ropoinmain lfamathair.

2829 ISsac *f*ridead n-aissi,
glead gnima glangaisse,
badluim degóir, dramm datta,
basenóir dall dinerta.

2833 Rogaid s̲éire foramac
cenleire, linib legart,
*f*orIssau cofargbad ail,
cotarddad abenn*ach*tain.

2837 Bai Rabecca iccloistecht *f*ri̇s,
ingen Bathúail ceneislis,
coruc ahoscor coglan
dochosnom nabennachtan.

[fo. 26 a. 2.]

2841 INhed bái Issau ictr*i*all immach
'sin sliab iarf*i*r frifiadach,
doluid inben tr*i̇*ahet n-og
cotrét nooisce Iacob.

2845 Goromarb menn moeth immaig,
rodṁberb fo*f*eth dolubaib,
gnim d*i*an coṅglére imracht
corothriall sére d'Is*a*ac.

2849 Rofuaig crocenn inmind mói*r*
tr*i̇*abáig imlaim n-Iacóib,
fochosmailius lama Issau,
gnim dana ciarb'immargú.

2853 Rolathair coluath, lith n-og,
amathair dolacob,
asraracht centreithi tr*a*cht,
cotarat s̲eire d'Issác.

2857 Tan ruca*d* intsére dron
coIssaac diachubuchol,
richt Issú sluagach, slicht n-óg,
bahuamnach laIacób.

2861 ꞌFail sunn sére sainglicc sláin

---

[1] Perhaps *connanacair*, as there seems a punctum delens over *d*.
[2] MS. dambram.   [3] Written as a correction over *-thuicṡiu*.

Ω   [IV. 3.]

duit, ameic airdirc Abráim [1],
laIssau saergrínn, srethaib sluaig,
lat'ma*c* n-oebind *con*-ilbúaid.'

2865 'Nician bai hIssau icseilge,
manidgau dó triachoemcheilg,
mochthánic astsleib isgle
mase thuc insérese.'

2869 'ISme dorigni inseilge séig
*for*sinché*t*naleirg dontsléib,
fuair hifocus, gleiri gair,
adbar seire dom' athair.'

2873 'Nabi icimrigi *for*huáid,
ameic ingini Bathúail !
nithu Issau semnach naslóg,
*ach*t istú int-enga*ch* Iacób.'

2877 'Nacathaig fr*i*m, asruith ran,
aathair, am*ei*c Abram,
frit' seirce ṅg*r*aidgr*i*nn ismé Issau,
fritt niráidim immargau.

2881 'Tuc huait fr*i*imdel n-achtach
dam doláim dialáma*ch*tad,
cofessur cogle ingnim n-óg
inhe [Is]sau no inne Iacob.'

2885 'Gia dobér molaim it'laim,
nichel, atu hit' choemdáil,
ataigen, istú rommalt,
tren dogní mochumtabart.

2889 'Doma*c* Issau [2], irgna buaid,
ocus ingen binn Bathuail,
doig ambith foaengne gle,
coir doib ciabtis cosmaile.'

2893 'Bess isshé Issau, slicht n-og,
bess noconhé Iacob,
bess isglé m'esbaid im'gaes,
bess ismé fil *for*togaes.'

2897 Senfoccul sein ochéin móir,
laca*ch* sruith, laca*ch*senóir,

nimedar mall immasech,
*ach*t corbdall bidamarsech.

2901 Duni truag, docharda, dall,
loburda, lubrach, lanmall,
olcc athairsin imgaes ṅgle,
iarscaichsin achétfaide.

2905 'Tomail inséire soer, sláin,
anoeib, am*ei*c ain Abraim !
hith dochuit fr*i*t' gnássad ṅglain,
duit ropsásad sainemail.'

2909 Dorumalt Isáac iarsain
inséire cosobarthain,
tuargaib adflaim at*r*aig
isródail abennachtain.

2913 Linib glang*r*ad, cruth imracht,
e*t*r Abram is Isaac,
inbennacht targbad dontslóg
cotarddad do Iacób.

2917 Dasechtmbliad*na*, cenbaes mbroin,
iss*ed* bái in-aes Iacoib,
cain adrann ca*ch*tucht rothecht
intan ruc inpr*i*mchinnecht.

2921 Huair dorat inséire sáim
diaathair doma*c* Abraim,
arbuamun abráthar diabrath
nifitir cid dogenad.

2925 Asbert fris amathair maith :
'heirg *for*teched riat' brathair,
caemgnim caindelb[d]a cengr*a*in,
cotreib lainderda Labain.'

2929 Luidis Iacob conabuaid
dothig Labain me*i*c Bathuail,
bacain condolbtha cenbrath
inbaid lommartha cairech.

2933 IArsain condasfuair immaig,
itoeb indliss lainnerda,
diingin congili andath,

    [1] MS. abaraim.   [2] MS. issac.

cenbini ocnigi acairach.

2937 Até batar ann foſeib,
fiadchuirib clann ocáireib,
imgil, cenglora, cengrain,
dſingin lola Labain.
[fo. 26 b. 1.]

2941 Roraid frìu ingilla combúaid :
‘cia airm sunn fil mac Bathuail,
brathair momathar, mod n-án,
fer dianidcomainm Labán ?’

2945 IArsin ferſat failti frìs,
riſin̄gilla cenciſlis,
luid indaranai, bareim ran,
diahinniſi doLaban.

2949 Atraig Laban, lŀníib gal,
’mach arcenn meic aſhethar :
ferais frais forſailti frìs,
dambeir frìnais diathegdais.

2953 Rothairgid Laban lán log
aringaire doſacob,
cach huan bec badubbrecc dath,
cach uan liath, cach uan alath.

2957 IAcob noſernad sreith
iſnahoimrib uiſcidib,
flesca beca, brecc andath,
arambelaib nacairach.

2961 Natreoit chairach immaſech
icſegad naſlesc finnglan,
datha naſlesc cotagaib
hed nobid forſnahuanaib.

2965 Tuc adiingin iarſein
Labain, lór cenimreſſain,
iarnathimgaire frìhail,
d’ingaire caire Labain.

2969 An-anmann cengnim caire,
radait auctair ecnaide,

Lia ligda, linib gial,
ocus indrigda Rachſal.

2973 Bái inailt incechtarde
ocnaſethraib sochraide,
an-anmann, cenmedra mael,
Bala ocus Selpha sochain.

2977 Robatar uli mále,
etir ſethra is hinailte,
cengrain, iarcomdeddaid choir,
icomlepaid oen Iacoib.

2981 Bertait cethri meic ſothri,
dó frìbríg bailcc ſoglanli,
ochtur[1] onaſethraib sreith,
cethrur onahinailteib.

2985 Cuit cachamna dib foleith
diaclaind choir inacomsreith,
feib roſern rí run cachcruth,
isferr dún andeligud.

2989 Semeic la Lia, lini[b] gial,
ocus damac roRachial,
rí bethra bailcc rodaſcar
cethra maicc nadacumal.

2993 Ruben, Semeon, Leui lor,
Isachar soer, Zabulon,
Iudas iarn̄Dia ce[n]terce (?)
ſé meic Lia liuchdeirce.

2997 Neptalim isDán dana,
dámac buadacha Bala,
Asser isGad, delbda dé,
da mac Selpha sochaine.

3001 IOſeph an, aurdairc ochein,
ocus inbán Beniaméin[2],
rogabsat cathairi gſal
damac rachaine Rachial.

3005 Dámac dec sin, cen[n]ach gráin,
Iacoib hui Abaráim,

---

[1] MS. uiii.   [2] MS. ben iaméin.

G 2

cona[n]dechraib inca*ch*threib,
conacethraib má*th*rechaib.

3009 Sechtmoga bliad*an* bai túaid
ifail Labain m*eic* Bathúail,
corothríall diathir, din cert [1],
conadibm*ac*caib dé[e]c.

3013 Tan tánic Rachial atúaid,
ingen Labain m*eic* Bathúail,
dorigni thargleo t*r*abrath,
tuc lea lamdeo áathar.

3017 Doluid Laban lonn 'nandiaid,
et*er*mag ischaill is[s]liab,
*con*dastárraid, cenchess ngle,
tess immedon intslebe.

3021 Maratehonnaire Rachial rán
ingen lainnerda Labain,
luid as f*or*leith, lathar ndu,
ama*l* nobeth fr*i*idnú.

3025 Dorat Rachíal chorcra, chaem
lamdeo aathar sís fotaeb,
roclos agol, rochlai dath,
ama*l* mnai beth iclamnad.

3029 Romert Laban, linib gial,
indaban f*or*srabi Rachial,
nirbobés leo, luth n-alta,
lamachiad mna lamanta.

3033 Ferais Iacob combúaid
failti móir f*r*ímac mBathuail,
conarlaic do, congrad gle,
siriud slán nasaccr*a*ide [2].

3037 Huair nafuair alamdeo ann
bai inbangleo nar'imgann,
tuargabad leo f*or*sinmaig
carnn comluga iscomchotaig.

[fo. 26 b. 2.]

3041 Carnn inchotaig sin lac*ách*

cennach*n*dfl cocaid cobráth,
et*er*chlainn laind Labain lóir
*ocu*s clanna Iacoib.

3045 Aingel De thimgair ca*ch*slog
bai lcimguin fr*i*Iacob,
rofersat cath, comul ngle,
cenbath arfut nahaidche [3].

3049 Rodbi int-aingel saer, nisneid,
Iacob sechbil asceith,
isós*a*in [4], aidbligthc [5] inscél,
roa[i]nmnigthe Isra*he*l.

3053 Luid techt con-ascadaib húad
oIacob, cain int-imlúad,
coIssau soid, basliucht ngle,
dobith doib 'nanbráthirse.

3057 IArsain rotharngert Issú
cain glanb*er*t, nihimmargau,
ambith cenances, nadchres,
'na cardes, 'nacomathches.

3061 Cenolcc, cenfingail, gnim ngle,
iartimnaib nambrátharse,
cenmeingg, cenmebuil, cenbrath,
cendebuid, cendolbanrad.

3065 Meicc Iacoib, ilar ambla,
hit meice sethar doDina,
Sechim m*a*c Ammoir, t*r*abrath,
romarbsat lucht achat*r*ach.

3069 Dásecht mbliad*na* bai if*us*,
forecht riagla, fochádus,
corothimart, cota mert,
dó thochta iúr n-Egept.

3073 Ri doraega, digr*a*is gair,
Iacob húais sechabráthair,
*con*id diaclaind, crichid scel,
dáthreib dec mac n-Istah*e*l.

3077 Mac-tharngeriaid De donim

---

[1] MS. cért.   [2] MS. saccr*a*ige.   [3] MS. nafaithche.
[4] MS. hisoshain.   [5] MS. aidbligthi.

bagart glangeltaid coemdil :
isbreo osbri nan-abb n-án,
inrí dorat doAbrám.
    Rí dorat d'Abram insin.

XXVII.

3081 Dorarngert Iacob coglan
    diaclaind inlin robatar :
'bethi uli frífessa feig
hirrichtain lessa Ioseiph.'

3085 Foidis Iacob, gec congreim,
Ioseph arsét coSechçim,
cain céim fodiud óthreib,
combiud éim diabrathreib.

3089 O rosiacht coSechim slán
Ioseph 'coambai incél comlan,
fofuáir ann fer, forom ngle,
icimthecht achonaire.

3093 Roiarfacht dó infer féig :
'can dodechad, cid notheig ?
cid condaige, adbul gair,
nocia foratai iarair ?'

3097 'Dodeochad m'oenur¹ om' threib
combiud donabuachaillib :
amscith, amtrramain cachthóir,
foriarair mac n-Iacoib.'

3101 'Meicc Iacoib, congloir glain,
mased hitái 'coniarair,
isnaraidaib rodoscar
atat imthaebaib Totham.'

3105 Dodechaid Ioseph iarsein
corocht Totham coabrathreib,
assan 'nalaim, luath aruth,
marclach fuirri dobiud.

3109 Arachind tinolsat dail
meicc Iacoib hui Abráim²,

roraid cachdib ris 'mosech :
'innhe seo int-aislingthech ?'

3113 'A bráthriu, fegaid fornglóir,
nádenaid ni basécóir,
cia nomthoirsed ni dorath,
ni foirbsi notaiscérad.'

3117 'Monuar nocomaith dochial,
aIoseph, ameic Rachial,
rot robaeth cengáes nglinne³,
derb rotogaeth t'aslingge.'

3121 'Anromidair moDia dam
etir doinib intalman,
ni chumaing nech uaib trrabáig
athormach nachadigbáil.'

3125 O shunn atches ochein móir
fís doIoseph mac Iacoib ;
rommiscnigsetar fosmacht
abrathir trra imformat.

3129 Luid colón doib isinslfab
Ioseph conglor, conglanmiad,
cocrait 'nambrathreib abrath
dial-lathreib conaragad.

3133 Rofóemad leo abás fosmacht
menisoerad morígmac,
nirn-anacht airdmes roclos,
nochairdes no condolbos.

3137 ISsindinbaidsin amne,
iartimnaib ríg noemnime,
    [fo. 27 a. 1.]
doEgept conglor, congraig,
luid lucht mor dochennaigeib.

3141 O recait fríu forsinmaig
Ioseph ossar, ambrathair,
bafó líth luidi, luad cert,
combo fríth itúaith Egept.

3145 IAsse mac Sechis, slicht ngle,

---

¹ MS. monenur.   ² MS. abraim.   ³ MS. nglinni.

batoissech nacennaige,
diabrathrib fein, febda tríall,
isse dorúacell[1] Iosiaph[2].

3149 Putrífaris, forom cert,
issé baherri Aegept,
tuc arIoseph, diamba imbrait,
tríchait leth n-unga n-argait.

3153 Aes Ioséph intan rorith
hitír n-Egept fría[3] derbdith,
congaes gelbda fochucht chert,
secht mbliadna derbda déec[4].

3157 Dásecht mbliadna, baivaid becht,
bái Ioseph itír n-Egept,
cotoracht[5] atúaid iartain
colacob conamaccaib.

3161 Batar icachtaib iarcein
fosmachtaib huaislib Ioséiph,
doIacób, bagnimrad cert,
rofirad feib dorarngert.

   Dorarñgert Iacób coglan.

XXVIII.

3165 Ri conoebi oscechthreib
   rofaidi ríanabrathreib,
cengoe, cengaili, gnim cert,
combóe fodaire in-Egept.

3169 IArsain rorith, babúaid becht,
frítoisech ituaith Egept.
cachmaith buan combai dó ífus
dorat dó auagcommus.

3173 IArom rodacar aben[6],
intigernaí doruacel,
tríaaslach n-imthach fochlith
dorimgart 'nacomlepaid.

3177 Roraid fría ingilla coglan :

'nihetragim dala ban,
ocus mé indaire centreóir,
m'oenur itirib anheoil.'

3181 Roradi fris inben blaith :
' natabair laim frim doraith :
anf dobiur duit amne
fail mor nech lasmadbuide.'

3185 ' Aben, bendacht fortgnúis ñglain,
nachamluaid dot'baethbriatraib,
inhed bambeo, buaid ñgelbda,
nifellub form'thigerna.'

3189 Roscrutai inben coleir,
uair naderna ingilla aréir,
forsinñgilla ñglan cenchol
cinnas doberad baegol.

3193 ISeed roscrutai inben baeth,
ónarabi ifus inlaech,
ingilla dothecht nachthan
le coseotu istech talman.

3197 ' Tair lim dodeiscin mosét
agillai, nihinmarbréc,
oslaic reom aglas dontaig,
aIoseph caem Cannanaig !

3201 ' A fir, tair remum istech,
narbamcrímnach comrairgnech,
uair nadigthim, fri set slán,
istech ñdorcha m'oenurán.'

3205 IArsain luid Ioseph istech,
nirb'anhumal imrisnech,
nifitir inmnai diabrath
combai iarcúl nacomlad.

3209 Huair forfemid uascachcruth,
iarñglerib, aðentagud,
doIoseph, bagnim n-etig,
imforbart fair forecin.

---

[1] Written as a correction over rochennaig. [2] MS. ioseph. [3] Written over cen. [4] MS. deac.
[5] MS. cotorś : over í is written ⳰ acht. [6] a written as a correction over in.

3213 Atrullai uaide immach,
assalamaib lomnachtach,
rohéige inben nert acind,
roscar friféle firthind.

3217 Tarraid ag fodofre tróig
doIoseph án mac Iacoib,
achor hicarcair, gním ṅgann,
fosmachtaib iṅguforgall.

3221 Ardri búan betha broenaig,
connic buaid cach primoenaig,
cengaili arcli cotangaib,
ri conoibi oscachoentreib.
        Rí conoebi oscechthreib.

XXIX.

3225 Doarfas fís, foromm cert,
doForann, dorig Egept,
nifrith dó cosúidib srath,
diadrúidib nech dosfucad.

3229 Nifrith frigeirchert osmaig
Eigept conafortúathaib,
ecnaid no drui no súi snéid[1],
nech dosfucad coglanréid.

3233 Badebthach Foraind friathúaid
corogail rolaind rorúaid,
        [fo. 27 a. 2.]
fridruidib duithib cachtreib,
friasuidib, friaecnadeib.

3237 Batar fri sothochta serc
dácomalta icrig Egept,
sechcach fridálaib[2] cachtreib
'nagradaib, 'nachomarleib.

3241 Friatoil togaig, friaig thaig,
'nachoraib, 'naglanchocráib[3],
indarafer d'Egept comblait,

araili glechert d'Affraic.

3245 Batar cenancess rochlos
'nachardess, 'nachomaltos,
babráthair máthar, mod ṅgle,
cechtarde dib diaraile.

3249 Gaid rí Affrici doib, delm n-óg,
combad tadchrethi dodergór,
feib sogabtais oscachrainn
acht coromarbtais Forainn.

3253 IArsain triallsat folaimm fair,
forForainn, forsinn-ardflaith,
indarafer feimdeth gail
arba d'Egept aathair.

3257 INfer aili d'Affraic áin
fricathslait cairi comlain,
tarmlaic acholainn fricath,
tarmmairt Forainn domarbad.

3261 Rohirgaibthi lasinrig,
rodirgnaithi fodimbrig,
fofuctha icachtaib cocfan
isincarcair colosfaph.

3265 Doarfas aisliṅgthi dóib
'sindaidchisin fochetóir,
hicacht carcrach crimnach [   ]
basnimach amenmandrad.

3269 Ruc Ioseph doib congloir gle,
breith cóir foran-aslingthe :
feib baderb tarbaid triabrath
baatnlaid rochomallad.

3273 'IMmárach indarafer,
nibagrádach, crochfaider,
biad araili, slanaib síd.
iṅgrádaib icondardríg.'

3277 Bae inri, foglámaib gne,
dodálaib aaisliṅgthe,
dondleo lerggach, nirṁbai bin,

---

[1] MS. ssneid.   [2] MS. frídalaib.   [3] MS. cocracráib.

baſergaċh ſṛiadegdáinib.

3281 Atchúaid do int-óclach, gnim ṅgle :
'nabi ſorsnim th'aisliṅge :
ata 'sincharcair cenchess
duini t'apthaib tuaslaicſes.

3285 'Fer ruc breith ſorſís, ſorruth,
ſorndís bámar icumriuch,
ſeib rotharṅgair achſall chain
[is]samlaid ſorcoemnacair.'

3289 IArsain tucad ſograd cain
Ioseph án asincharcair,
ſiadshúag Eigept, amra bainn,
combai iſrecnarcus Foraind.

3293 Roiarſacht Forainn ſadein
dó fiadintslúag coglanléir :
'nirbatruag, innis doscel,
ciatuath duit no cíacenél ?'

3297 Atchuaid Ioseph corath,
coſossad, coainmnitach :
'nicóir gó fiadríg coṅgráin,
atúaid dam, acrích Cannáin.

3301 'Nihed domthahair ſograd,
m'athair bahúa doAbrám,
int-Abram adrann ochein,
nir'bunad ſann doChalldéib.

3305 'Ata hitarṅgeire ochéin,
sain, a Forainn conglanchóil !
bidlán de inbith bladmall, bán,
donDia dian-adrann Abrám.'

3309 'Tarſas' dam fis, ſúaim n-amra,
romloisc gris ahetarba,
nech nosſuaslaiced, ſuam cert,
niſuar d'intliuchtaib Egept.'

3313 'Aisneid inn-aislingthi n-an,'
arIoseph alainn imnar,
'cluinem uait centris, cenilas,

indſís cinnas dotarſas.'

3317 'Andommarſas, ameic raith,
duitsiu dalſas cechṁbithmaith,
diambera breith ſír ſorsein
nibia dſl ſorth' airmitein.'

3321 'Bidbreth ſír beratsa, aſlaith,'
arsé, arIoseph inbithraith,
'gním gle ſríollblad cechcruth,
cendolbad, centuscurnud.'

3325 'Secht ṁbai metha tarſas dam,
secht ṁbae caila, clú n-ingnad,
na secht ṁbae caela, clú gle,
duatar na secht ṁbae remrae.

3329 'Secht punainn lána dogran,
secht punaind seṅga, saeb dál,
na secht seṅga, ba truag tra,
duatar na secht granmara.'

3333 'Cocúala inguth 'coarad rim,
cluinti, a Foraind nadandind,
[ſo. 27 b. 1.]
ismor indrún, ruathar ṅgle,
fíl ríathur it'aisliṅgthe.

3337 'Tabair domenmain cenbrath,
delgnaid docachintliuchtach,
bidlán bith ſonelaib bla
doscelaib naſissisea.

3341 'Diambera breth ſírí fair,
ſorsinn-aislingthe n-ingnad,
indmass domuin dotrega,
dohúaig ſein abithdoéra.'

3345 'IN ſer ſoil beras breith ṅgle
cocoir ſorsinn-aislingthe,
cendoimme diss nambrig ṁbrass,
roinne ris doſlathemnas.'

3349 Cor'ſaillsigder duit cenchess
int-aisliugthe laind landes,

---

gnim cadla, agillai cengr*ain*,
attaig Dia n-amra n-Abraim.

3353 'Rotbia límm airmitiu intslóig,
rotbia gr*ad*, rotbia onóir,
maſſraid duit ácachcruth
indfissiu doſuaslucud.'

3357 'Tuctar dam gr*emm*ann cencr*ád*,'
arsé, arIoseph cosoergr*ad*,
'ſeib tarṅgir dochomrad cloth
cocomlan diacomollud.'

3361 'Rotbia lim gr*eim* Dé ſodéin,
rotbia m'ordan coglanleir,
gr*í*an *ocus* esca 'mole,
muir istír, dru(ch)t isdathe.'

3365 Atchúaid Ioseph dó cogle,
doFor(ai)nn ahaislingge,
*con*adlumaib dluthaib dein,
[is]corunaib riagaltaib.

3369 Macán Iacoib cosinrath,
bahé inliacoir lainn luágmar,
ósglaindírge 'nagnim cert,
rogab airrígi n-Egept.

3373 IN*t*-aislinge luágmar, lín cert,
bahuathmar lasluag n-Egept :
am*al* teidm torainn atass,
ſíss doForaind doarſas.
    Doarſas ſís, ſoromm cert.

XXX.

3377 R i tríarath doraiga ochéin
tr*í*aimcasin réid roréil,
combai Ioseph, lín asloig,
ósEgeipt uasail ardmóir.

3381 Secht ṁbliad*na* lana mole,
sommá, slána, sonaidé,
ógab Ioseph gloir garta
coaimsir namórgorta.

3385 Fotroirgell, bagnim cialla,
Ioseph cocenn *sech*t ṁbliad*an,*
nagebad, cidmor insmacht,
etach, nahor, nahargat.

3389 Nigébed Ioseph nachfiach
onatuathaib *ach*t madbiad,
caiṅgnib cainib, ciniud cert,
diadliugud doríg Egept.

3393 Rothinolad lais insain
naſuair fr*í*sna *sech*t ṁbliad*naib,*
'naduinib trénaib daingnib,
innaindsib eradblib.

3397 Dosrocht gorta garbda, garg,
dosrort ſr*i*ſodla ſodard,
rodascr*í*n cenchoimsi cruth,
roslín toirsi isderchainiud.

3401 Doratsatar uili arbiad
tuatha Egept doIosiab,
cidmór rothechtsat ſosmacht
et*er*or ocus argat.

3405 Doratsatar ſéin dondríg
an*d*oire dochinn ambſd,
natiastais aidid ṅgorta
innalainib lomnochta.

3409 Rosbiath Ioseph sechcac*h*claind
sloig fer n-Egept imForaind
ſogne riagla, ruathar n-án,
ſr*i*ſ*é* c*óic* ṁbliad*an* comlán.

3413 Rosbiathastar fiadcac*h*sluag
cenrad ſr*i*Forainn findrúad,
s*é* c*é*t dec mili, m*o*d ṅdil,
arſichit cet domilib.

3417 Ce[n]mothat dala dligid
aes dana ocus primſilid,
druid diana doca*ch*maig,
cruitti cíſara, clesamnaig.

3421 Cenmothat mogaid, m*o*d cert,
sluag soraid ſr*í*timthirecht,

ísmna bana, buidnib blá,
meicc ána ocus ingena.

3425 Cenmotha insluag roslin mairg,
natuath trúag ascechoenaird,
tietís iarn-elluch fosmacht
dochennuch itír n-Egept.

3429 Rí rombennach oscach maig,
cenon, cenolcc, cenerbaid,
gorbomál cach maige móir
Ioseph án mac Iacóib.

[fo. 27 b. 2.]

3433 Ruiri richid, rigda gáir,
crichid cachcuirid comláin,
areli fricath oscách blái,
inri triarath doraegai.

Rí triarath doraega ochéin.

XXXI.

3437 I Sindara bliadain, luad ngrínn,
ór'gab ingorta gerthind,
huid clann Iacoib, bagnim cert,
doluaig bíd itír n-Egept.

3441 IMrulat dargarbaib[1] gelt[2],
iartirib amraib Egept,
il-lurg intslúnig, trúag atli,
cosintuaith imbái int-ardrí.

3445 Roslín mertain, rosgab cess,
diafechtaib otir díles,
cenergna n-eolais, centreóir,
cenbérla itirib aneóil.

3449 Roptar sním aig[3] iarsétaib
diangnímaib, diambaethbétaib,
fiadnasluagaib oscechmaig,

truagaib, tursig, dércóintig.

3453 Meirtnig rostacht amenma,
rosnart fochacht comfedma,
cennech diabreith, leo baceist,
cosinn-airríg an-atheisc.

3457 Lotair triamedon intslúaig,
broccaig, naconnim comthrúaig,
congabsat foss, febda fír,
hifrecnarcus indardríg.

3461 Foidis techtairi tind huad,
aracenn cogrínn, coluath,
amal atgeoin ingnim cert,
airri airtmitnech Aegept.

3465 Tinsit andúine fotrdig,
fillsit glúine fochombáig,
roslecht diadúis diadoss[4],
fiadagnúis 'nafrecnarcus.

3469 Roiarfacht doib, derb roclos,
Ioseph congloir, cenamlos:
'raid[id] afír dúir forngair
can duib no can tancabair?

3473 'Cid condnaigid 'narmbrúig bras,
cenairig, cenífreolas,
cenbérla fritlad relta,
amal áes ndian taiscelta.

3477 'No maraes mbraith foraig thaig,
bis ochathraig dochatraig,
censcribenn lib, línib drech,
censcela ríg no ruirech?

3481 'Nimtha forsamail sunn se
acht mad aes braith ísligthe[5],
no álebbaire loittit smacht,
no brécaire icbrecairecht.'

3485 'Donrímmart gorta congrain
attuaid acríchaib Cannáin,

---

[1] Over dargalaib. [2] Over gart. [3] Over miscnig.
[4] *Sic.* Snould it not be *reslechtsat dia ndúis, dia ndoss?* [5] MS. íslidte.

fríarn-adlaic uaig, huar'crích cain,
feib tecait sluaig fer ṅdomuin.

3489 'Fonrathaig tir Caim ochétu
arn-athair badoChaldeib,
roalt cengrís gaibt (*sic*) cengrain,
bamac Isaic meic Abráim.

3493 'Bráthir sinn huile martám,
lín arcuire 'sarcomdal,
icgaire arn-athar naċthan,
ismac aile arṁbrathair óssar.'

3497 'Masofír[1], fríheraim n-án,
forṁbith iarmui doAbram,
tucaid huaib etere ṅgle
fritichtáin doridise.

3501 'Tan tissaid arcúl nachtan
lib diatf inbrathair ossar,
forbia forn-eitteire fein,
isdogéntar forn-ogreir.'

3505 Riandúla doib forafecht
diatfr conacennaigecht
il-laim indairrig fríandail
doratsatar Issachair.

3509 Roraid Ioseph, scél cenchess :
' dogress dogen forṁbithless,
inceċhuair formbia farṅdail
uaimm duib árDia n-Abaraim.'

3513 IArsin dochuatar diatfr
feib fosruácar cendimbríg,
rofucsat frítascaid tróg
ascaid arDia doIacob.

3517 IArum rancatar diataig
soera, slana, somenmnaig[2]:
dosfarraid maith fogloir glain
flaith lóir 'sindarabliad*ain*.
ISindarabliad*ain*, luad ṅgrínn.

XXXII.

3521 Roattlaig Iacób án
diaChoimdid, bagním com-
lán,
feib fuair achlann, glanlír cert,
fáilti laairrig n·Egept.

3525 Feib rostríall fochaiṅgnib ciúin
in-iathaib aidbli aniuil,
rosnalt cenbét osceċhmaig
dosrat forsét sainemail.
[fo. 28 a. 1.]

3529 Feib dosfuc forcúl, nicress,
óscaċhmúr conamorless,
atichtain buidig diatig
isdiaruirig roatlaig.
Roatlaig Iacob án.

XXXIII.

3533 Dorigset comarli cóir
maccrad amra Iacoib,
andul iarfithisi fecht
doridisi itír n-Egept.

3537 Dochuatar iarsétaib slain,
cenbétaib cethirn comlain,
cotren tluachtar dareaċhtír
coruactar cosinn-ardríg.

3541 Fuaratar colór cenhír
fáilti mor icondairrig,
feib bamellach laceill cóir
rosṁbái cennaċh fochetoir.

3545 Gabais Ioseph escra n-úag
atnaig il-laim fir diasluág :
tabair tríahaccail diambrath
isaccaib naCannanach.

3549 Nidimraig lotar diatfr,
nibdardimdaig dondairrig,

[1] MS. Mafofír.　　　[2] MS. somennaig.

feib roellacht doib cechtriall
bai ambennacht forIosiaph.

3553 Tan batar naifni arinmaig,
amal bid mfli onchathraig,
rodloṅg, nimebul diadail,
drong dremun dian-irgabail.

3557 Nibtar foichligthi fritóir
rocro[i]chligthi fochetóir,
tuctha colúra donmaig
foracula donchathraig.

3561 Tuctha coneoch rostechtai,
'nacimmidib cumrechtai,
batrúag afatal cenbríg
combatar fiadinn-airrig.

3565 Frisrogart int-airrí dóib
roraidi friu fochetoir :
'truag dodail farcuire ṅgle
farṅgabail uili icmeirle.

3569 'Uair lib[si], ni lathar ṅdil,
inmeirli cenimressain,
infarcin clothach asbiur
forcrochad cosinn-oenfiur.'

3573 'A airri Egept cenchess,
rosatglechert friarlanles,
niclothach dot'búaid, dot'blaid,
·   trúaig dochrochad cenchinaid.

3577 'Niheol dún, ciacol fogréin,
dur dron doBeniamein,
fonralaig mairb mesetha mir
dodalaib indescrasin.

3581 'Fortgellam cech ṅduis, din cert,
it'gnúis, aairri Egept,
arn-idain, fiadtestaib Dé,
dochinaid indescraise.'

3585 'Tucaid dochind forn-anma
uaib aitire n-eramra,

farn-ósarbráthair fodéin,
dianid comainm Beniaméin [1].

3589 'Éirgid [2] iarforsetib snéid,
isleicid Benieméin,
huair isleis, lith [3] cesta ṅgle,
frith escra naEgipte.'

3593 'Ossar naclainne, gnim ṅgle,
fir foxal fainne fíre,
issé isdiliu diarslog
liarn-athair, lalacób.

3597 'Guidmit ní, menipgrain lat,
dii, aairrí nahEgept,
cia rondairane dot'réir,
coronsaera Beniemein.

3601 'Mad marb duini fonim glass
dochumaid, isgnim n-amnas,
bid marb Iacob fodein
diachainiud Beniemein.'

3605 'A maccrad Iacoib áin,
frigartrad dochlainn Abráim,
cenchlothchobair, cennach ṁblaid,
dorochrobair forcinaid.'

3609 Rorelsat ascel cenbríg,
roslechtsat fiadinn-airrig :
'fortgellam Dia, dana de,
darslana onchinaidse.'

3613 'Tabraid forcobais centláis,
rad forais riandig tiugbais,
failsigid fornech nith ṁbras,
dorinnsid gnim n-imamnas.'

3617 'Ciambadlonnbrass digal Dé,
fornn bacomadas friarclocnré :
coir ciaroncrinad colár
icinaid artargabal.

3621 'Ronbaidsemmar, bagnim trog,
rocraidsemmar Iacób,

[1] MS. beniamin.   [2] MS. Heirgib.   [3] MS. liith.

romertsam coem diarṅgnáthaib,
rorecsam arn-oenbrathair.

3625 'Atmora arcinaid donbrath,
nidarn-idain diarsócrad :
     [fo. 28 a. 2.]
tríallamm arn-aided, scel ṅgrínn,
tiaganm fochlaideb ṅgérthind.'

3629 'Nirbochoir dam forṁbádud,
fota ataid in-imgábud,
targa fortacht De fortóir,
achiniud amra Iacoib !

3633 'Bidbann buada forarṅdáil,
ahiarmhui uagdai Abraim !
gengnim ṅgessi, tríadil ṅgair,
iss messe rorecsabair.'

3637 Rodosmachtaigset foalaim,
roattlaigset acomdáil,
sníset cocóir acainti,
rochisset armorfailti.

3641 'Fuapraid cotenn, nibartroig,
eirgid arcenn Iacóib,
cenlen, islethan forcert,
tren fortrethan in-Egept.'

3645 Ri dafuc atúaid iartain
Iacob conamaccalb,
dialotar fodess forfecht
foainm Ioseph in-Fgept.

3649 O sunn rancatar fodes
coIoseph hicomaithches,
ani badech docaᴄhthreib
dorat Ioseph díabrathreib.

3653 Robai Iacob, bagnim cert,
censním itírib Egept,
malle fríachlainn conamblait,
dábliadain arsechtmogait.

3657 Mori coragrad ochéin
dofuca Abrám oChalldéib,
hé cotnarlaic iarcóir cheirt

doib anisin dorigset.
Dorigset comarli cóir.

XXXIV.

3661 O shunn atbath Ioseph án
     nisṁboe sacre nosaergrád :
fir Egept, comeit cloine,
dosratsat fothromdoere.

3665 Rodosdairsatar diaréir
iarn-ec indamrai Iose[i]ph,
daire amlaid, eraim ṅglé,
nitharlaid forbith buidé.

3669 Mor dochlainn, batrog [inscél,]
beirthi dislog Israhel,
cosuilib dessaib, deilm ṅdil,
conbenᴅais assacennaib.

3673 Mor daceᴄhulcc, nabucert,
fodaimtis fosluag n-Egept :
nibai dóere badteinné
comarbdais aprímgeinné.

3677 Ciarbothromm andoire dacht
robae anDia 'coafortacht :
inmet fordiṅgtis intsluaig
forbartais incaᴄhoenhuair.

3681 IOseph mac Iacoib áin,
meicc Issaic, meic Abaraim,
dorumalt, fririagla recht,
deich fichit bliadna in-Egept.

3685 Dochuaid forcel, cluithi cin,
forslicht sen súithi soerdil,
facbaid dámac, maith aṅgraim,
Mánnases ocus Efraim.

3689 Dorumensat caᴄh fosmacht,
fosrugensat fir Egept,
diambúaid, diammathius, díamiad,
cosinn-uair atbath Iosiaph.
     O shunn atbath Ioseph án.

XXXV.

3693 Rogénair Moisi, mod ngle,
    in-amsir natromdóire¹:
rolad, ciarbochain achruth,
ass hisruth Níl diabádud.
3697 Conafuair Termod, gnim cert,
ingen Forainn rig Egept,
'condsruth, icinnlat alám,
cainbe fial, forssaid, findnar.
3701 IArsin colorngart diamnaib
conotuctáis asintráig
inmac mbec incrotha glain,
uair dorat Dia foamenmain.
3705 Rodacar Termod iarsein
feib caras cách aoengein,
coron-erail, bacain glonn,
baforgo diadegaltrom.
3709 O shunn roalt combatrén,
diall friclaind mac n-Israhél,
dochuaid ifat fiadcachclaind,
narbomac d'ingin Foraind.
3713 ISsu cenlen, lúad nglanna,
cenathair trén talmanna,
forfailtig gnim gle cachthuir
'sindaimsir irogénair.
Rogénair Moisi, mod ngle.

XXXVI.

3717 Cotranic lá forsinmaig
    frioendiis icimsergáin,
indaranai diachlainn cheirt,
araili badoEgeipt.
[fo. 28 b. 1.]
3721 O shunn atgeoin, narbotrén,
infer dochlainn Israhél,
bahe ingnim garb ceuchcrt,
romarb infer ahEgept.

3725 Rofitir intúath cogle
fer domarbad doMoise,
feib leir dorigned cocert
atchuas doafrrig Egept.
3729 Forfúacart Forainn cocert
forferaib amraib Egept,
nabeth dó dín innachdu
acht abas no ahinnarbu.
3733 Dodeochaid Moisi forfecht
forteched riasluag n-Egept,
iartfrib, iarslicthib srath,
cofarnaic indingenrad.
3737 Cofuair slog mór forsinmaig
dogillaib isd'ingenaib,
icimmain chairech fosmacht
dochum topur istiprat.
3741 Ocdéne natrebthach tren
imslessaib slébe Coréb,
bamor angair forsinmaig
icdail usci diacairchaib.
3745 Dessid Moissi, bamod ngle,
forochair naconaire,
snimach, saethrach, bec anert,
aoenur, icsfrimthecht.
3749 Moisi batrén incachdáil
dochiniud clainni Abráim,
nicheil ceol ngle ngnimrad nglicc,
is doréir De cotránic.
Cotránic la forsinmaig.

XXXVII.

3753 Robatar ann, cainig cain,
    'coacáirib hitimmarcain,
in-immblib intsluaig comblait,
dsingin inprimsacairt.
3757 Roraid friMoisi, mod nglan,
iarsain indaraingen:

¹ MS. natromdaire.

'cid nacharcobrai, dín cert,
ahóclaig út ahEgept?

3761 'Atarſail cenduine¹ trén
arn-oenur in-etarlén,
immunn-us*ce* n-uar, ca*ch*cruth,
ata inslúag icarsárgud.'

3765 At*r*acht Moisi, m*od* ṅgle,
nipuhéirge meraige,
cotarat cobair trein tr*a*it
dohingenaib int*s*acairt.

3769 Rogartatar leo diataig
Moise amru ca*ch*n-armaig,
con-éicsitar ascéla
dian-athair cenimséna.

3773 IN sacart sluinti gaissi
roſer failti ſr*i*Moise,
aracruth, aracheil ṅglain,
arfortacht diaingenaib.

3777 Rofastai i[n]sacart iarsein
inaoentaid, in-oentreib,
iartimnu indríg, ruathar ṅdil,
dorat [dó] apr*i*mingin.

3781 Hiclemnas intsacairt cenlén,
ifichaib slebi Coreb,
dorumalt Moisi, m*od* ṅgle,
ann tresraind aaimsire.

3785 Noemrí nime, nert ce*ch*sluaig,
coemcli cenbini bithbuaid,
ri betha borggaig cenbrath
rosnordaig² ſeib robatar.

Robatar ann cainig cain.

XXXVIII.

3789 Báe lathi Moysi immuig
isleib Choreb 'coachairib,
conidnarlassair inrí

atathlassair teintidi.

3793 Ri roſorcoṅgart amne
for*i*nac n-amra, ſorMoyse,
roraidi ſris, ruathar cert:
'isſerr duit dul in-Egept.'

3797 Roraid Moysi, monor ṅgle,
'nituidecht ſr*i*' ſorngaire:
roſetar ſein, ſebda bainn,
amſer ecraite doForaind.'

3801 'Heirgg lamobrethir ſorſecht,
arcenn intsluaig in-Egept:
notnoibſaider ſiadcac*h*claind,
notsoerſaider ſorForaind.

3805 'B*e*ra³ uaim comartha lat,
notsaerſa ſorecomnart,
*con*a*ch* ſil ni n-uag ſonim,
coni tichtain ſr*i*'menmain.'

3809 Fofuair mor dobuáid cenbrath,
mor n-ecnai uaig *con*-ógrath,
con-uaill, bamór ṅgaissi ṅglé,
ſoſuair Moise, bái lathe.

Bae lathi Moisi immaig.

XXXIX.

3813 R i dorat ſleisc rﬁblaith rﬁbalnái
il-laim Moisi m*e*ic Amraſ,
[fo. 28 b. 2.]
diar'lass indrub, rígda scél,
imrún ríg isléib Choréb.

3817 Rí rorádi codána
ſriMóise taidbsiu alama,
i[n]darahuair di baclam,
induair a*ll*e bagléglan,

3821 Rí dorat sain ſr*i*sam lái
doMoisi, dom*a*c Amrái,

---

isamlaid sain, ségda insmacht,
' dog*ress* dogensa to*l*ortac*h*t.'
3825 IN ri rofa*l*di *fr*itóir
dochlannaib aibni Iacóib,
dochath labrethir ṅDe dil
*fr*iForann conadrúidib.
3829 Rí rochart Moise *l*or*f*echt
coForann, cor*l*g n-Egept,
cotar*l*aiced uad cenlén
clanna amra Israhel.
3833 ' Manistar*l*aice coluath
meicc Isra*h*el, l*l*nib tuath,
*f*óid*f*et mor ṅdigal dishain,
'mod*f*l*f*at uad aré*c*in.'
3837 Ri *f*otat huili naslo*l*g,
isshé artuire dergoir,
ninlen cloen, nago, naceist,
ri dorat dó inṁblaithfle[i]sc.
Ri dorat fleisc ṁblaith.

XL.

3841 R aidid Moisi fiadca*h*clainn
iarsain iarum *fr*iForainn :
' lessaig dosluaig *f*ein *f*oleith,
lei*c* uait athuaith dinCh(o)imde[i]d.'
3845 As*b*ert Forainn, *f*orom ṅgle,
natibred doib asaere,
co*f*ess*ed* cia bad mó nert
anDiasom no dia Egept.
3849 Dogniat druidi indr*l*g,
tr*i*abrichtu ainble anf*ir*,
nathracha colúaith don*f*laith
dolbsait a*f*uath d*l*a*f*lescaib.
3853 Dorigni Moisi, mod ṅdil,
in-anmaim indrig donim,
labrethir ṅDe fiad*f*lathib,
d*l*a*f*leisc combaglenathir.

3857 Nathir Moisi *f*uabrad cath,
*fr*i*n*athracha nandrúad,
istig arbelaib indrig
dodas*f*uaid cos[in]n-oenm*l*r.
3861 Gabais anathraig dolár
Moisi fiadintaig *l*omnán,
noscroith, nodosai i*f*leisc,
lasinslog, robomorcheist.
3865 Moisi minn osbetha barc,
hua Iacóib meicc Isaac,
aaithesc glan, gnimrad ṅgle,
isdoreir De roraide.
Roraid Moisi fiad ca*h*clainn.

XLI.

3869 B ahuamnach Forainn amne,
iarsin roraid *fr*iMoise :
' maith limm dula doib *l*or*f*echt,
masomaith latuaith n-Egept.'
3873 Dodechaid Moisi diathig,
atreib Forainn *l*orúabrig,
conhécaid coglan inscél
dodagdainib Israhel.
3877 Ama*l* dochuaid Moisi uad
*f*orcoṅgart cuce inmorsluag,
dorat *f*oh*l*r *f*orca*h*smacht,
rol*l*n d*l*mus isdasacht.
3881 As*b*ert Foraind censena,
*fr*i*a*chlanna, *fr*i*a*chenela :
' *f*ortuatha De, torum ṅglé,
tabrad ca*h*tormach ṅdoére.'
3885 Batar toirsech intuath trúag
*fr*iMoisi aran-imluad ;
' ac*h*t furail saethar is[s]macht
nifuaramar ni du*f*ortacht.'
3889 Radid[1] *fr*iu Moisi combúaid :
' nabid *fr*ibaisi ṁbeltrúaig,

dal De donessai cechrainn,
bidtressai indás bág Foraind.'
3893 Ardrí Egept, ilar ṅglonn,
ri góach, guinech, garblonn,
batarb tnu frigleo, frícath,
aned babeo bahuamnach.
Bahuamnach Forainn amne.

XLII.

3897 Ri roráid friMoisi cotrén :
'abbair fríclaind n-Israhel,
dentar leo, lathar ṅgle,
uan d'idpairt cachoentige.

3901 'Uan firenn bliadne insein
cengaili ṅduib no temein,
afuine forgris cechcruth,
cenachnáma dobrissiud.

3905 'Frithalid inn-uan cenlocht
doidpairt incachoenphort,
ahithi istig cenni immach,
cossaib cenn isinathrach.
[fo. 29 a. 1.]

3909 'Menibe istig, torum ṅgle,
dodoenib lin ahithe,
tact nech ammuig onachdruṅg
cach uaib inahiallacraund.

3913 'Lalubai lachtoc, luad ṅgle,
laharán nemdescaigthe,
bachla forláim, línib ell,
forcressa forn-imthimchell.

3917 'A ithi forsessam sain,
ahfuil fofarn-aursannaib,
diaforraib, fuidel foleith,
aloscud duib iteneid.

3921 'A denam dogres insein
docach oen incach oentreib,
doforaithmet, monar clecht,

fortuaslaicthi aEgept.'
3925 Atat inmuirig fotráig
doruirig nimi noclnáir :
dorat mór ṅdígal hicrí
forrigab ri roráidi.
Ri roráid friMoisi cotrén.

XLIII.

3929 Ri dorat mor ṅdigal tren
dosairad mac n-Israhel :
bamaidm torainn forcechmaig,
forForainn conathuathaib.

3933 Loscainn riasca, reim ṅdata,
cuili, biasta, brecnata,
bolcgach, lasruth fola fann,
dorcha, tene [1] istorann.

3937 Plag naprímgeinne huili,
etercethri ocus duine,
gol cecha clethi, gním cert,
rochlos lafíru Egept.

3941 Ri dorat nadeichplaga
forthu fríhuair combaga,
nílac rognf iarcóir cath,
inri dorat mor ṅdigal.
Ri dorat mor ṅdígal tren.

XLIV.

3945 Rolcicset dilmain uadaib
'nandirmaib, 'nammorslua-
gaib,
samlaid dochotar forfecht
cosetaib amraib Egept.

3949 Cethrichet tricha triamnaib,
indóiri doib dobliadnaib,
in-Egept daill tairbert tren,
dochlaind airdeirc Israhél.

[1] MS. teneď.

1   [IV. 3.]

3953 IArsain scarsat fridóire
Egeipt con-ilur clóine,
iarmbliadnaib[1] coriagail raith
trichat iarcethricétaib.

3957 Dorigset sét, sliucht combuaid,
cenbét ahEgeipt sairtuaid,
cengrissa, bacain intsluaig,
doRamissa, doSochuaith.

3961 Ri ragmas dasfuc trianert
adoire amnas Egept,
dorat nel impu fride
istor tened cachn-aidche.

3965 IN tene icloscud intsluaig
Egeipt 'sindaidchi adhuair,
innél dorcha doib fridé[2]
combruissitis acairpdé.

3969 IArsin roraidset colainn
sluaig fer n-Egept friForainn :
' tiagam forarcul cenlén,
lecamm uain claind n-Israhél.

3973 ' IN dia asdech forbith búan
dorat meth forarmorslúag ;
atá ic[c]athugud cotrén
darcenn clainne Israhél.'

3977 Asbert Forainn fergach friu :
' nileicfem arlaesechu,
conostucam lenn imbrait,
latoeb arn-oir 'sarn-argait.'

3981 Dochuaid Forainn conasluag
'nandiad imMuir romra Ruad,
nasluaig remi rosatr[i]uin
ocus Forann fohfrdiuid.

3985 INri dodasaer iarsin
arForaind cona airbrib,
triamuincinn Mara Romuir
dosfuc innan-irchomair.

3989 IN muir mór, comflib scel,

triastuc Dia claind n-Israhél,
rodáil rí grene cenrainn
forformnu féne Forainn.

3993 Báe Gaidel friglegelt cain
in-Egept 'sindamsirsain,
dobreth Scotta fiadeachclainn,
ingen airmittnech Foraind.

3997 Atroebaid Gaidel combúaid
dula dó indegaid intslúaig,
uair bafaith, friglea scél,
uamun Déa mac n-Israhél.

4001 IArsain dochuaid Gaidel Glas
il-libuirn lir lethanbras,
fuapraid meirge mara maill
arhuamun ferge Foraind.

[fo. 29 a. 2.]

4005 Luid Gaidel cain conabuaid
iársain sechIndia sairthúaid,
corogab tir, torom ngle,
in-insi Deprofane.

4009 Luid ondindsi, cretais slúaig,
Deprofane sel siarthuaith,
bái 'nafichaib lín mbliadna
fonaerichaib Caspianda.

4013 Robaided ann, arim chett,
dodegdoinib fer n-Egept,
coic cét rig rán, regtai rainn,
immonn-ardrig, imForaind.

4017 Lin intsluaig cenmotha sin
nifitir nech an-árim :
nochinned foreachdine
arimbed ahilmile.

4021 Ri tarlaic Muir Romuir ruad
forForainn conamórsluag,
nitherna leo diatfrib
cid oenfer dohilmilib.

4025 IAmandamnad, gnim glinni,

_____
[1] MS. iarmbliandaib.   [2] MS. friden.

iarmarbad ap*ri*mgindi,
nicheil ce*ch* sui, srethaib slecht,
cosin rosmbái rosleicset.
  Rosleicset dilmain uadaib.

XLV.

4029 R i tuc claind n-Isr*ahé*l ass
       intan rommol inmorchlass,
cenmna, cenm*a*ccu, *fr*ícath
s*é* cet mili fer n-armach.

4033 O*s*hunn rosiachtatar tír
roattlaigset dond*a*rríg,
at*er*nam iarńgábud cacht.
iarmbádud andergnámat.

4037 IArsin túargabad inchlas
domolad De bacomdas :
cansatar, badeoda intlus,
hili uli cantemus.

4041 Siur doMoisi, Maire már,
iarsain rosephain timpán :
rochachain ceol doríg nél
labantrocht m*ac* n-Isr*ahé*l.

4045 Ri rán rodluig riasinslúag
adruimni dogba dubrúad,
rí oscach*b*rí conem nél,
inri tuc claind n-Isr*ahé*l.
  Ri tuc claind Isr*ahé*l ass.

XLVI.

4049 B atar buidig doDia dron
       iart*er*nam doMuir Romor,
robdar dimdaig D*é* f*o*rruth
oshunn rancatar dithrub.

4053 ' Truag doD*í*a donrat im-m*er*t,
nach*a*nrelic in-Egept :
donfuc iars*é*taib cech*c*ruth
diarn-*é*caib isindithrub.

  ¹ MS. Ccenbiad.

4057 ' Cenb*i*ad ¹, cenlinn, lethan locht,
cen*é*ta*ch* beos arbithnocht,
ronl*í*n bochta, ronbás bath,
dogena ingorta armarbad.'

4061 Ri roráid *fr*ìu aurdairc dul :
' inhed bethi 'sindithrub,
nocho*f*orbia immaig *no* taig
airchra b*í*id *no* etaig.'

4065 Ri rodosas donmaind blaith
oc*us* indiall en imthlaith,
inlind *fr*íatoir asce*ch*maig
do*f*uc doib asindailig.

4069 Srotha índithruib, delm n-ada,
ciabtar nemi nemnecha,
lacach, ciatserba slassa,
doibseom batar somblassa.

4073 Dorigset sét, sliucht combuaid,
al-lam chle *fr*ímuir morgluair,
siarthúaid darca*ch* fich *fr*ífeth,
focr*i*ch n-amnais n-Amaléch.

4077 Gnisit cathu croda ríad
frisluag n-uathmar n-Amaliach :
dorochair mór n-arma*ch* de
tall tr*i*acrosfigill Móise.

4081 O roláset ár intsluaig
Amalech aurdairc adrúaid,
imsliab Sina, srethaib socht,
rosuidigsetar lońgphort.

4085 IArcathaib, iarnithaib n*i*ad,
*fr*íclainn n-*f*raig ² n-Amaliach,
isl*é*ib Sina, sluagda ańgal,
fobannaib buada batar.
  Batar buidig doD*í*a dron.

XLVII.

4089 D oarfas gnim n-i*ń*gnad doib
       isleib S*í*na fochétoir,

  ² MS. nairaig, with a dot over the second letter.

fiadgnuis intslúaig ¹, torom ṅgle,
daig derg dermor teintide.

4093 IN[n]í dodechaid donim,
dodiṅgnaib richid rindgil,
coformaig recht sainglicc slan
forciniud n-airdirc n-Abrám.

4097 Rí rogart caini gnima
Moisi lais islíab Sina,
    [fo. 29 b. 1.]
cendig, cenbiad, bamod úgle,
cocenn cethrachat lathe.

4101 Rí doridnacht doMoisi
deich mbríathra glana gaéssi²,
iarsrethaib ríagla, reim ṅdil,
dothinchosc inmorpopuil.

4105 Dothidnacul rechta reil
cenimracul tríaglancheil,
inri thánic donim glass
cotimnaib doib doárfas.
        Doárfas gnim n-iṅgnad doib.

XLVIII.

4109 A nhed robai Moisi istsleib
       nochosrala fordagceil,
dorigned leo, nir'gnim coir,
oedam deligthi dergóir.

4113 IArsain, bamessu cechscél,
dothúathaib mac n-Israhél,
etcr firu ismná cenrath,
andul huili diaadrad.

4117 Diultud forríg n-aṅgel n-úag,
bamor ingnim donmorsluag,
ocus ahithi ind[í]eoir gairb
fiaddeilb indócdaim hermairb.

4121 Ferggach fríu Fiadu bacoir,
fríclainn n-cngaig n-Iacoib,
cotarmart tairbert intslúaig

fothuinn talman fríoenhúair.

4125 Gorognid Moisi iarsin,
forsinRíg connaiṅglib,
coroléiced dó achosc fein
'satimargain diauagréir.

4129 Manibed Moisi, mod ṅgle,
asbcrt inRi orddnide,
óenfer díb frígleo nagail
nafaicbed beo fortalmain.

4133 Fiadgnuis Dé, badiada túr,
icfoglaim ríagla isrigrún,
isleib Sina[í], slíucht ṅgle,
aned cian robai Moise.
        Anhed robáe Moisi ist[s]leib.

XLIX.

4127 F orfócart Moisi fonert
       forsinsluag bái 'nacoimthecht,
iarsin frire teora n-úar,
coromarbtais inmorslúag.

4141 Conar'choicled, croda gair,
nech amáthair no athair ;
no diabráthair, bág comblait,
no diachaim, no diacharait.

4145 Roshort Moise, monor ṅgle,
etcrcethri ocus duine,
etcrfiru ismaecu ismna,
dosrat fochlaidiub diglá.

4149 Rumcnm[n]aiged lais iarscin
indelb dindór derg demcin :
doridnacht doib, nirbothruaṅg,
tríanambiud donmorslúag.

4153 Dorimnai Día, torom ṅgle,
acosc censil comairge,
iarn-urd gaissi, croda cacht,
isfor Moisi forfócart.
        Forfócart Moisi fonert.

L.

4157 Dotharraid teidm duairc dóib,
   iarcein dogalur medóin ;
  bamarb sochaidi dontsluag
  dondimsruth roenach roruad.

4161 Ri roraidi friu coglé :
  ' denaid nathraig n-umaide :
  turgabar fricrann corath
  uasinslúag frisirsellad.

4165 ' Ciphe ardoscé donmaig
  incrann ocus innathraig,
  biatslana cachandénat,
  dogalur nihepélat.'

4169 Figuir Crist atbeir annsain,
  dodeochaid diartesargain,
  tuargabad fricrann corath,
  is dararcenn rocrochad.

4173 Cibhé frisaiccidar ann
  Issu Crist cumtachta arann,
  rambia nem, nassad ndaingen,
  imbithoentaid archaingel.

4177 Sloig sil Adaim doceehdu,
  eternoebu isphecthachu,
  ili huile, comgrad ngle,
  atá acomdal friMoisi.

4181 Manbad ruirig nimi nair
  conic cachsuilig sográid,
  balór d'huathaib oscechmaig
  donatúathaib diatarraid.
   Dotharraid teidm duairc doib.

LI.

4185 Ri roráide friu cenlén
   friclainn n-amrai n-Israhél.
  conderndtais doib eclais nglain
  ocus indarcc testemain.

4189 Dias doib frisóirsi slecht,

fricerdachl, friprimgoibnecht,
[fo. 29 b. 2.]
Adiar adma irdaig múr,
isint-amra Ithidún.

4193 Dotreib Leui, lat[h]ar ndil,
doreir indrig donoemnib,
sechtmoga fer, fobaid fecht,
friacobair, friatimthirecht.

4197 Cetnagnim gnisset marchloc
dabach humai istudloc,
con-ilur delb, lethan lecht,
trethan derb trifer ndcec.

4201 Gnim tanaissi, tadbat ruin,
admat adfét inscriptúir,
eterfiru ismaccu ismná,
bacc iairnn cechoenfir iarma.

4205 IN tres gnim, roglé cenchol,
tegdas Dé tabernacol,
nir'bu dín[n]im laDía ndil
conamslib mírbailib.

4209 Cethramad gnim, indarc úag,
cain imracht fricach n-imlúad,
ór delgnaid, dín docachthreib,
amal cachscrin n-ildelbaig.

4213 Ri dororainn dóib, babúaid,
inn-eclais n-orhuill noebúaig,
etirfot, cenchaillti cert,
etirairddi ocus lethet.

4217 Tricha cubat, comul nglé,
etirlethet isairdé,
coica cubat, fochucht cruth,
innafut frisuidigud.

4221 Cláraib cainib crotha glain,
slánaib, soeraib, sodelbaib,
iartinnrud tairchil cachgreim
dofidrud saindil secheim.

4225 Cuairt cethrochair, cumtaig grál,
nirbodrechrothail dermár,

cathclái gelbdai, gním n-ogdai,
fachlái febdai forordai.

4229 Rí rosorddaig clethaib clar
dosforgaib srethaib soergrad,
rodascinn fríhergna alt,
dáchlar dec ségdai sescat.

4233 Dáchlar déc 'mondorus ndron.
caintomus cenimmfordol:
cethriclair déc, derbdair scin,
serntair immonsenisteir.

4237 Tri cláir fichet incachsliss
clichet cenag, cenanfiss:
dáchubat, nidechelt tair,
bid il-lethet cechoenchláir.

4241 Cethricláir fosummib dé
inhuillib naecalsé,
feib dorumat, rigda rad,
trichubat incech oenchlar.

4245 Se fotha dec, derb cenlocht,
ar sechi fichtib doarggot,
eturru islar, lith fríbaig,
dáfotha dib cech oenchlair.

4249 Airddi nafochrai[1] folt
huasnafothaib findruini,
cubat fríſut alame,
cenimforcraid n-imhairme.

4253 Dorus sneid sair segdai máil,
solus frigrein cain comláir,
cenardgrain gním, cian cachcruth,
intsanctair 'nafiriarthur.

4257 Cethriclair comlain, gním ngle,
o[c]congbáil nasanctare,
cofothaib fiadtuathaib treib
conafuathaib forordaib.

4261 Altoir frídorus antuaid
fríloscud n-edpart noebúaig,

altóir aurgnaidi 'nadess
fríaurnaigthi nadimchres.

4265 INprímaltoir cosindrath
frignimgart gloir roturcbad,
cechthucht foardbilib óir
baharddidir ucht Aroin.

4269 Deil telchinni tíar istair,
anniab amal chorcarglain,
dírge cechtolgdail tailce
fráorgbáil nadrumslaitc.

4273 Tuiri tren diriuch dolar
frísiniud sruthi soergrad,
fondrumslait déin derbtha slóig,
cotrìbdelhaib dec dergóir.

4277 Coluid tríasindrummslait druin
fríuidmi nasuanemuin,
fair tuas cenlen, laid lorda,
én uais con-aib forórda.

4281 Coroiset lár dicechleith
fornaclaraib hicomsreith,
gníthi ondrumslait immach
sithbi n-anart n-ildathach.

4285 Oenanart tairsiu anechtair,
coemthoracht ciacomnertaid,
frísnima seirgthi sóeba,
frignima, frígarbgaetha.

4289 Clar diargut, gle cenmeth,
cechtarde nadaprimleth,
[fo. 30 a. 1.]
iartuidmidib, togach tóir,
sechtmoga folach ndergóir[2].

4293 Frí sreng doib, frícuimrech ngle,
nan-anart coir coimtige,
bacan dron dergoir togaig[3]
dochur forcechm-oenfolaig.

4297 Suidigdir tairsib immaig[4],

---

[1] The r is written over l. [2] MS. ndergóir (the second mark of length in a later hand).
[3] MS. togaid. [4] MS. immuig.

diataibsin donaslogaib,
slessa sct frisella slog
tricessa dec dodergór.

4301 ' Dénaid fritarba cechdruing
arcc amra, demin forgaill,
'monfleisc,'moanmaind,monoringle,
imnoleedai taiblide.

4305 Cethricubait, comol ngle,
dobith ifut naairce,
atri 'naairdi, mod cert,
ocus adó 'nalethet.

4309 Cethridrolaim diór dron
asindaire diahimmarchor,
dádrol treothu, derg angne,
dondor amra forloiscthe.

4313 Delb hiruphin forsindairce,
dindór bilarcháin imtháirc,
cofathaib niam, nassaid gle,
coscathaib ascfath scailte.

4317 ' 'Sintsanctáir suidigter lib
indarc noeb cona aidmib,
isanart sroil, sreth centair,
eter inslog 'sinsanctáir.

4321 Cocétlaib griannaib cechcruth,
cocliaraib, con-airfitiud,
con-orthonaib, cocóraib,
comolbthogaib dermoraib.

4325 Flesc Moisi, flesc Aróin aith,
cenlaisi, línib ollgraid,
coica n-unga n-óir gleglain
cechtarde nadaflescsain.

4329 Flesc maith Moisi, monar cert,
rofer foraesa aEgept,
nathir doilbth[e], delgnaid cruth,
derbaid forafiruachtur.

4333 Flesc Aróin, baamra dúis,
gradgloir glanna fiadgelgnúis,
foblath bil bolaid noibe,

fothorud cechdegmoine.

4337 'Sindlestar lán cosinmaind
se cet dior centádrainn,
hisinprimchaindelbra choir
tri cet n-unga nderb ndergoir.

4341 Secht nibenna buana, búaid ferb,
forsinchaindelbrau cruanderg,
gnitis dindor gle glanna,
forsinbitis secht sutralla.

4345 Cuich gela cuairt cennachcleith
suig frisreba suairc sainred,
intu nobruindis bannae
nosuildis nasutralla.

4349 Secht cet unga 'sin meis móir
cocethricrossaib dergóir,
furri adó sechtmogat sla
d'aran remúir nemdesctha.

4353 INcaindelbra 'sindleith tess,
cain, caindelbda, cendimes,
inmias atuaid, tairethi rúin,
cosnabargenaib remuir.

4357 Ilar nacúach, nacód cass,
ilar lestar lór, lannmass,
ilar mias menmaib mórdaib
cosnadelbaib dergórdaib.

4361 Dior huili, ilar ndelb,
condruinc, ni mod n-inderb,
nastaba, tolaib gestal,
stomacha istuslestar.

4365 Srethaib sutrall, soillsi scuir,
frisoimsi 'sintabernacuil,
caindelbrai gelbdai glordai
ité delbdai dergórdai.

4369 Forlassad coléir dogres
ola ocuscheir fochomlés,
iarnauerchur fridídnad,
cenherchur, cenairdíbdad.

4373 Tech fricomdail cechtharbai.

cenchomraid, cenchomlabrai,
cenfáilti, centoirsi traig,
soillsi eterlá ocus adaig.

4377 Tempul diada, dín cech áin,
tegdais rodígrais rocháin,
friacallaim De, sunn sel,
fritinchosc, friforcetal.

4381 Nachastathigi aes baeth,
mná no meicc no laine laech,
naciñged sét asossad,
acht aes fírien fírfossad.

4385 Aés trúag, aes deoda dessa,
athláich ocuslaichessa,
sluaig sin súaire, dúaire, tolaib gair,
impe 'mocuairt díanechtair.

4389 Tiagat 'sindeclais folí
aes óg, sacairt, leignidi,
[fo. 30 a. a.]
isáes humal, ceim forais,
farn-athirge, farñglanchobais.

4393 IN chlass inchleir, bacert cóir.
toirnet coleir dondaltóir,
tairismig, nibatlúamnaig,
athé feta, forhúamnaig.

4397 Gaibed cach agreimm tarbái
doreir Aróin meic Amrai,
glaini glethig friacacairt,
friabrethir inprimsacairt.

4401 'Dentar lib iarmbes cechcuir
dogres isintabernacuil,
edpart matinda, mét bla,
ocus idpart fescorda.

4405 Bolud naluba ascachthoeb
latorroma inSpirta Noeb,
clu con-áue frignassad,
fríslane, frisirsassad.

4409 Ri roráid fríu : 'sernnaid sreith
'mondeclais dicachoenleith,

forson reilgce corebaib,
doanartaib oengelaib.

4413 'Dorus indindliss fodess
cain set solus narb'imchress,
frituttacht Dé, deoda nuall,
friathigid namorsluag.

4417 'Nabid forn-aittreib, mod ncim,
eterchrann caiñgil isgréin :
set inSpirda Noeb foleith
frñauttacht, frñathigeid.'

*n-éim
Cf. 1541, 5263*

4421 Bid amne indeclas folí
feib dosrorann int-ardrí,
uascachmaig rodasderscaig
cenforcraid, cenimthesbaid.

4425 Ri dosrat forfaglaib recht
dosfuc ahfathaib Egept,
ishé mal naslog, slan síu,
inri ran raraid frfu.
     Ri roraidi fríu cenlén.

LII.

4429 Ri roráid fríu aithesc n-uag
dohorddogud forsinsluag,
immonn-eclais n-ena n-aird
trítreba docachóenaird.

4433 Trítreba condóni anair
greni fríturcbail toebdein,
isatrí dondleith aniar
frísreith, frifuiniud fírian.

4437 Trítreba dondleith andes
cencleith frífeba fírles,
isatrí tecrais cech rhbuaid
frísinn-eclais afírthuaid.

4441 Ri roraidi fríu triarath,
fríaiffrenn, frícclebrad,
treb Leui lerol cengreis
im-medon, immonn-eclais.

4445 INdaramac d'Ioseph án

Mannasse mſlib ol[l]grád,
dessid iarndligud Dé de
in-inud trebe Leue.

4449 Rí dorat Áarón fosmacht
combahe baprímsacart,
ocus Moisi, mo cech n-ail,
itoisigecht inpopail.

4453 Ri betha buirr, buan ablat,
ri domuin [   ] dorosat,
ri oscach ríg, cengleo cert,
ri roraid friu inn-athesc.
    Ri roráid friu athesc n-úag.

LIII.

4457 **B**a formtech iarsain inslóg
    friMoisi ocu[s] frihArón,
imdliged sacairt, sáer smacht,
ocus immontoſsigecht.

4461 Atrachtár iarsin codian,
triadiumus istríanriad,
in-agaid Moisi, mod n-án,
Core, Abiron, Dathan.

4465 INri rodígail insain
forru fein forasluagaib,
rosloisc tene, tolaib gal,
ocus ros[s]luic intalam.

4469 Atraig insluag diarb'gnath cath
diambas arrodis brathar,
con-erlatar, lin atuir,
coríce intabernacuil.

4473 Rosnort int-añgel cogle
arherge doib friMoise,
cethrimili dec dontsluag
lacet toisech ñdian dermuad.

4477 IN-agaid mac n-ammra n-án
triallsat cath calma comlán,
intslúaig 'nasrethaib 'mosech

sech baſeochair, baformtech.
    Baformtech iarsain inslog.

LIV.

4481 **R**aidid Moisi frisinsluag
    arnabetis forimluad,
flesc cachatreibi cengeiss
dothabairt leo dondeclais.
    [fo. 30 b. 1.]

4485 Nech assa flesc, buan bolud,
úraigfes foalantorud,
toimled dodeoin De, din ñgle,
ord saer nasacerdóte.

4489 Clannaid Moisi doib cechfleisc,
batuaslucud domorcheist,
flesc Ároin, amra bolud,
rothaitni folantorud.

4493 Rooirdned Aron insain
isacerdóti in phopail:
dorairned diumus namborb,
roairbered cechfodord.

4497 Mosi mórglan, moltais máil,
targai inslograth 'nas[ó]erdail,
clethaib cialda, gair cencleith,
iarrethaib riagla ráidid.
    Radid Mosi frisinslúag.

LV.

4501 **R**ocluned cach, clu cengeis,
    tan teged Áron d'eclais,
dó dicechleith, deoda tſí,
cantais céola clucíní.

4505 Ado secht ñdeich, comgrinn cóir,
tuidmide dronmind dergóir,
ocus ubull dondór gle
eter cech dá cluicíne.

4509 IArnacumrech, cumnech gloir,
dichocholl huillnech Aróin,

K

iarnacrechad, c*ri*chid cruth,
iarsrethad, iarsuidigud.

4513 Aron baamru ce*ch* n-ail,
saided 'sintabernacuil,
cen*t*athair diag*ra*d fogl*ó*ir,
'nachath*á*ir dr*u*imnig derg*ó*ir.

4517 IN chathair ch*ó*ir, cain acuch*t*,
cen*t*athair donp*ri*msacurt,
l*ó*r duis fiadca*ch*drui*ñ*g dein,
adruim f*ri*sintuiridein.

4521 Dothairced ca*ch* dib ad*á*il
doce*ch*leith immonsanct*á*ir,
senad sruithi, s*ó*erda sl*ó*ig,
dofuctais recht iscanoin.

4525 Achethri meic, monor *ñ*gle,
Aroin uasail meic Am*ra*c,
bitis f*ri*gartgl*ó*ir, cain cach*t*,
osalt*ó*ir n*ó*ib nan-edpart.

4529 Sl*ú*aig nasacart, srethaib gr*á*d,
ca*ch* dib 'sadruim f*ri*achoemchla*t*,
dondeclais noeb barnasse,
f*ri*cumtach nac*ó*emclasse.

4533 Nafogr*a*id ann f*ri*andeochair,
nadeochain, nasuibdeochain,
f*ri*annad caindle, gnim cert,
f*ri*tairbe, f*ri*timthirecht.

4537 INslog b*i*id if*u*s frifeis
doce*ch*leith immonn-eclais,
s*é*olaib soid*ñ*geib, suilgib srath,
c*é*olaib cuibdib rochluined.
Rocluined ca*ch*, clu cengeis.

LVI.

4541 BAmertnech Moisi, m*o*d n-uag,
f*ri*hilchai*ñ*gni, f*ri*imluad,
f*ri*aforcetal asce*ch*cruth,
f*ri*asrethad, f*ri*asuidigud.

4545 Friorddugud caich fom*á*m,

is f*ri*immad an-ilgrad,
f*ri*cuibdigud fogl*ó*ir glain,
f*ri*atinchosc, f*ri*atimmarcain.

4549 Fr*i*ambid co*ó*g, forecht run,
f*ri*sreith iarslecht nasl*ó*gd*ú*n,
fohuamun D*é*, dind arthl*u*s,
cenh*ú*abur, cenimmarb*u*s.

4553 Dorat achliamain cogl*é*
comairli maith doMoise,
' guid dondR*í*g reil, reim fobaid,
nech dontsluag dot'imchobair.'

4557 Rogaid [Moisi], monor *ñ*gl*é*,
iarsin forr*í*g nair nime,
corothogad nech dontsl*ú*ag
diachobair f*ri*ca*ch*n-imluad.

4561 INri doraiga tr*i*arath
asintsl*ú*ag f*ri*sid sonthach,
f*ri*etargle*ó*d cai*ñ*gen *ñ*glicc
d*á*fer d*é*c istr*í*fichit.

4565 Sessiur derb dib doca*ch*treib
dob[r]ithemnaib bronngaethaib,
f*ri*cocairt cai*ñ*gen, gnim *ñ*gle,
f*o*rb*é*laib morglain Moise.

4569 Ca*ñ*gnib gleraib, gloraib cacht,
ardib trenaib tocomrac,
laMoise modmar cenmeth,
sech bamolmar, bamertnech.
Bamertnech Moisi, m*o*d n-uag.

I.VII.

4573 ISnasabbotib sacraib,
isnafelib f*í*rn*ó*ebaib,
tictis d'eclais, tola tr*é*n,
sloig m*ó*ra m*a*c n-Isra*he*l.

4577 Ticed ca*ch* dib doca*ch* leith
con-edpartaib diaChoimdeid,
[fo. 30 b. a.]
batar hili sl*ó*ig ascuir

fritóir dontabernacuil.

4581 Ticed ann Moisi combúaid,
cathbarr gaissi cach morslúaig :
basainigthi sechcechngnuis
flal glainidi friagelgnúis.

4585 Cid dondeclais, cid dodáil,
cid dochertchlais achomráid,
diis arsechtmogait, mod cert,
bahé lín bíd 'nachoemthecht.

4589 Cenócdaine, cenaes mbaeth,
acht toga fer flal, fírgaeth,
friatimarcain, cuibdi cacht,
frituigli, fribrithemnacht.

4593 Dochoistecht fritimna trel,
fri hidna, fri forcitel,
sreba naslúag ascachthreib
tictis isnasabboteib.
ISnasabbotib soeraib.

LVIII.

4597 Forcongrad Moisi maith, mór,
cenbaisse braith forArón,
darcenn intsluaig, tolaib smacht,
dul doerdducb nan-idpart.

4601 Atraiged Árón friandail,
coslánóg isintsanctáir,
baceim comlan comgraid ndil
icomdail inglanaingil.

4605 Tairced int-angel donim
icomdail Aróin imdil,
con-innisenn dó cenlen
adlaice macc n-Israhél.

4609 Aisneided Arón foleith
doMoisi cenimthesbaid
mor doathescaib idnaib,
dochétlaib, doglantimnaib.

4613 Aisneided Moisi cenchleith
diathuathaib, diadagdoineib,

connachbeth díb nachsluag sen
digsed huad cenforcitel.

4617 Condechaid coglé centair
d'acallaim Dé 'sinsanctair,
briathar bunaid, bág cenbráth,
huair bacubaid forcongrad.
Forcongrad Moisi maith mór.

LIX.

4621 Ri rosbiath iarn-urd ri[a]gla
frite dáfichet bliadna,
isindíthrub, digrais scél,
dithreib dec mac n-Israhél.

4625 Ri thuc doib inmaind donim
frituara tarbaig, nderbdil,
ocus indiall ón diadéoin
conabetis cenhurféoil.

4629 Ri thuc doib sruam usci uair
asindailig reil, rachruaid,
cechblas bamaith leo fonim
fogeibtis forsnuscisin.

4633 Nadáthuaith déc centrebad,
mnáib, maccaib istrénferab,
soillsidir ingrein alf,
inri réil rodasbiathái.
Ri rosbiath iarn-urd riagla.

LX.

4637 Maire ingen Ammrai ain,
finngel frisamlai soegráid,
mor dul d'ulcc doromnat aclú,
robá icformait friabrátriu.

4641 Rosgab claimi, rosoi dath,
fiadroscaib nasluag sonthach :
menbad Moisi, monar ndein,
atbelad dinchlaimisein.

4645 Duini delbda, togu drong,
banscal fedbda foretrom,

cen aliud imgaissi gné,
siur maith doMaisi Maire.
        Maire ingen Amrai áin.

LXI.

4649 Oshunn rosiacht inslúag
        coArnon n-airdairc n-ad-
        rúad :
    foidit uadib dreimm tríablad
    diatunthaib dothascelad.

4653 Rodosterbaiset foleith
    oenser glicc dicachoentreib.
    rodasfaidset forset slán
    dochuairt imericha Cannán.

4657 Corofegdais leo cenbrath
    inmór immed achathrach,
    aslúaig imtarláin diangail,
    imtarilerda acóraid.

4661 IMtartaicthig atrebthai,
    imtarimdai an-ilchethrai,
    imdar ilarda alubai,
    imtar cáine aclarbrugai.

4665 Oshunn dochuatar forsét
    nochostarraid nachoenret,
    coruachtatar, monor ngle,
    cocenn cethorchat lathe.

4669 Huair rofegsatar intír,
    etermin ocus anmín,
        [fo. 31 a. 1.]
    tancatar cencredim cruth
    foraculu dondíthrub.

4673 Mór n-ergal, mór n-erbach n-úag,
    mor torrelmach frïimluad,
    ismór cath ngarbron rochacht,
    coArnon orosiacht.
        Oshunn rosiacht inslúag.

LXII.

4677 Gabsat aCoimdid[1] dothair
        fiadambriathrib'nammordáil:
    ' farñDía doforfuc forbrath,
    cian atá ocforñbrecad.

4681 ' Fuaramar tír n-uar n-aiñbtech,
    acgarb, anmín, etortech,
    con-ilur droñg, trén athbach,
    con-immud ahillnathrach.

4685 ' Con-ilur achorad cruaid,
    ocus coniurt ammorsíuag,
    con-armaib grandaib, glassaib,
    conñgaib, conhernmassaib.

4689 ' Cocuradaib gleraib cath,
    coturadaib trenmiled,
    conacathrachaib calmaib,
    daiñgnib, deimnib, dithoglaib[2].'

4693 Rotríall Satan asoimled
    arecnach ammorchoimded,
    indna trúag triamuin roscacht,
    timna Diabuil rogabsat.
        Gabsat aCoimdid dotháir.

LXIII.

4697 I Arsin rohimclóe inscél
        laléssu ocus l[a]Caléb :
    ' gó thairic dóib ascachdu,
    nachascreitiu abrathriu !

4701 ' Fuarammar morthír mainbihech,
    toichthech, trebthach, iltairthech,
    con-ith isblicht, baso fecht,
    cofín, comil, cocruthnecht.

4705 ' Memais remaib forcechtuáith,
    bidforcoscraig conglanbuáid,
    bidlib huili, linib bla,

---

[1] MS. achoimdid.   [2] MS. deimnim dithaglaih.

eter tír iscathracha.

4709 ' Cosétaib saidbrib slánaib,
con-ardib, con-ildanaib,
tírib, túathaib, tolaib dál,
feib rotharṅgered d'Abram.'

4713 Cia roscuibdig morf ran
roscuibrig focacht commám,
rola nel dicachtreib toi
iarsin inscel roimchlóe.
Iarsin roimchlói inscel.

LXIV.

4717 I Arsin tarmairt moDia dil
frisintúaid n-engaig n-anbil,
coro[s]sluiced talam tenn
acor foleittreib lethglenn.

4721 Raidid fríu Moisi cenlén,
menbad Iessu *ocus* Caleph,
amal én 'mon-iadai sás,
noragdais huill oénbás.

4725 Sét cethrachat lathi lán
fail oshunn cotir Cannan,
rigfidir sét bas mo de
cocenn *cethrachat* ṁbliadne.

4729 Nocorfa nech dib aréc
donadib trebaib d[e]éc
cocrich Cannan, *crichid* scel,
acht mad Essu *ocus* Caleb.

4733 Tír Cannain cofairgi fraig
nista daréis an-ecnaig,
acht marannait, airdairc dul,
formeic iarforn-adnacul.

4737 Rádid ² fríMoisi iarsein
moDia déoda baderbdein,
toimlid forre marcachsruith
dogress ingnais indíthruib.

4741 Menbad Essu, immaid raith,

¹ MS. Radidid.

ocus Caleph cóir, cial[l]maith,
atabairt fo thalman ² tlacht
iarsin moDia dil tarmart.
IArsin tarmairt moDia dil.

LXV.

4745 D ochuáid aclu *for*cachleith
coscélaib atrénmiled,
corolín cechtuaid toirsi
arhúamun am-mórlo[i]ṅgsi.

4749 Dodeochaid *cách* dicachtreib
cosinsoerslúag n-anaichned,
sluag cechthiri, derb colar,
con-ilur mili Moáb.

4753 Rosgab crith grain[n]e atcha
etir tír iscathracha,
robaid brig nasluag nasreth
cengnim, cengail, cengasced.

4757 Tarchomail *cach* cumtaig arg
cosinslóg scrig serbgarg,
nifríth dib tuath trelmach, trén,
gabad friclainn n-Isra*h*él.

4761 Tinolsat dóib, torum ṅgle,
cethricatha coimtide,
[fo. 31 a. 2.]
Seon, Bassan, badbda slóg,
amra Moáb isAmmón.

4765 Memaid remib, ruathar ṅdein,
*for*snacethrib slógaib sein,
cirtis cerpaib incath cron
*for*leccaib arddaib Arnón.

4769 Dorochratar ann frígail
*for*snaslébib slamdergaib,
sessiur sescat cet frilar
ar *secht* mílib, bamorár.

4773 Ri dosfuarggaib, uathmar ail,
cathaib cródaib comramaib.

² MS. fothalmain.

aclú ccnchiabair cec*h*leith,
iarsin iarmaib dochúaid.
　　Dochuaid aclu *for*cec*h*leth.

LXVI.

4777 Foidit huadib Balám *m*bras,
　　　badrui, bacóir, bacomadas,
diam-mallachad dica*c*h*bla
tr*i*abrechtaib adruidechta.

4781 Doluid *for*agabrai gluair
Balam ahucht inmorslúaig,
*co*nnágabdais cle fr*i*caih,
cotuaid Dé diamallachad.

4785 Doluid a*n*gel Dé diatr*a*ig
arcinn Baláim baethbriatr*a*ig,
na*ch*areilic siar nosair,
asindf*i*ad hitarrasair.

4789 Gabaid *for*bualad aheich
Balám baeth dice*r*hoenleith,
*co*nid arlassáir indláir
dondaithiusc airdairc imnair.

4793 'Cenombuala fobagaib
lat'feirg, lat'bruth, aBaláim?
nimleic a*n*gel Dé na*ch*leth
*co*nachlaidiub derg tened.'

4797 Forcongart tóisech intsluaig
*for*Balám cenna*ch*glanbúaid :
'asinbaile atái tr*i*abrath
deni uait ámallachad.'

4801 Asoslaic Balám agin
fr*i*athesc n-alaind n-imdil,
uran uair balán dorath,
nirochan ac*h*t bennachad.

4805 Tuargaib Balam aguth *n*gluair
darasargud inmorslúaig ;
diamb*en*nachad, monar *n*gle,
*for*seimdes ahergairc.

4809 Nirás na*ch*nduine dalbda
commu*s* huili aaurlabr*a*,
isderb is lam'Choimdid cain,
rodelb nem *ocu*s talmain.

4813 Macc Bcoir, bág *m*buiden *m*bras,
baleor plág fr*i*ag n-amnas,
forset saer, deochair tr*i*ablait,
uair bafael feochair foidit.
　　Foidit uadib Balam *m*bras.

LXVII.

4817 Ri rosheitte, ri rosbiath,
　　rí dodassáer aranriad,
isindfthrub fr*i*sith sain,
cethrídeich doib dobliad*n*aib.

4821 Ri dorat comarle úglaein
doMoisi cona slúagaib,
diatír *ur*chach cennachcacht
iarciunniud acethrach[a]t.

4825 Ri roraid riu uasce*ch* cruth :
'mithig dúib techt ondithrub,
cosintír saer suthach sain,
dorairñgered doAbram.

4829 'Eirggid *for*set dobartaig :
nabid uamnaig, imeclaig :
messe *for*snaera arca*ch*cath,
etirdered istossach.

4833 'Ciambat ilardai naslúaig,
ciamtar imdai indríg rorúaid,
nigebat fr*i*b *for*nachmaig
icathaib, icomramaib.'

4837 Ri dorát doib biad bacet
dona dib[1] trebaib deéc,
arri óchéin, glan alí,
ishe inri reil roshétl.
　　Ri rosheti, rí rosbiad.

---

[1] MS. d*ri*ib.

LXVIII.

4841 'Cluinid mothimna doléir:
  narbardúrcridig [1] dochcil,
  nadénaid *tr*iu, ruathur *m*bras,
  cuibdi, cardes *no* clemnas.

4845 'Lam *fr*ĭidal *n*glethech *n*gal,
  *fr*ĭcthech, *fr*igúfǒrgal,
  censaint, cenaccobur *n*glé,
  maini caine cocéile.

4849 'Cengail, cenecnach, gním cain,
  cenetrad, cenduinorgain,
  honoir tuistide, dreim *n*glan,
  serc Dé *ocus* comnessam.

4853 'Cométaid iarn-urd ríagla
  inchaisc *ca*chaoenbliad*na*,
  ochoicid déc, isdin cert,
  cosinn-oen *f*ebdai fichet.

  [fo. 31 b. 1.]

4857 'Foirbthi, fcidli, *f*eth cenchel,
  foglaim ocus*f*orcitel,
  ladeichthimna, *t*or*um* *n*glé,
  cometaid recht n-imdíbe.

4861 'Ladechmada [2], derbtha bí,
  primiti ocus *pr*ímgeinni,
  honoir doDia, dig*r*ais gair,
  dog*r*es isintab*er*nacuil.

4865 'Cách conaalmsain iartain,
  iar*n*dligud, iar*n*dut*r*achtaib,
  isiarrúnaib c*r*ídi chóir
  dog*r*es iconglanaltóir.

4869 'Nadermaitid timna *n*Dé,
  idna huimle aurnaigthe,
  niburn-ecnaigid Dé dil,
  nib*f*or*c*étludaig, cluiníd.'

  'Cluinid mothimna doléir.'

LXIX.

4873 Orddaigid inn-eclais n-uaig,
  dog*r*es immedon intsluaig,
  se sluaig rempi, rígda gair,
  *oc*us *s*é slúaig 'nadegaid.

4877 Nocolaimed nech dontslúag
  macc n-Isr*ahé*l *f*ri[i]mluad,
  dochois nalaim, comrac cuir,
  *fr*iclar dontab*er*nacuil.

4881 Treb Leue colini th[é]ol
  immoneclais cenanshéol,
  *fr*ăimmarchur osce*ch*cruth,
  *fr*ĭasrethad, *fr*ĭsuidigud.

4885 Muint*er* nasacart *f*osmacht
  ocimmarchur nan-anart,
  batheisreite, srethaib srath,
  immonn-eclais dianechtair.

4889 Drong na*n*deochain, derb laca*ch*,
  *fr*ĭimmarchor curtínad,
  cosna*f*uilgib, bam*ed* *n*gle,
  cotuidmib nadrumslaite.

4893 Sluag nasacart, sochla dal,
  *fr*ĭimmarchur nacoemclar,
  coca*ch*cumtuch, cain allí,
  conafothaib findruini [3].

4897 Senad nasruithi foleith,
  am*al* bite 'nacomsreith,
  iartimnaib De tiagait de
  d'immarchur nasanctáre.

4901 Achethrima*ice* conamblait
  Aron indhuasalsacairt,
  iarn-urd ríagla, ruathur *n*glé,
  *fr*ĭimmarchur nahairce.

4905 INdarc huasal osintslóg
  iarnacumtuch dodergór,
  *con*aaidmib, aidble bainn,
  cocilurnn lán dodegmaind.

---

[1] Written as a correction over *dochuirdig*.   [2] The *-da* is in the margin.   [3] MS. findruine.

4909 Arón amra, ard agair,
bahuasalsacart húasaib,
deichtimna De, digrais bes,
forabruinnib dobithgres,
4913 Treb Leue col-lînib cest,
nocodlegat atairmesc,
friairdiu domuin, dîn cloth,
fricaińgniu, fricathugod.
4917 Na aurraind tîri natúad,
na imfognam rige rorúad,
na snim no saethar, sliucht ńgle,
acht dliged an-ecailse.
4921 INri rosnordaig, reim n-uag,
etereclais ocus slúag,
indeclas diareir cogle,
insluag doreir naecailse [1].
4925 INdeclas conagradaib,
sruithib slógaib saerdanaib,
airbrib alaib uascechmaig,
ardib anaib ordaigid.
Orddaigid inn-eclais n-uaig.

LXX.

4929 Rádid Moisi menicc dóib,
huair basnimach, sruith, senóir,
'Iessu mac Nun, nassad ńgle,
fortoisech darm'essese.'
4933 Mosi mac Amra, meic Caid,
meic Leue, meicc Iacaib,
meic Isaic, meic Abraim óig,
meic Thaire dil, meic Nachóir.
4937 Meic Reu rocháin, rúathar ńdein,
meic Seruch saer, meic Ebeir,
meic Sale sláin, srethaib gal,
meic Fallech, meic Arfaxad.
4941 Meic Sem sochraid, srethaib iath,

meic nair Noe, meic Lamiach,
meic Mathussakm óscechrot,
ocus meic huasail Enóc.
4945 Meic Iareth, tomthaib tríath,
meic maith molbthaig Malalfal,
meic Cainain, meic Enos ail,
meic Seth saindil, meic Adaim.
4949 Adam mac Dé, dińgnaib dál,
dorimgair Fíadu findnar,
gle cocachn-eladain n-óig,
sé senathair armorslóig.
[fo. 31 b. 2.]
4953 Dorumalt Moisi, mod mass,
in-oitid, in-oclachas,
iarn-urd riagla, rethaib recht,
dáfichet blíadna in-Egept.
4957 Dafichet aili comblait
iclemnus inprimsacairt,
os sléib Choreb, grata bainn,
forinnarba óForainn.
4961 Dafichet aili, deilm n-uag,
do 'sindithrub riasintslúag,
iartimnu ríg nimi nel,
ocimthus mac n-Israhél.
4965 Se fichit blíadan insain,
cenforcraid, cenimhesbaid,
saegul Moisi, mílib rann,
feib leir adfet inscríbenn.
4969 INri rongart lais immach
Moisi críchid glantoisech,
conruc leis ontslog forleth
onduáir thanic aamser.
4973 Oshunn roscarad fríaslúag
Moisi con-ilar imluad,
nibae dib nech lasmadbecht
aadnacul no hetsecht.
4977 Mac Ammrai baardrí intsluaig,

[1] MS. -si.

combáig baldai, combithbúaid,
crích aaissi, derrit[1] breth,
Moisi menice noráded.
　　Rádid Moisi menic doib.

LXXI.

4981　Lín afer fír ferdais feirg
　　　frícath croda claidebderg,
secht cet dec tricha, dcilm dil,
arsecht cetaib domílib.

4985　IShé lin doruaraid díb
diatuathaib cenimmirím,
iarn-ec an-athar, cechcruth,
iarnandíth isindithrub.

4989　Mairb huili isdithrub insin,
an-athir, as-senathir,
cenoenfer mbeo fonim nel
acht ma[d]hEssu ocusCaleph.

4993　INri rodastraeth tríafrois
hicinaid an-immarbois,
rodastroeth tríachetfaid ngairg
cin indecnaig 'sindoenaird.

4997　Deithbir badchosc docach sain,
cobrath tríabithu samlaid,
donech frignim, cetlach ngle,
baeth an-óenach nasruithe.

5001　Cenárim mogad nachthreib,
maccaib, mnáib no ingenaib,
oscechmaig frigaethgail gnim
lainib laechaib alánlín[2].

　　Lín afer fír ferdais feirg.

LXXII.

5005　Ri rooirdnistar mac Nún
　　　Essu, con-immud hilrún,
corb'hé bahárdri dontslog,
icdul darmaige[3] Moáb.

5009　Ri roráid frihEssu n-uag :
'heirg frilessu namorslúag :
frithail cocalma, gním ngle,
catha garba, geintlide.

5013　'Suidig naslúagu 'nasreith,
bil impu docach oenleith,
nigébat frit'gnuis ngráddai
buidni borba barbardai.'

5017　Ri dorat sainhsamlai slain
forclainn n-airegdai n-Abráim,
ambith cencessu, cenchacht,
cein bae hEssu itoissigecht.

5021　IIEssu cocoscor congrad
dosrat fochoscor coemnár,
iarmaigib Moab, mod mass,
cosruth n-Eordanain n-admas.

5025　Trífichit míli iarsét,
trichoic mili laglanchet[4],
cet mili morfesser múad
docachoenleith donmorslúag.

5029　IIEssu fodiud, dclm n-uag,
triur dorosern inslúag,
cenlen frisrethad sechtar,
coimthrén 'coan-imnertad.

5033　Cia nolindais forru inmag
slúaig cechthiri, tolaib gal,
rianothuathaib[5] codinnim
nomaidfed forilmílib.

5037　Ri roróidig doib sét slán
doascnam tíri Cannán :
cossaib tirmaib, digrais scél,
lotar darsruth n-Eordanén.

5041　Dofucsat leo asintsruth,
fricorgud, fricertugud,
lasinslog, balór n-cire,
cloch mor cach[a]oentreibe.

---

[1] MS. dérit.　　[2] MS. alallu.　　[3] Written over tiri.　　[4] In margin: uirorum.　　[5] MS. -aid.

5045 Ri rianadúilib, delm n-úag,
ri bias beos iarmbrath bithbúan,
rí uas gréin, isgle roscar,
inrí réil rooirdnistar.
          Rí.

LXXIII.

[fo. 32 a. 1.]

5049 Ri rodaslín dobrig brais
clanna Israhél admais,
corosirset acricha
immaigib imhEricha.

5053 IArsain rosernsat ascuir
árteclammad amorchruid,
insluag lonn, lín an-athbaig,
san chan immonprímcathraig.

5057 INchathir cumtaig datha
frifrithalim n-ilchatha,
dosrimchelsat, derb, dana
secht muir tróna, dermára.

5061 Secht stuic rosophain inslúag
immoncathraig frámluad
corolegai, lathar úgle,
mur cechlathi sechtmaine.

5065 Lucht nacathrach conálí,
hili, huili, ilmíli,
doreir De trocthas cachngail,
dochotar fogin claideib.

5069 Acht mad Rab, amru gnímaib,
nitherna dontromdígail,
dothréon natrúag nithuaraid
oenfer donamorslúagaib.

5073 Ri dosfuc forso[i]rthib sláin,
adoirthib díthruib dermair,
reim n-an cenag, iarset sir,
inrí rán rodaslanlín.

          Ri rodaslin dobrig brais.

LXXIV.

5077 Tinolsat tor tolach talc
corad comfossad comnart,
arcind túaithi Dé dochath
secht tuatha Cannán cathach.

5081 Clanna Cannan gniset cath
fríhuaith Dé, dúr rodelbad,
coroclaithe fobrig bróin
icríchaib broga Bethróin.

5085 Tan turcbad Essu adiláim
friCoimdid nime noebnáir,
nomaided incath granna
forsecht tuathaib Cannána.

5089 Tan bascith lais, lathar ngrínn,
adilaim icrosfigill,
dossleced hIessu fríathoeb,
foramuintir bafírroen.

5093 Dorónsat toisig intslúaig
comairle nglicc conglanbúaid,
rosuidigset folama
dicloich tróna dermára.

5097 Romebaid incath iarsein
ocus roscail indimguin,
nirb'hanad díb, derb inrad,
coralád huili andergár.

5101 Coromarbtha na secht ríg
conasluagaib, slocht[1] ndirim,
cechoenfer beo, torgbad dail,
dochiniud clainni Cannáin.

5105 Doaitne ingrían frísinslóg
dondleith aniar darGabón,
nisgluais rosmbai innatass
fritrae dálathi lanmas.

5109 Tarrasair intsoillsi dil
iartimnu Dé donoebnim ;
fir sluaig Cannain comtarmairb
nirosluaid asindoenairm.

---

[1] o written over i.

5113 Andorigni Dia donim
dofertaib, doadamraib,
ardainib fríhuair rhbáge
atdirecraí, díárme.

5117 Na *sechí* rig réil, reim ruanaid,
congail géir commórslúagaib
buadaib, bagaib, brigaib blat,
tuathaib, tírib tinolsat.
    Tinolsat tor tolach talcc.

LXXV.

5121 R oraind Essu, airdirc scél,
    dosluagaib mac n-Isr*ahé*l,
indíraind déc, deilm dána,
*sechí prím*thuatha Cannána.

5125 IMraind atíri d'espaib
dorigset mor d'imresnaib,
*conidcrann*chor roscoraig
for*nat*uathaib dermoraib.

5129 Cetnacr*ann* iarcuimnib cein
babúidnib Benieméin,
isnadálaíbse iarséol
intánaise laSem[e]ón.

5133 Suidid intres, bagnim cóir,
lasfl suilig Zabuloin,
incethramad, gnimraid gr*ai*d,
laclaind n-irglain n-Isacháir.

5137 INcuiced cr*ann*chor, gnim gér,
laglanthor cinid Assér,
insess*ed* [crannchor] iarscing
dochlainn noithig Neptalim.

5141 INsechtmad cr*ann*chor laDán
iarcertr*ad* glannchor comlan,
int-ochtmad glanbda, gnim ñgr*i*nn,
laciniud n-amra n-Effr*ai*m.
    [fo. 32 a. 2.]

5145 INnómad laGád cenchess,

conág fr*i*sruth anaitdes,
indechmad cr*ann* d'Iudas diadcoin,
isroga rann laRubeoin.

5149 Treb Mannase, mflib gne,
rorannadside hicerde,
fr*i*sruth aness fofuair gr*ai*m,
al-leth n-aill tuaid icEffr*ai*m.

5153 Treb Leue, colinib scél,
fothírib mac n-Israhél.
cennachñgaile, *congr*ad glé,
fr*i*socre, fr*i*sacerdote.

5157 INdeclas nóeb conaairc
rodosuidigthi in-ocnailt,
fr*i*silad saincomnart slán,
fr*i*taircomrac acomdál.

5161 Secht pr*ím*thuatha Cannáin cain
fallain conafortuathaib,
et*ur* sessu nasluag soimm,
dorigni hÉssu inglér*ai*m[1].
    Rorainn Essu, airdirc scel.

LXXVI.

5165 T reb Iuda, treb Semeoin séim,
    ocus treb Beniamein,
siarthuaid ontsruth tana thren
cocr*i*cha mara Torrén.

5169 Lethtreb Mannase centáir,
tr*e*b Effr*ai*m, tr*e*b Issacháir,
atuaid cc*ch*ñdiriuch dontsruth
fr*i*siniud, fr*i*suidigud.

5173 Treb Neptalim, noithech scél,
ocus tr*e*b áibnech Assér,
cc*ch*cruth rognisset ambuaid
dontsruth rosinset sairthuaid.

5177 Treb Zabulon slaides feirg,
ocus tr*e*b Dán daigerdeirg,
acuir fr*i*glanaige ñgluair

---

[1] MS. ingléram.

omuir Galaile sairthúaid.

5181 Treb Ruben, treb Gaid nadchress,
fograd frisruth anairdess,
nocomeirtnech amasse,
ocus leithtreb Mannásse.

5185 Dondleith anair dothreib Dáin
sernait sreith slébe Lebáin,
fríslatbrig slaidi sluaig sréin
icaccrích uaig Israhél.

5189 Annaneos, nuall nadchres,
Sidarios, ruad riges,
Echeos, glere cengráin,
trísluaig sin slebe Lebáin.

5193 Ebron, Gassear, Masheal már,
Gabaa, Gesseon, Galád,
sé cathracha attaig úaig
clainni Israhél adruaid.

5197 Ri dosfuc trínadíthrub trén
istrisi[n]dsruth n-Eordanen,
ri cougart cóir cotagaib,
dorotacht doib cechoentreib.

Treb Iuda, treb Semeoin séim.

LXXVII.

5201 R i dosfúargaib tríananert
adóire huathmair Egept,
ishé rodasidaig, sliucht slán,
forcrichaib clainne Cannán.

5205 ForFelistín oscechmaig,
forNathsared, forGalaib,
forArabia conaslóg,
forMoáb is forAmmón.

5209 Forbrugaib Abethib ban,
forsrethaib naSamratán,
fornamaigib, mod cenlén,
san chan im sruth¹ hIordanén.

5213 ForZeb, forZebe, sliucht n-án,

---

forPsalmandra, forIsmál,
forsliab Sióin, rethaib rad,
forGalad, forIosophath.

5217 ForAmalech oscechdruñg,
forAssur is forTirum,
forMadian mín, mod glanna,
forCisson, forSissarra.

5221 Forfiliis Loth, línib gial,
forEdom, forhIdumiam,
forAmorreorum, reim n-án,
forGebal isforBassán.

5225 Fortír hGeth, forCarmill cron,
forTerebinthe, forTabor,
forGalgala rochar Dia,
formaig Messopotamia.

5229 Fortírib na[n]ingen n-úag,
Selfaid frítindrem tromslúag,
Malaa, Melcha, Egia án,
Micha ocusTersa tonnbán.

5233 Forglinn n-Ammrai, amrai rád,
cétna adbai doAbrám,
forSeon slanda naslóg,
forSamara, forBethrón.

5237 ForhEricho, aurdaig slog,
forGilune hglain, forGabón,
forriathur Cedróin cenbreic,
forsliab n-amra n-Olaueit.

[fo. 32 b. 1.]

5241 F(or) ca(ch) tuaith trein,derbcenlen,
rogabsat meicc Israhel :
doreir Dé, bagnim cenchol,
rolethsat darsindomun.

5245 Otha Alaxandir ain,
aness oAffraic imslain,
fothúaid cocrích Med isPers,
rorigset acomaithches.

5249 Dondleith anfar, aith cenlén,

---

¹ Written over *niord* in 'imerich híordanén.'

otraig mór mara Torrén,
fosrugensatar comblait
sair cocrich n-orda n-Eofrait.

5253 MoDia tricc frisrethchor slamm,
rí conic trethnu torann,
ri condathaeb oschrí chain,
rí centathair dosfuarcaib.
    Rí dosfuargaib trianert.

LXXVIII.

5257 Rí rodasáer uascechmúr
    arcechn-irgail, réim rogúr,
connachasclai cath no crech
aned bai Essu atoissech.

5261 Robris for trichait cath crúaid,
ruc acoscur anglanbuaid,
con-ilur muirech, mod neim,
cotrichait ruirech roreil.

5265 Oshunn báth Éssu mac Nún,
atoisech tolaib tromthúr,
liunsatar cach dib foleith,
rodiultsatar aCoimdeid.

5269 Fichi bliadan ocus chét
aés Éssu meic Nun rian-óc,
cor'hadnacht, fograda grrim,
inTamara, isleib Effraim.

5273 Ri robai riambetha bann,
dorigni retha retglann,
conrotaig cechñgrád hicrí,
inrí rán rodasaeri.
    Ri rodasáer uascechmúr.

LXXIX.

5277 OShunn roscarsat, gnim glé,
    friadrad rig noebnime,
rodasbate plág dibaid,
dosrat focachtromdigail.

5281 Dosrat cenbaide fomnad
fodóire, fobithfognam,

Gussán garg, crodu cechnia,
toisech Mesopotamia.

5285 Ocht mbliadna doib, toromm [n-án],
fodubdoire doGussán,
conastorslaic uad triablait
Nathanel amra aurdairc.

5289 Rodasdáer coleir colór
reil ri naMoáb Eglón,
cotuc Ógeth huad triachath
arécin iarnamarbad.

5293 Rodasdáersatar diambríg
Sissarra ocus Iabín,
condossaersat dicechthracht
Diborra ocus Barác.

5297 Fosrordingsetar codfan
Amalech ocus Madfan :
gle rodasaer Gedeon cain
lafortacht Dé donoebnim.

5301 Diatarfas indlassar lór
asindailig réil romór,
diafer broen forincnai ñglain
diambai tart forsintalmain.

5305 Ort trifichit mili mas
artribcetaib, gnim n-amnas,
inidapad Oreb de
Psalmanae Zeb [is] Zebe.

5309 Bai clann Israhél cachtreib
fodóere, fodeirmitneib,
cenbuaid, cenbrig, cenbaeg ñiblat,
friarig osunn roscarsat.
    Oshunn roscarsat, gnim glé.

LXXX.

5313 Bretha doGedcon glan glic
    deich meice ocus trifichit,
rosnort acht oenfer, baliach,
ambrathair Abimeliach.

5317 Acht atrula int-ossar uad

Ionás toxal natromsluag,
bagnim truag dodaiṅg d'aes raith
atascomaiṅg foroenchlaich.

5331 Ilardai atoisig ceċhtḣreib,
nibtar foismid foroensreith,
Tolia, Ior, Ioipti óg,
Abisson, Abigilón.

5325 Ri rosdilsig doée thricc
nónbur dóib istriḟichit,
foroencloich cuchtai, cain blai,
isann ructhai ambrethai.
          Bretha doGedeon glan glicc.

LXXXI.

5329 Genair dothreib Dán, delm
          ṅdein,
Samson slan, sochla, saergein,
mac Manúail, mind mordais máil,
dochiniud amra Abráim.
          [fo. 32 b. 2.]

5333 Dochuaid assathír immach,
huair badelbda, diummussach,
cotuc mnái n-uallaig, trúag gnim,
dithuathaib naFilistin.

5337 Ní rosaisneid nech fomeirg,
gnimrada Samsóin slegdeirg,
feib lor doranic, tuc ṅdein
mór doceċh hulc ochlemnaib.

5341 Trisluag nasinnach, sliucht ṅglé,
doloscud nafinemnae,
trḟasinfidba cnáma crúaid,
dian-erbailt mfli morsluaig.

5345 Trḟasinfodb [   ] ṅgell ṅglan,
trḟasinceist cruaid cáin comram,
trḟadoirsi, tarbach clissiud,
nacathrach doforbrissiud.

5349 Dian-erlai uadaib diatreib

tren asnatricumrigib,
trḟanan-indriud centlaihe
cosluagaib ceċhoenrathi.

5353 Mori reil rígda raihmar
dorigní firt n-imathlam,
diambai icselach naslúag
Samson slan, serig, slamrúa(d).

5357 Diambai in-hitaid osindleirg
ocslaide inchatha cródeirg,
dia rodáil dó Dia dig
dolind glan asindflaccail.

5361 Dianmert fodein truag cumma
dobrrad amormuṅgga,
bade bai andith iartain
andegdoenib in-oentaig.

5365 Samson slattra slaidi slúa[i]g,
ba mál machta mac Manúail,
nifrḟh amacsamla sain
isindamsir rogenair.
          Genair dothreib Dán, delm ṅdein.

LXXXII.

5369 Genair gein airmitnech án
          Samuel óg, etlai, imnár,
mac Elcanna, glan abbeirt,
ocus mac Anna ambreit.

5373 Alcanna, críchid agréim,
deNamatha ósleib Effraim ;
Anna, bási aben combúaid,
máthair sainsemail Samúail.

5377 Basui, basacard [1] sruit[h], saer,
bahalgen, craibdech, glanácb [2],
bafaith humal, ennac, óg,
friforcital namorslóg.

5381 Rí dorat digail iartain
forhEli conamaccaib,
Samuel iarsin, srethaib smacht,

---

[1] The second a is written over e.   [2] MS. glan báeb.

sechbafaitli, baprimsacart
5385 Oshunn báth Essu combúaid
coamsir saindil Samúai(l),
nibae dib cotacoimsed
doprímfaith noprimthóisech.

5389 Ri dasfuargaib, milib scel,
fortirib mace n-Israhél,
diathuaid batrénfer badrech [1],
rogénair gein airmitnech.
  Génair gein airmitnech án.

LXXXIII.

5393 B ahuallach forDagon[2] dían,
diahídal immid anr[f]an,
arc Dé cuce rian-ócaib,
iarsligthib, iarprímrótaib.

5397 Diatardad dígal cotrén
fortirib mac n-Israhél,
icind Hele conachlaind,
dochuatar huile imbadbraind.

5401 Diatorchair dib isinchath
trichet mili fer n-armach,
imdámac Hele andiis,
Ofne ocus Finees.

5405 Diarucsatar leo indairc
Filistín feib dosrimthairc,
línib gelglor conangrain
dothempul dérmor Dagain.

5409 Or'siacht coDagan diathaig
airc inCoimded cumachtaig,
dorigni dé min islúaith,
rochlaemchlai gne 'sindoenúair.

5413 Mór domilib, buiden mbras,
dorochair dib, delm n-amnas,
rodosnairg Dia, toromm ngle,
arairgabail nahairec.

5417 Cid nahí naherbalt díb
rodospianta fodimbríg,
lotar forru immach, mod ngle,
conara an-imthelgthe.

5421 Arce indríg reil rígi áir
morchoimded nime noebnair,
robai ann fogris grada
secht tnís caine comlána.

5425 Tuargabad indarc corath
fordiócbáe cendomnad,
al-loeg fogaile cachta,
até caine, comblechta.
  [fo. 33 a. 1.]

5429 Rochumrigthe leo dondairc
cuibdigthe feib dosrimthairc,
fuath lochad[3] landai lordai,
fuath nan-ainne erordai.

5433 Ri rosnordaig nadibai
cosinn-airc cenimmarbae,
iarconair chóir, crichid scél,
cotarrasair forambel (?)[4].

5437 Batar ann túatha frífeis
dianidainm Bidsomieis,
dosrinolsat, toga ngle,
doimcassin nahairce.

5441 Acht chena insluag, lathar ndil,
dodeochaid diahimcasin,
trífichit fer, feochair glóir,
bamarb uadib fochctóir.

5445 Cáeca mili, medar n-úag,
iarsin bamarb donmorslúag,
dontúaith dathglain, dine ngle,
imchathraig Bidsomite.

5449 Bidsomite fo[i]dit scél
cosluagu mac n-Israhel,
cotissed nachslúag dib de

coluath arcenn nahairce.

5453 Dodeochatar natúatha
cuce, caine, comlúatha,
d'fáilti fria, cenait n-uabuir,
frihairc indrig roruanaid [1].

5457 IArsin cotucsat hifén
indare docharraic Abél,
arg*ra* de delbais cc*h*cath
cotegdais Aminadab.

5461 Elizor*us* rigdu rath,
dochinud Aminadab,
fr*i*cacart cáin, caingen ńglé,
bahé sacart nahairce.

5465 INdare amra, ilair blad,
in-adbai Aminadab,
robai *fich*it mbliadan mbind
isintúaith Cariath[i]arim.

5469 Corodmbroe rí betha bailce,
rodelái tr*i*agertha comthaile ;
badremun degr*a*ch dochath,
sechba menmnach bahualla*ch*.
        Bahualla*ch* *for*Dagon [2] dían.

LXXXIV.

5473 Oshunn dorúacht indárce úag
darmórtíri, darmórtuath,
meic Isra*hé*l, cosreib sáil,
rothinolsatar oe[n]dáil.

5477 Friinnarbu n-idal n-él
dothirib m*ac* n-Isra*hé*l,
dorinolsat, srethaib srath,
combátar huili imMesbad.

5481 Roráid Samuel, snímach scél,
fr*i*sluag n-frach n-Israhél ;
' doforfua digal cc*h*maig
icin *for*n-idal n-ańgbaid.

5485 ' Manichuirid húaib coluath
ilar forn-idal n-ollmuad,
derb dofo*r*fua digal tinn
oríg nime náir nóebfind.'

5489 Doratsat réir ńDe cc*h*dú
me*i*c Isra*hé*l fiadchainchlú ;
rodosslechtsat doDia díl
iarsin cenadrad n-ídaíl.

5493 O shunn atchuas iarfír
doshíagaib naFilistín,
dodeochatar *con*acath
cucu corice Mesbad.

5497 Roraidsetar, érim n-úag,
meic Isra*hé*l friimlúad :
' corob linni búaid donchath
guid inCoimdid c*u*machta*ch*.'

5501 Adropart audpart tr*i*arath
isrogaid coduthrachtach,
Samúel dorig nimi nél,
darcenn clainne Isra*hé*l.

5505 INrí thuc inn-arce forcul
immu*s*racht [3] darcec*h*mórmúr,
incec*h*airm, cec*h*dú, cendín
dorat maidm *for*Filistín.

5509 Ri dorat digail cendín
forslógaib naFilistín,
oscec*h*thracht fr*i*sratha smacht
indare oshunn doroacht.
        Oshunn doruacht indarc úag.

LXXXV.

5513 Ohel, Abía, erctha buáid,
dámac sain segda Samúail [4],
nibatclithemail 'moscél,
brithemain m*ac* n-Isra*hé*l.

5517 F.coltchinn [5] eat fr*i*gním ńgann,

---

[1] MS. roruanaib.   [2] *o* written over *a*.   [3] MS. imimm*u*sracht.   [4] MS. samuél.
[5] MS. Ecoltchitchinn, with dot over second *t*.

frigubreith, frigúforgall :
badimdaig díb, tola trén,
sloig mora mac n-Israhél.

5521 Linib treb dál, tola ṅglé,
otha Dán coBersabe,
dochum Samuél cosindrath
dodeochatar coRamath.
[fo. 33 a. 2.]

5525 Gadatar doDia, delm n-úag,
isgadatar doSamúal,
fricathu, fribruth, fribríg,
conábetis cenoenríg.

5529 IArfacht dóib Samuel frisreith :
' cid ta[ch]thi Día forcoimdeid ?
fortse isferr cechríg ráin,
ardruire nime noebnáir.

5533 ' Fónmissi robriss recht réil
foirb ritecht darbforn-amréir,
arforfelmáine cenlén,
adegdáine Israhel l'

5537 IArsin roraide inslúag
an-athesc fir friSamúal :
' frímmad ṁbrig ṁbuidenn ṁbla
niruibem cenríg ṅdóenna.'

5541 Rooirdnistar Samuel faith
Saul mac Cis conglanbaig,
frisoerbríg ṅdúasaig, deilm ṅdil,
dooenríg [   ] uasail.

5545 O shunn rogab ríge rúad
Saul digrais daigermúad :
rodaslin galma ocus glóir
clanna ámra Iacóib.

5549 Connabetis cenrig rain
gádatar huili ahoendail :
romiscnigset, mílib scél,
Abía ocus Ohél.

Ohél, Abía, eretha buaid.

¹ leg. n-ammail?

LXXXVI.

5553 Nás ri Ammón, aurdairc rád,
dorat smacht forsluag Ga-
lad,
cosúilib dessaib teṅnaib
dogait asacoemchennaib.

5557 Conaclannaib rosdocraid,
gnim naṁmail ¹ fodubroenaib,
cocoicthib trenaib trommaib,
cocroicnib díaṅglédrommaib.

5561 Rogáid slúag Galad cogle
forNas ossud sechtmaine,
dus infoigebtais fonim
nech donech an-imditin.

5565 Foidit atechtairecht trúag
coSaúl is coSamúal,
dus infogebdais nert n-óg,
nos-ainsed forslúag n-Ammón.

5569 Dolluid Saul iarsét sen,
sécet míli, cenimlén,
ocus tricha míli mass,
doslúagaib n-Iuda n-amnas.

5573 Rodobris coslattra slán
forNás cath calma comlán :
bahé achetnacoscur ṅglé
iarnagabail ir-rige.

5577 Doluid Sául, gléraib cath,
cotúatha n-Ammon n-engach,
tor troeta tríath, sas naslóg,
roiad imNas ri Ammón.

Nas rí Ammon, airdirc rad.

LXXXVII.

5581 Coscur n-aili trén túargaib,
diar'maid forsnamorsluagaib,
con-iṁmud muirech, mod n-án,

riaSául, rian-Ianothan.

5585 Diatancatar cucu intslúaig
Filistín feochair¹ fírchruaid,
nicondilgud *acht* *con*gail,
diandibdud, diandianarggain.

5589 Dodígail Náais, noithech ág,
forSául, forslúag Galad,
cocath gér geimlech, gnim n-óg,
icoemthecht ne[i]mnech n-Ammón.

5593 Díarmide daigrech dín
drong daigrech naFilistín,
tricha mile cairptech cath
issé mili fer n-armach.

5597 Lotar lín ateglaig dein
bagním dedgair coanaimteib,
dámfie laSaul slán
ismfie laIonathán.

5601 Cofopartatar inslog
naFilistín, nan-Ammon,
corálsatar og glanóg ágrínn
forAmmon, forFilistim.

5605 Macc Ciss óragab ríge
robris formór n-ilmile,
rosindre iarcoscur glé,
dorigne coscur n-aile.
    Coscur n-aili tren túargaib.

LXXXVIII.

5609 Fecht dodeochatar otír
fianna feoch[r]a Filistín,
sluaig sin sirden frislait srén
dodilgen *mac* n-Israhél.

5613 Arim asluaig, slicht cenchol,
línib atuath, atromthor,
secht mili fer, ferr *cech* ngail,
con-armaib, *con*gascedaib.

¹ MS. foechair.

5617 Tinólsatar, tola tren,
slóig mora macc n-Israhél,
    [fo. 33 b. 1.]
bahuamnaig triamnaig diatraig
combatar uili in-oendáil.

5621 Cororaid moRí noebnar
sech *cach* n-oen friIonathán,
condig*sed* iarfoimsin² fir
do'rfaicsin sluaig Felistín.

5625 Dochuaid Ionothan forleth
aoenur 'saarmiger,
coromarb díb, díni ñder,
fichi mili fer fortrén.

5629 Ri dorat digail, delm n-án,
forígaib rian-Ianothán,
o[M]achim, comflib slóg,
cocrich n-iraig n-Achilon.

5633 Nir'línaib fer, formnaib snas,
lainib ligdaib, ler n-ernmas,
nisnacht osbrí brigda brass,
acht moRí rígda rinnmas.

5637 Rucsat réim, rod rainni sloig,
dochlod clainni Iacoib,
fribríg bert, fricumtach ngal,
otír fecht dodeochatar.
    Fecht dodeochatar otír.

LXXXIX.

5641 Ri roraid friSamúel súg
con-erbarad friSaúl,
condechsad lín athor triath
cendil d'argain Amaliach.

5645 Conátuctha lais ambrat,
étach, nahór, naargat,
atairbirt uili frilár,
etermnái isfer, badergár.

² MS. iarforoimsin.

5649 Centáin cethra, cengraig cóem,
centróetu muc foroenróen,
connátuctais leo coatech
almai gabur nachairech.

5653 Dodeochaid Sául iarsein
cosindneoch fuair diócaib,
coroslig seirgib selggaib,
díglaib demnib drumdergaib.

5657 Tri cét míli, maith inscél,
doslúagaib mac n-Israhél,
ocus deich mili, mor mbla,
diocaib treibe Iuda.

5661 Rosaraig Saul nasluag
ani roraidi Samúal,
tuc leis toirti attír natráth,
ocus tuc ríg n-Amaliach.

5665 Togach rohiccad infiach
friAgach, friAmaliach,
osbri niblaith abríg buan
inRi roraid friSamúal.

Ri roraid friSamúel súg.

XC.

5669 Badebthach friSaul slán
Dia deoda, declrach, dermar,
diar'anacht Agach, rad nglé,
diar'sáraig aforngaire.

5673 Samúal cenanad[1] rosiach
coAgach rig n-Amaliach :
rochind aaided n-ada
fochlaideb inGalgatha.

5677 Rí roraid friSamuel faith
athesc n-inclithi n-imtlaith :
'inn-ined Sául, slicht síd,
deni lat oirdned Duíd.'

5681 Ri doraega, rúathar nglé,
Dauid degmac Iessé,
or'bamac slán secht mbliadna[2]
dorat fográd chomchialla.

5685 Rí betha binn, búan ablat,
arcrúan ngrinn, arclithcomnart,
dondindlach sainti 'masech
acht badimdach, badebthach.

Badebthach friSau[l] slán.

XCI.

5689 I Nrí dosfuc sechinslóg
Abimelech[3] coMoób,
aben isadámac, cain blá,
dialuid oBethil Iudáe.

5693 Abimelech, censíl mbrón ;
Nóemi, Mallcón, Cellcón,
Orbba friluth, líth ngarta,
ocusRuth Moabdita.

5697 Dodechaid huide fata
Ruth rochain Moábdita
laNóemi, mílib bla,
cotoracht Bethil Iuda.

5701 Rooentaig[4] iarsin friBoz
mac Salamoin, nirb'anfost :
húaide rogenair iarcéin
mac diarbochomainm Obéid.

5705 Salamon slan, srethaib séis,
bahiarmhuasede Fares :
Fares friglanail, gnim nglé,
bamac Tamair isIudae.

5709 Ruth máthair Obed, rád ngle,
Obeth athair Iessé :
Iessé, cendimess díth,
baathair díles Dauíd.

---

[1] MS. cenauag.   [2] MS. mblianda.   [3] MS. abimebech.   [4] S. Roentaid.

[fo. 33 b. 2.]

5713 Duíd togu dodelm glé
bai fechtas ichingaire :
dofarraid leo, lan dogail,
coruc caerig diacháireib.

5717 Cororaith foróenaib ríad
Dauid aoenur 'nadíad,
tríagradaib achoiblid chain,
cotarraid inleoamain.

5721 Coforbart Dauid dána,
coleomain nalonnbága,
cotuc tríaláeschur cenchleith
asachráesluch incáireig.

5725 Rofersat cumleng ńgradach
Dauíd 'sindleo lonndbágach :
tressiu Dauíd, tolaid crích,
lafortachtain indardríg.
INrí dosfuc sechinslóg.

XCII.

5729 R othinólsat slúag[ad] sír
tuatha feochra Filistín,
con-hilur mbuada, mor scél,
cotuatha mac n-Israhél.

5733 Con-immud sleg ocus slúag,
conniurt curad claidebruad :
batrén roindled leo insain
dian-inred isdian-argain.

5737 Dodilgenn androńg ńdalach,
amban, amac mórgradach,
diacor diacríchaib, mod cert,
diafichaib aforaithmet.

5741 Sinsit cenerbrón donchath
inslóg dermor diummussach,
congabsat lońgphort ńglám ńgle
forlár glinne Tríbinthe.

5745 Eterfocus ocus chiáin

dorigset huili comtriall,
intsluaig cendil, tolaib tlacht,
diatuaithtir rothinólsat.
Rothinólsat slúagad sír.

XCIII.

5749 T ucsat leo trénfer n-frach
diarb'ainm Gola garbgní-
mach :
nirb'fer suairc sochraid oslóg :
bahéo duairc dermór.

5753 Matud mógda merda mend,
mor d'étuch aimthimchell,
inaairdde, adbul deil,
secht ferchubait core sein.

5757 I.urech imme, garb achruth,
fricomrac, frícathugud ;
cóeca dochétaib uńga
robae innacomthrumma.

5761 Bái slind [1] agae fiadcachdruńg
secht cét uńga doiurn,
cocraunn chain, críchid, cumma,
remidir déil damchuńga.

5765 Ahiallacrann humai glain
otha aglúine cotalmain :
dohiurn glass rochummad,
cathbarr immachertmullach.

5769 Claideb gér garbda 'naglaic,
méit claidib garmna comthailc,
scíath forachliu, niclithi,
balethiu indá damseche.

5773 Fer cachlaithi lais il-lén
dislógaib mac n-Israhél,
nifríth díb oenfer foleith
folilsad arái ńgaisc[e]id.

5777 Gola granna congail glua[i]r,
dána frítola tromsluaig,

¹ MS. islind.

frìsrengal nirb'súaire asmacht,
batrénfer duaire tí thuesat.
     Tuesat leo trénfer n-irach.

XCIV.

5781 Giabdarilarda[i] intslúaig
     clainni Israhél adrúaid,
rosgab crith, gléraib ellach,
riańGola ńgér garbgrennach.

5785 Dosrat hituaim immondeil,
roscacht cenhuail, cenergail,
glerden roscnái sechcachńdáil,
trénfer cechlae diandigbail.

5789 Rolin toirsi, rogab ferg,
Saul slisfota slegderg,
fer cachlae laiss, ciarbobin,
domarbad diadegdáinib.

5793 Saul mac Ciss croda, ger,
ri cóir clainni Israhél,
rogell aingin centmeth
frióenfer dafińggebad.

5797 Dosrat frìsním, serig sel,
cendín demin diatairchel,
trúagdai garbdai cennachtlí
ciamtaramrai ilardai.
     Giabdarìlardai intslúaig [1].

XCV.

5801 Dodeochaid Dauid amné,
     ossar clainne Iessé,
isindinbaidsin othreib,
'sin slog colón diabrathreib.
     [fo. 34 a. 1.]

5805 Cocuala incóe, nua[i]]laib nél,
bóe forsluagaib Israhél,
acomruc désse cenchath,
fer cach lae dísb nomarbad.

5809 Roiarfacht Dauid cenchlcith
isinphopull diabratreib :
'coalog dobeir no ciarath
inrí dondfiur nombffad?'

5813 Atchuadatar inbráthir,
briathraib bithib bithblaithib,
doDauid, cennf iarcul,
feib léir rodgellai Saul.

5817 Rogellai Saúl mac Ciss
ahingin cendil ń-indliss,
lacachmaith do doberad
dondoenfiur dafińgebad.

5821 Dauid dualach, tolaib gal,
bahé inset sluagach salmglan,
badcecair taidbsen diadrech
isinda[i]mser dodechaid.
     Dodeochaid Dauid amné.

XCVI.

5825 'Regatsa,' arDauid cenlén,
     'coSaul rig n-Israhél,
cotuc aingin cenclith
is coromarb incóraid.'

5829 Gabsat acharait cechcruth
achose isa chairigud :
diabraithrib robogábud
alabrad noaimrádud.

5833 Roraidi Dauid cotren
fiad dagdáineib Israhél :
'dińgebsa [2] infer hut dontslóg [3],
istábar dam adaglóg.'

5837 Rogellai Saul iarsain
doDauid cenimresain
aingen dó, demin scél,
agrad sechclainn n-Israhél.

5841 'Ainige fris, foglóir glain,
ameic Cis chóir comramaig !

---

[1] MS. instlúaig.   [2] Read fingébsa?   [3] MS. dontslóg.

cendimiad imchoible cruth,
coſſrian diaſſrugud.'

5845 'Róthiat limm anige intslúaig
fotheisc sainigthe Samuáil,
ſeib thorgaib bríg imratha
ſom'ſorgal ſein ſír[ſ]latha.

5849 'Fnech Ioseph uasce*ch*du
Moisi, Iacob isIessu,
henech ſodeoid osce*ch*dáil
uaisliu doib Dia Abaráim.

5853 'Huaim daitſri*cech*ñdáil,delm ñglé,
ſrū'laim, ame*r*c Iessé,
ſrisotharſa dochor cain
a*ch*t coromarba incoraid.'

5857 'Muirſetsa Gola, gním ñgle,
bihé cora arcardine,
biaid mobríg bág ſorassa,
doreir morig regatsa.'
'Regatsa,' arDau*i*d cenlén.

XCVII.

5861 L uid cenlurig, lathar ñdein,
Dauid arcinn indſirsin,
cengae, censcíath, cloithi bann,
cenchlaideb cſar, cenchathbarr.

5865 Rogab eóic clocha cengr*s*in
atraig intsrotha dermair,
dodosrat ſein ſr*i*buáid [   ]
innathéig n-uaig n-áigarda.

5869 Gabaid cloich díb, bagnim ñgér,
sróid huaid isinn-aer,
roben Gola iclethi achind,
corocht conice ainchinn.

5873 Doluid Dau*i*d cucai iarsin,
gaibid dó achlaideb ſessin,
cotuc achenn tr*i*agail ñgúir,
combóe ſorbélaib Saúil.

¹ MS. Luig.

5877 Dau*i*d cenbini adreth buáid
oruirig nimi nocbuáig,
nitrúag dluige rſanadreich,
baluath luide cenluirech.
Luid ¹ cenluirig, lathar ñdein.

XCVIII.

5881 A trachtatar nadaſlúag
donchath croda claidebrúad,
doimruachtain cinn icenn,
doimthuargain cocomthenn.

5885 Friſúrad nañgrúam ñglora*ch*
nacúrad, nacruadchorad,
colin añdroñg ñdſan ñdaigrech,
bátar ciai ic[c]omclaidbed.

5889 Ri dorat tr*i*all ſorsincath
riañDau*i*d ñdian, dássachtach,
coroemid incath cendil
ſorslog ſaelid Filistín.

5893 Bai crú garb darcorp centlí
icath glinni Treibinthi,
diatorchair dib, toromm ñglé,
séssiur c*ó*ica coicmile.

5897 Slúaig naFilistín ſonél
ocus slúaig mac n-Israh*e*'l,
[ſo. 34 a. 2.]
nírbuchian ſr*i*ginol ñgal
tinól dſan atrachtatar.
Atrachtatar nadaſlúag.

XCIX.

5901 O shunn romebaid incath
rſanDuid cosinmó[r]rath ;
atb*e*red inslóg cogúr :
'ſerr comor ² indá Saúl.'

5905 Ocmolad Dau*i*d, delm n-uag,
sechSaúl, sech inmorſlúag,

² .i. Dau*i*d.

babind acéol ńgrinngel ńglé
innan-ingen n-Ebraidé.

5909 INtan baóenmſli aig
ocSaúl conaslúagaib,
deichmſli mora, mordíth,
dorochratar ocDauíd.

5913 Tinól Dauíd diluth glan
friherud nahairmiten,
cetheirtréin tairbbig foleith
dichairdib, dichomdíneib.

5917 IArsin tuc fobríg buadaig
ingin Sáuil srethsluagaib,
Míchol mór, mó cách ńgaine,
dohinchaib nandagdaine.

5921 Or'ort Gola, cruach golach,
diambái inslúag 'coamormolad,
lammac croda [   ] cońgail
baduairc laiss aimcasain.

5925 INtslúaig indruirig combríg
inmuirig immonn-ardríg,
bafaelid cach dſb dialuid
incath oshunn romebaid.
          Oshunn romebaid incath.

C.

5929 Dorigensatar sid slan
     Dauid ocus Ionathán,
farriaguil Dé, ſochucht chain,
fríaré hiſut asaegail.

5933 Dorat Ianothán iarſír
huad aheirriud doDauíd,
eter etach fríríad rath,
etr gae is[s]ciath ischlaideb.

5937 Rochinnset acotach cáid
cennach cocad imchomdáil,
cidolcc, cidmaith, tríabith sír,
etir Sául isDauíd.

5941 Duthracair Michol cenmeth
abráthair, aairchinnech,
ambith icairddes cendíth
Ionathán ocus Dauid.

5945 Bái Dauíd ſoglórai grad
iarcórai friIonathán,
innathig ſomſad, ſecht ńgúr,
octríall dothecht coSaul.

5949 Rogab Michol, medar ſír,
cotrebar tinchosc nDauid :
' nidechais fríslemna scel,
corſg n-ergna n-Israhél.

5953 'Náteig cotdiss, agass glé,
comac Ciss cencommairgé,
babaeth meni adair rún,
nátabair toeb friSaul.'

5957 Doluid Saúl frisnúad sid
coluath dothegdais Dauíd,
fríairsin Dauíd ifus
cenaigsin, cenſurachrus.

5961 INduair dodechaid, tarm trén,
ri croda clann n-Israhél,
ann dothaet Dauíd, delm ńgúr,
immach forsét coSaúl.

5965 Sernai Saul insreth sláin
imthreib ńDauíd commórgráin :
roiad marnathraig, níth ńglé,
imchathraig meic Iessé.

5969 Mar'tchuala Míchol inmbreis
conrúala insluag 'montegdais,
rothinól dintoirt tachtai
nalſnbroit, nahanartai.

5973 Dor'imthas, bahé ingnim cass,
ambé findchass fíramnas,
rosuidig cosuairc naslaimm
immuacuaird immoncerchaeill.

5977 Conderna ſúath ındſir de
colúath innagaethrige,

feib ba bés bith icétlud
dogress doib foainétgud.

5981 Rogart asdorus immaig
smacht solus Saul sáergein,
roraid comall, monor ńglé,
'infail tall mac n-Iessé?'

5985 Roraid Michol, mín aguth,
friSaúl diachennsagud :
'menipcél críntaig dochath
mochen tíchtain degathar.'

5989 'A Michol merda, menmnach,
gelda, genbda, comdelbach,
taet 'mach fochléire cachta
doché[i]le, dochomalta.'

5993 'Aní condnigi, amric Ciss,
achlí gaili ceneisslis,
  [fo. 34 b. 1.]
atá sunn, cennach glíim ńglé,
etir daláim th'inginé.'

5997 'Ciabeith dolám, lathar ńglé,
dardrochmac n-an n-Iessé,
ninanais fritindremm tinn,
ahingen Achinoym l'

6001 'Cidnech badmó miscais lat,
arí [I]srahél con-armacht,
tissed ríandígla fom'guth,
nirígda duit mosárgud.'

6005 'A Míchol mer, menmnach, mas,
ahúa engach Athemas,
nítbia frit'dil ńdogra ńder,
rígdomna mac n-Israhél.'

6009 'A meric Ciss fort'glonnaib gaib,
nabris fordochommorgeib,
na'báid triaderbága trén,
cenn n-erbága n-Israhél.'

6013 'O dorala, rúathar ńglé,
frim'thala mac Iessé,

duit, abé féne fechtach,
nibacéle crídserccach.'

6017 'Americ Ciss clechtaig, gnim ńglé,
nahettraig mac n-Iessé,
tairínn thogail gnáthaig ńgil,
nasárnig dodegingin.

6021 'Násáraig Ionathán uais
coṅgail gnáthaig, corochrúais,
cenolc. cenna[i]nces, cendíth,
rogab cairdes friDuíd.

6025 'Nasáraig Samuel fáith finn,
congab grad núalnar, náebdind,
nasaraig cengáisi ńglór
Máisi, Ioséph, Iacób.

6029 'Nabris báig n-airech noláech,
noainech nafer fírgáeth,
nagnáthaig ni assia doscél,
nasáraig Dia n-Israhél.'

6033 'Cia dobertha dam frímthóir,
abrn, cél n-unga ńdergóir,
argais galais no gart ńgle,
nianais mac n-Iesse.

6037 'Rodonanacht Dia donim,
cain glanalt cenimresain,
fográdglunn, cenchúairt ńglassa,
dochúaid uait donfabullsa.'

6041 Foruirecht Míchol nanníth,
cendul indegaid Dauíd,
corocht Dauíd, reim iarruth,
icéin in-oen nandithrub.

6045 IArsin adcocrat cencrad,
Dauíd ocus Ionathán,
cor'chinnset cenchíthu cess
tríabithu 'nambíthchardess.

6049 An-6entu dogress cerhcruth,
atóebtu cendíscailiud,
fofiadnaib indinngnaib gal,

iartimnaib dorigéntar.
Dorigénsatar síd slán.

CI.

6053 Bái Dauid 'sa druim fritraig
fecht fiadindríg 'sindrígthaig,
focháinbuide nandroñg ñdál,
in-oenṡuidi isIonathán.

6057 Luam laidi fochaini cruth,
gengaili ocairfitiud,
dondríg, dontslúag, centeidm tind,
icseinm athimpáin téidbind.

6061 Dauid indratha, réim saer,
bafotha flatha fímoeb:
sephain scol salmda osbla,
baceol n-amra n-adamra.

6065 Basegunn séim ascechmud
archruth, archéil, archoibliud,
lasinsluag sóer, so[i]smert sid,
bind leo coistecht friDauid.

6069 Ciarboairfitiud lacách
linib tairchitul ñdermár,
iarsét slemun, sechinslóg,
dochoid Demun iSaól.

6073 Sreeis Saúl uad insleig
forDauid isindrígthig,
triáchlár cruaid itoeb achinn
robidgc ingái gluair gerthind.

6077 Atraracht inslúag istaig,
batoracht núall integlaig:
indar lacach gae indríg
robáe triamedón Dauid.

6081 Atraracht Ionathan ard
coruc reim ruanaid rogarg,
cor'idnacht Dauid, toem ñglé,
uad coóen nafidbaide.

6085 Rochathaig cogarg, combríg,

friaathair, frisinn-ardríg,
rañgab guba, rochlói cruth,
ardula diasarugud.

6089 Ferais Míchol debaid tinn
friSaul, friAchinoim,
nochor'bo choimsech acath,
batoirsech, batromdebthach.
[fo. 34 b. 2.]

6093 Ferais inslúag athber ñgúr
forsindríg ruam, forSaúl,
adul censamṡúgud sid,
diasárugud imDauid.

6097 Mac Sauil slaide glonn ñgal
badúscud lonn leoaman,
rosoer cenchíabair cachta
achlíamain, achomalta.

6101 Ri rodnanacht forsinmaig,
cenámare ondleoamain,
hé rosáer cenbuide indríg
isintsuide imboe Dauid.

Báe Dauid 'sadruim fritraig.

CII.

6105 Dorigni Dauid, deilm n-án,
comarle ocuslanothán,
imdul cencleith frigail gúir,
cenbeith itegluch Saúil.

6109 Roraidi Ionathán fris:
'Saul natabair d'eisleis,
an fri'gairm ifail sunn sel
naclochi dian-ainm Ephel.

6113 'Cofesser friselba síd
inmaith frit menma indardríg.
indeil dúrchathach natres,
no'ndúthrachtach fri'amles.

6117 'Dotrua comarda uaim,
bid sodamna¹ fri'banbúaid.

¹ MS. bidsodomna.

imdul r[e]ut, reclit ṅgúr ṅgle,
nothecht arcúl dorise.

6121 'Fochuriub uaim saigit snéid,
féig friglaineilc frit'glanchéil,
airct rosso, réim corath,
cid icéin nofaicserad.

6125 'Mad hicein chiṅgges cenchess
ber cheim cinnes dot'lanles :
menipcfan frisoirchi sain
toirchi codfan d[o]rígthaig.'

6129 Dochúaid Ianothán istech,
cosindríg, cosinteglach,
condessid censil ṅdogra
innasuidiu rigdomna.

6133 R[o]iarfacht Saúl frisním
d'Ianuthan scéla Duíd :
'ciabaile ifail, delm ṅda,
dofer comtha comdána ?

6137 'Ciabaili ifail immaig
drochmac Iesse aṅgbaid ?
nithoracht fiadnachdruṅg tra
sunn in-oen naláasa.'

6141 Atchuaid Ianuthán, án aig,
dondrig rán innarígthaig :
'dochúaid, cendechel, deilm tra,
diathreib, doBethil Iudá.'

6145 Roráid Saul frisnuad sess :
'cia istslúag nádigni m'amles,
tan istursu rogni inse,
adrochmeic namerdrige ?'

6149 Dochúaid Ionothán immach
combái formúr nacathrach,
feib nognathaiged cendíth,
dús inrathaigfed Dauíd.

6153 Focheird cenlén onmúr 'maig
airchur trén forsinn-ailig,
segda, sodalbtha, slicht ṅglé,
icomartha cumnigthé.

6157 'Máta nech iconcloich thall,'
arIonathan nírb'imgann,
'orthad colúath, táet cotricc,
isléced uad insaigit.'

6161 Rí roleth brat nimi náir
imthoebu talman tonnbáin,
ocus grén ṅgúir conalf,
diaréir cachduil dorignf.

Dorigni Dauid, delm n-án.

CIII.

6165 L uid ass Dauíd, tolaib rath,
cengác, censciath, cen-
chlaideb,
iarcálaib garb rogáel gail,
fácaib aarm 'sindrigthaig.

6169 IArsin dochúaid fochucht cacht
coAchimilech sacart,
cotormalt leis, gle[f]re guir,
bargena réile remfúir.

6173 Cianchacht imchaṅgnib cuirperíad,
roiarfacht Abimeliach,
doDauíd r'iarfacht cucht cain,
'indatglain lucht dotheglaig ?'

6177 Dorat Dauíd teist iarfír
ifrecnarcus indardríg,
cencomrac dó frímná imne
re trílá is teoran-aidche.

6181 Robái cenglorai, cengeis,
claideb Golai 'sindeclais,
fríbrig mbladailc fiadcachslóg,
iarnathabairt doSaól.

6183 Roráid Dauíd ciarbodalb,
'olcc dul icéin cendagarm,
fríala indrig, rúathar mbras,
domrala triatinninas.'
[fo. 35 a. 1.]

6189 DoAchimilech nirb'folith,

rofer fáilti friDuid,
ocus doridnacht do immach,
claideb Golai gér golach.

6193 IDumeus atchúaid inscél
doSaul ríg Israhél,
Dau*i*d colucht rabolíach,
rochaith bíad Abimeliach.

6197 Nitrúag fúair fáilti fosmacht
Dau*i*d icsluag nasacart,
ocus ruc cenloga leis
claideb Gola ceneisleis.

6201 Luid Saul ce*ch*thucht iarmbrath*i*
corágaib lucht nacathrach,
ort slúag nasacart cenclith,
coiciur arcethrifichtib.

6205 Rosnort iarcétrud agleo
in-étgud, ephud líneo[1],
labruth *m*brathlaig, bág amné,
'sinchathraig dian-ainm Noué.

6209 Acht itrulai oenfer díb
corice tegdais Dauid,
Abiathar conablait,
macc Abimeliach sacairt.

6213 Romiscnig Saul, gnim ǹglé,
Dau*i*d mórm*ac* Iessé,
cofor*congr*ad lais, lethan scél,
nabeth forcrích n-Isr*ahé*l.

6217 IArnafocra dom*ae* Ciss
Dauid nitharat eisleis,
cenna*ch*techel dochuaid ass,
ruc atheged coAchess.

6221 Roimraid cá*ch* fiad indríg
intr*ath* dodeochaid Dau*i*d,
'innhé seo inclí glanna
Dau*i*d ri natalmanna?

6225 'IN doso[m] labras inslúag
nan-ingen n-amnas n-adrúad :

'ort Dau*i*d derb deichmili,
ort Saúl serb óenmíli[2]?'

6229 IArsin rongab galar gér,
fr*i*sním calad nirb'imthrén,
corochumscaiged achíall,
cotunscanad (*sic*) ca*ch*n-anríad.

6233 Cororaid Achis tr*i*asním,
niharaithis forDau*i*d;
'berid uain cenmíad imma*ch*
induini ǹdían ǹdásachtach.'

6237 Luid Dau*i*d, linib aslog,
hit[í]rib minib Moab,
con-aes lathair, con-aig thaig,
coamáthair is coathair.

6241 IArsin roaittreb coog
indess im-Maffa, im-Moób,
brig bladmar rogab Maffa
pr*i*madbar indfirflatha.

6245 O roathain fiad inslog
aathir forrig Moob,
folsr*ahé*l, ilar crích,
iarsin ass doluid Dau*i*d.

      Luid ass Dauid, tolaib rath.

CIV.

6249 Saul iarselaib fr*i*sním
dorat meball forDau*i*d,
diatardad Míchol fogr*e*is
doAlathi mac Lais.

6253 Roráidset coleir coluth
amuint*er* fein fr*i*Saúl :
'biaid nech imbánugud Dé
dofárgud[3] m*e*ic Iessé.

6257 'Digelaid doDia ce*ch*cruth
fort fein, fort'clainn, fort'chiniud,
Dau*i*d fr*i*dalgud nachdil
dosargud 'mochetmuintir.'

6161 Tuirid natuath tinach trén,
ilar nuall mac n-Israhél,
cotrethnaib iarsrethbruig súg,
bátar debthaig friSaúl.
Saul iarselaib frisnfm.

CV.

6165 Bóe Dauíd ré mór foleith
fofuacru, foinnarthaib,
fodichruth, foclére grém,
indithrub slebe Carmeill.

6169 Icailltib Séb, srethaib sleg,
imrulaid Dauíd tonngel,
isleib Sfon immallé
isindithrubaíb ainge.

6173 Secet caini gascid glain
diocaib friimmargail,
doDauíd iarfir frifraiss,
bahé alin foraloṅgais.

6177 Bantrocht coem, corcarda, cóir,
conatimthaigib dergóir,
droṅg n-ingen, droṅg ṅgilla cert,
friatindrem, friatimthirecht.

6181 Friseilg, friṅadrad fogréd,
cenmeirg fricfallrad comlán,
comafein húathmair cenlén,
fortúathaib mac n-Israhé l
[fo. 35 a. 2.]

6185 IMsliab Carmeill docachleith
cengarbgrém friachomaithcib,
bamenic nodechrad dáil
imchethraib n-aidblib Nabáil.

6189 Nabál iCarmill rochlos
gabál gremma icomaithcheos,
balcbethraid osbetha blá,
aittrebthaid indithrubá.

6193 Abigail, glan agréimm,

     ¹ MS. nádchélar.

ben Nabáil slébi Carmeill,
set suthach, slicht nádchelar ¹,
banscal crutha*ch* coemtrebar.

6197 A almai aidb[l]i cenmeirb
imCharmill doca*ch*oenleirg,
mfli dogabraib frigleith,
teoramili docháireib.

6201 Dochúas oDauíd coathech,
inbaid lommartha cairech,
coNabál frigabáil ṅglé,
diaglanáil imfeis n-aidche.

6205 Araburba fríaig thaig
isarchumga amenmannraid ²,
Nabál sin slebi Carmil
rofemid immoenbargin.

6209 Coic muilt, dacét ṁbargen ṁbil,
dacét mfas dochaTicib,
daphaitt fína, iarset sid,
ruc inben lee doDauíd.

6213 Cethrib cétaib gilla cain
iarsétaib friinmargail,
conarmrath tánic 'nadáil
Dauid domarbad Nabáil.

6217 Ferais inben fáilti fris,
friDauíd cennach n-eisleis :
' cucut tucsam forset sain,
nifailmet darth'airmitein.'

6221 ' Manithorasta modáil,'
arDauíd frimnái Nabáil,
' imbarach 'sinchamair chain
nobfad Nabál cenanmain.'

6225 Nabal nemnech, gemlech, crín,
atúb tadail dorofln :
'sindechmaid lá, líth cenchol,
bamarb Nabál aoenor.

6229 IArsin tuc Dauíd cendáil
Abigail mnai Nabail,

     ² MS. amenme*n*mannraid.

dosrimthos dó Dia donim,
con-innmos, *con*-innilib.

6,333 INrí robennach sechćách
Dauíd fríhellach n-ollgrád,
secht dé badichmaig cendíth
isdíthraib imbai Dauíd.
Báe Dauíd ré mór folcith.

CVI.

6,337 Sephi[1], niptar seccle slóg,
atchuadatar doSaól,
'Dauíd dichmaig, doig notcheil,
'narñdíthruib, 'narnderriteib.'

6,341 Doluid Saul, nisuail sain,
lín aslúaig conaarmgail,
frígním ñgúr cu*m*taig catha,
combái ict*ar* indithruba.

6,345 Rosuidiged longphort leis,
bagním comnort ceneisleis,
rosainig cosrethaib sét
f*or*maigib nacairechtrét.

6,349 Fofúair fiaddínib athuir
huaim itírib indithruib,
frígnim cinti achuirp ca*ch*cruth
luid inti diaimthelgud.

6,353 Dauid cotr*i*ath[aib] darb'bai
bái in-iarthur nahuamai,
tréin iartimchul daire daill,
conaféin, conafairaind.

6,357 Roráidset fr*is*, réim cendíth,
amuint*er* féin fr*i*Dauíd,
'feib tharñgert duit, rem cenbrath,
innossa rochomolnad.

6,361 'An-dorarñgered ochéin
dorairbered fot'huagróir,
iscían inbúaidsi fosmacht,
isindúairsi doroacht.

Ziphaei, *I Reg. xxvi. i.*

6,365 'Mór intuicthiu oDía dil,
duitsiu, aDauíd toebgil l
osdálaib tharaic tríablait
fot'lámaib dodergnamait.

6,369 'Gaibther doclaideb ger glé
dot'reir, am*ei*c lessé l
naroa dál derbdroñg immach
Saúl slan serblonn sirthech.'

6,373 Atraracht Dauíd iarsin
ocusrochoisc amuintir,
badechrad fodćtgail dúir
doletrad étaig Saúil.

6,377 Dodécaid féin, febdai glonn,
Dauíd delb dreim [   ] dodroñg,
cor'letair, gním ñdetlach dúr,
inn-ćtach bai imSaul.

6,381 Cia dochuaid Saúl immach
asinduaim isinteglach,
[fo. 35 b. 1.]
rogaba fr*i*glamma gné
nimbai samái laSephé[2].
Sephi, niptar seccli slóg.

CVII.

6,385 Dolluid Dauíd dána dúr
aidchi sáma coSaúl,
coruc agái cu*m*nech cóir,
lacúach ñdruimnech ñdergóir.

6,389 INgái robae itóeb achind,
maroen fr*i*chúach coemgr*i*nn,
ruc Dauíd, bagéire gúr,
indédesin oSaúl.

6,393 Manbad omain Dé donim
glé fr*i*ca*ch*comul cóemdil[3],
fr*i*sretha sell nagr*e*iss gúir
nob*er*ad leis cenn Saúil.

6,397 Dorigni troich ñdorchaid dé

2 MS. lasephi.   3 MS. coemdil.

cotorchair icath Giluáe,
nimbál suidi saigthi síd
ondaidchi doluid Dau*i*d.
    Doluid Dau*i*d dána dúr.

CVIII.

6401 C ein bae Dau*i*d dichmaig, dil
     isdithruib 'coaimditin,
bacomaithech, glére glé,
Nabáil slebi Carmelle.

6405 Corothafind Saúl ass,
latochim abag ṁbladbras ;
luid fr*i*adintrén [1], narbodis,
itir ṅGed coriacht Achis.

6409 Dorat Achis, glórib crech,
inchathir dianidainm Siclech,
conatír, tolaib dliged,
doDau*i*d fr*à*prímhined.

6413 O roaittreib Dau*i*d dian
iSiclig conamormiad,
isé aainm oṡhain illé,
Siclech án nan-Iudaidé.

6417 Fecht dochoid Dau*i*d cengr*ei*s
dothecht slógaid laAcheis,
daraéissi tanic crech,
cor'ort, coroloisc Siclech.

6421 Nir'leicsetar leo nacein
Dau*i*d sluag naFilestein,
artess*ed* Dau*i*d nachdis
sofuacru uadib d'Achis.

6425 'Arnáronfuap*air* cosneid
mac Iesse me*i*c Obéid,
niraga linn Dau*i*d trén
dochath fr*i*sluag n-Isr*a*hé*l*.'

6429 Nirelic Dia Dau*i*d díl
dothuilled insulúagaid sin,
ór ishe sin, srethaib slóg,

fecht diaromarbad Saól.

6433 Tan dochúaid Dau*i*d iarsain
coAchis conasluagaib [1],
fúair adún ṅdonn iarnacrod,
Siclech, lomm iarnaloscod.

6437 Centech, centegdáis, delm ṅglé,
ceninnmas, ceninnile,
cenduine ṁbeo fonim nél
n'innisfed dóib na*ch*n-oenscél.

6441 Cenmná, cenma*e*cu, mét ṅgal,
cenór, cenargat n-allmar,
censoṡid fr*i*toirsi atr*ai*g,
tarmairt Dau*i*d ahaidid.

6445 Luid Dau*i*d indiaid intslóig
coroacht cosruth Pessóir,
cofuair fer d'aes indfechta
iarfemiud ahimthechta.

6449 Dó dobreth biad cenbrath
laDuid diacomnertad,
ruc eolas uair narboscfth
dochum intsluaig rianDau*i*d.

6453 IArsin dochuaid Dau*i*d ass
cotr*i*b cétaib, gnim n-amnas,
fogeib dacét cóir eachta
fós iarfemiud imthechta.

6457 Mebaid forru, bafúam fír,
forsintslúag mór rianDau*i*d,
cofárgsat centuili ṅdala
huili cruid aṅgabála.

6461 Gabais insluag raind indfaidb,
gluair iarnaṅgalais glégairb,
cenní dondíni bai ifu*s*
hisuidib fíri hiforus.

6465 Nirelic Dau*i*d, dalb tenn,
acht rainn nafadb cocoitchenn,
doib icein *con*gr*a*d cengr*ei*s,
cobráth combad beim forais.

---

[1] *Sic.* Read *dinn trén* ?　　　[1] MS. -ail.

6469 O dochuaid coAchis n-án
   fofuair maibius commorgrád,
   congail glé cech cluid rogníd
   doreir Dé céin boe Dauíd.
      Cein bói Dauíd dichmaig, dil.

CIX.

6473 Saul sfrach slaide sluaig
   basnímach iarn-éc Samúail,
   cosaibe fogaili gné,
   cennoibi, cenfáithsine.
      [fo. 35 b. a.]

6477 Mac Cis cenlíthaib folén
   forcrfchaib mac n-Israhél,
   rodlín snim sribgrínn, slicht ńglé,
   ohingrím meic Iesse.

6481 Bái mac Ciss icocud chían
   friDauíd conamórmfad,
   cotorachtatar otír
   sluaig fer fortrén Philistín.

6485 Dor'inól frí'bualad ṁbal
   sluagad n-Israhé'l n-armglan,
   aracenn, cengailib gne,
   forcláraib cainib Giluae.

6489 INdadaig riasincath ńgúr
   robai snim mór forSaúl,
   arnaconfitir tríarath
   cia fors'maidfid inmórchad.

6493 Dodeochaid Samúel iarsin
   coSaúl inn-aidchisin,
   con-erbairt fris, rád cenbrath:
   'notmairfider immárach;

6497 'Ocus dotrimeicc, mod cert,
   hit'chinaid, it'tairimthecht,
   ocus ár trog, díglach, trén,
   forslóg n-frach n-Israhel;

6501 'Ocus roscarad frit'scél

ardflaithius macc n-Israhé'l:
   t'imthacht fríafégad cofír
   doridnacht Dia doDauíd.'

6505 INri scaras gói frilír,
   coñgaib clói, glanas anfír,
   dorat adigla, deilm n-og,
   ruc breith prímda forSaol.

6509 INtrath rothaitne ingrían glan
   oscechtfan imdreich talman,
   feib bagnáth dóib dul dochath
   rogab cách achatheirred.

6513 Gnísit cath ciana, cét ńglonn,
   snisit frífiana ferdroñg,
   icath Giluae conaslog
   romarbad iarsin Saól.
      Saul sfrach slaide sluaig.

CX.

6517 Batar ocSaul mac Ciss
   morféssiur doclaind dílis,
   cethrimeic, monor n-ada,
   tríingena imglana.

6521 Melchisau, basluagach slán,
   Iessu, Ispas, Ionadán,
   Brígente, Merob medrach,
   ocus Michol mormenmnach.

6525 Achinoym amáthair mass,
   ingen amra Athemas,
   ocus Saúl, srethaib gal,
   nibochlethaib robatar.
      Saul sfrach slaide slúaig [1].

CXI.

6529 Síl Saul snímaich frisrén
   forclainn n-fraig n-Israhé'l,
   nirosliuna hed diacur
   acht madtreb Iuda ahoenur.

6533 Dorat Abner tríagail ńgúir

---

[1] *Sic.* This should of course be *Bátar oc Saul mac Ciss.*

rígi d Ispas *mac* Saúil,
*for*deichtreib tarraid areir
is*for*treib Beniemein.

6;3; IArndechraib dóib díni dé
debthaig immonn-ardríge,
centlí tarba, *for*aig thaig,
níptaramra oentadaig.

6541 Fosralaig cenrige rúad
or'sáraig Saul Samúal,
immanduinib duinnig dúir
níptarsúinig síl Saúil.
Síl Saul sutmaig *fri*srén.

CXII.

6545 Bae [dígal] deithbir doráith
     dirain *for*deichtreib dim-
     bláith,
lataidbsin fainni forúin
in-aimsir clainni Saúil.

6549 Rodoselaig cec*h*sluag saer
rodosdedaig fodubraen,
garbthenn dosrimmart cuairt cacht,
dosnarmchell cec*h* n-ecomnart.

6553 Rodastroeth cec*h* n-olc arhuair
rosglaed cec*h*locht cenlonnbuaid,
dosr'imgair arsec*h*cói cath
indinbaid robái indígal.
Bae dígal deithbir doráith.

CXIII.

6557 Rogab Dau*i*d, tola nglé,
     rígi n-ogda n-Iudaidé,
iarngormchath nangruad ngúr,
itorcha[i]r slúag imSaúl.

6561 Roaittreb in-Ebrón án
rochaitreb Cebrón comlán,
*for*treib Iudae, cengr*i*s nglé,

  ¹ Written over glunir.

---

sé mis *ocus* sec*h*t mbliadné.

6565 Fóidis Dau*i*d, censfl mbróin,
techt colspas mac Saóil,
cotuctha dó, saer sluinter,
Michol chaem achétmuint*er*.
[fo. 36 a. 1.]

6569 ISpas mac Sauil cenlén,
rogab ríge n-Israhél,
dafuc Michol, ciarb' olc leis,
oAlathis mac Lais.

657.3 Corucad doDau*i*d húad,
'arbuide n-Iuda n-ollmúad,
armbeith iarmbes hitóebtaid
dogr*es* innarslróentaid.'

6577 Bai cluichi garb, glinni glór¹,
*for*ochair linni Gabon²,
et*er*Abnér *mac* Néir nair
ocus Iob *mac* Sairb soeráil.

6581 Cethror arfichit coglé
doBeniemin is d'Iudae,
fochutr*um*mu cenclói clu,
dorochair 'sincétchuinnscliu.

65ª5 'Singleo thánaise iarnarím,
doócaib Beniemín,
dorochratar, t*r*aig *fri*t*r*aig,
trifichit artribchétaib.

6589 Romebaid incath iarsin
*for*Abnér conasluagaib
Asser *mac* Sairb, srethaib scél,
*con*id ann romarb Abnér.

6593 IOb badicerta cr*i*ch,
toisech mfltnechta Dauid,
macSairb, baglanger imgail,
romarb Abner 'nadígail.

6597 Banna *ocus* Recab, réim rúin,
marbsat Ispas *mac* Saúil:
*fri*sretha sell iarnadíth

  ² Lon written over buain.

rucsat achenu coDauid.

6601 Céiu báe Dauid forIuda trén
riaríge mac n-Israhél,
in-Ebron frignim n-airec n-íd
bretha secht maic doDauid.

6605 Ammon asinser, slicht n-óg,
Eleab, Abisolon,
Athenoias, frigart nglán,
Asfothías ocus Esrom.

6609 Rí dorát recht n-Iuda n-oll,
doDauid deoda drechdonn,
srethaib slánaib slógaib sid
congrádaib rogab Dauid.
    Rogab Dauid, tola nglé.

CXIV.

6613 Tinólsat dáil, derb cenlén,
    sruithred slóig mac n-Isra-
        hél;
iartimnu Dé, din cech síd,
dodeochatar coDauid.

6617 Doratsat rígi, réim nglé,
domac amra Iesse,
doDauid conamslib
fortúathaib, foriltírib.

6621 Rogab Dauid rígi ran
cechacríchi cocomlán,
othá Dán, frítola Dé,
coclár broga Bersabé.

6625 Arcruth cengaile imgaes,
arsáere, arairmitin,
nibái remi innachdú
ríg n-aíle bádadamrú.

6629 Lín amuirech, lín amál,
rím aruirech corográd,
lín aslúaig sláin frisár slait,
bamór indál tinolsat.
    Tinólsat dáil, derb cenlén.

CXV.

6633 Tricha bliadan, cenbaes bríg,
    iarn-urd rí[a]gla, in-áes
        Dauid,
fortir, fortalam, treb tlácht,
coragab fír flathemnácht.

6637 DoDauid centressi tra
sluinnit seissi senchassa,
fricethrachait mbliadan mbalcc
roríaglad afollomnacht.

6641 Ceth[r]icóraid, cóir andíth,
dorochratar laDauid.
Benedab, Séb, Góla cain,
isinfer cosé méraib.

6645 Cethrur nalúaided, laíded nglé,
laDauid mac n-Iesse,
Ethán delbda, tolaib rún,
Assaph, Eman, Ithidún.

6649 Agitophel, sód cengreis,
is hIssau Arachiteis,
dede cosinairdib (sic) síd,
daprímchomairlid Dauíth.

6653 Tan rogab airichas n-ard
Dauid daigermas derbgargg,
friåg n-úathmar, uascech bla,
baslán dotuatach tricha.
    Tricha bliadan, cenbaes bríg.

CXVI.

6657 Túargabad lais, lúh cenlén,
    prímchathir mac n-Israhél,
forsleib Sioin, srethaib sell,
cor'fothaig Hierusalem.

6661 Suidig forsléib, sossad slán,
Sion snéid, srethaib saergrád,
    [fo. 36 a. 2.]
rosmathig frítoir uasdinn
cathir coir fagabulrind.

6665 Tricha mili, mod cenhír,
lotar d'ócaib laDuíd,
arcenn nahairce congrad
cotegdais Aminadáh.

6669 Conaclasschétlaib glinnib,
conacruittib céolgrínnib,
con-organ cainiu clíaraib,
comáinib, comórmiadaib.

6673 Bai indarc forcuclaigi gell
'coatabairt diHierusalem :
tarall lám Oxa inn-airc ń-óig :
bamarb Oxa fochétóir.

6677 Úair dosfuargaib, rígda ell,
coslúagaib Hierusalem,
arcc Dé thargcai oscach traig
tucad lais donprímchathraig.

6681 Riasinn-airc noib, noithi mail,
liñgged arśailti ńdermáir,
Dauíd friáluth, líníb smacht,
amal druth icfurséoracht.

6685 Badcgrach rodéc immach
Míchol menmnach, meruallach,
forsinríg, reim cendochta,
baréil di ahimnochta.

6689 Rochúrsaig inrig fomeirg
corondúsaig fomorfeirg,
cotarat Dauíd, delm n-om,
amallachtain arMíchol.

6693 INcathir centomaidm tenn,
dían' comainm Hierusalem,
cain cumtach, clú cotagab,
oscachdu dofúargabad.
     Túargab[ad] lais, líth cenlén.

CXVII.

6697 Dauid cotrethnaib tor trell
forsrethbruig Hierusalem,
róriagla fodelba tlacht

tribliadna derba trichat.

6701 Rosrethaig tolgdail triath tenn
iartorgbail Hierusalem,
oscechdándíne droñg trén,
il-lánrige n-Israhél.

6705 Mespossad friattach n-án
mac baccach bae iclonadán,
dafuc Dauíd osdroñgaib
sechcách innabithcommaid.

6709 Ammon mac Dauid, delm n-án,
dorat forran forTamár ;
etir fer ismnái bacol,
isde báe amudugod.

6713 Abisalon, ni frísid,
romarb Ammón mac ńDuíd,
combái cendfamra fogreis
teorabliadna forloñgais.

6717 Muinter Dauíd, friúíd slóg,
fecht lotar coríg n-Ammón,
impu roger[r]tha atuinchi
is rober[r]tha alethu[l]chi.

6721 Nisreíic Dauíd, delm n-óg,
dían-imcasin donmórslóg ;
frían-athnugud, fríatogo
robátar inhEricho.

6725 Tuc Dauíd Annon mac Náis
ríg n-Ammón indig tiugbáis,
cotuc amind diachind chóir
irabi tallann dergóir.

6729 Roart Dauíd, glérib crech,
tír n-Ammoin forcechn-óenleth,
rodamnad cosáthib slóg
Ramath, cathir nan-Ammón.

6733 Teora bliadna, bochta bríg,
bói gorta in-aimsir Dauíd,
cotarmartad huili ambás
icinaid Ammonitas.

6737 Saúl robris cotach ńgér

Ammonita isIsrahél,
dosrat fochrúach cachta,
romarb slúag Ammonita.

6741 Aiṅgel¹ Dé tharic cech síd,
radid coglé friDuíd:
arnaraib dígal forslóig,
adfbad forsis Saóil.

6745 Doratta darcenn intsloig
morféssiur clainne Saóil,
dosr'idnacht Dauíd datta
ilámaib Ammoníta.

6749 LahAmoníta coataig
archomailliud inchotaig,
doréir Dé, sochlai senchai,
rochrochdai in-oentelchai.

6753 Sedba, Sobab, Nathan nár,
Salemon ocus Ibár,
Elessia lanmas cechdía,
Iafeig ocus Iabfa.

6757 Elizammama, aurdaig rád,
Elida, Elezeliáb,
clanna Dauíd, sretha snó sell,
bretha dó inHierusalem.
[fo. 36 b. 1.]

6761 Rí con-ammodair bith mbán,
rí con-allodaib² o[l]lmár,
rí coláinib lúathaib líth,
ostúathaib tuárgaib Dauíd.
Dauíd cotrethnaib tor trell.

CXVIII.

6765 Tinolsat deimni teclai
slúagai sergi Sirecdai,
cotolcaib nator talc, trén,
doorgain mac n-Israhel.

6769 Dodfbad tuath itraiti,
dochrínad uad Affraice,

colindrud natríath, torm tenn,
dohindriud Hierusalem.

6773 Forrogellsat iarfir fecht
noragtais itír n-Egept,
cobrath natargtais díatig
cor'airgtis Alaxandir.

6777 Focart dóib Dauíd derb drúad,
fosropart inserb slegrúad,
combátar lanaib lerggaib
donasrábaib srebdergaib.

6781 Ort dib Dauíd, delbda drech,
deichmíli derbdai traigthech,
ocht cét córad carpat cruaid
cethorcha míli marcslunig.

6785 INrí doruásat cechríg,
rí cenguásacht, cendimbríg,
ríaṅDauíd trén derbdai raind,
dosrat hirén romadmaim.

6789 Slúag naSerda, sretha droṅg,
fríTúam febda faebarglonn,
lethnaib, lúathaib, lúardaib lac,
trethnaib túathaib tinólsat.
Tinólsat deimni teclae.

CXIX.

6793 Rothráeth natúatha díana,
dosrat fogláed comríada:
tríalonnbruth nambríg mbassa
rol-lin tondgur diummusa.

6797 Dorairchel ilar tiri
cuaird gairbthenn fochoemríge,
Dauíd, ciarbo deoda doss,
dorigni mor d'immarbos.

6801 Dia rorained³ lais lín slog
bái focumachtu clannmór,
diatuc inmnái dorímid,
diaromarb atrénmílid.

---

¹ MS. Aṅgle.   ² MS. alladaib.   ³ Sic. Read roáirmed?

6805 Dáinib, dínib, tolaib dind,
 máinib, milib ammórmind,
 glé roscacht *tr*ágr*á*in, *tr*íacath,
 dosrat *t*ot*r*áig diatr[o]ethad.
            Rot*r*deth natúatha díana.

CXX.

6809 O*n'*fáided Íob, bátrúag scél,
        d'arim sluag *ma*c n-Isra*hé*l,
 otha Dán, *fr*íthola Dé,
 coclár broga *B*ersabe,

6813 Nóimis lána, lathar *tr*ícc,
 isoenlá tesbaid difichit,
 *fr*íriad robalcc natr*í*ath tenn
 cotor*acht* Hirusalem.

6817 Dorigni Íob dondríg ráin
 inslóg dorim 'narf[g]dáil,
 cóir adfét deserc Dé díl
 *tr*íchet dec dóib dimilib.

6821 Ocht c*el* míli foroen recht
 díní nan-óentreb ñdéac,
 treb luda arfír, adfet scél,
 *cói*c c*el* mlli fer *t*ortrén.

6825 IArc*ach* n-áraim díb aruair,
 coslánaib sid *fr*isrethbúaid,
 róráid ' innia, núall cenlén,
 torraim Día slúag n-Isra*hé*l.

6829 ' *M*enisb*en*nachad Íob án,'
 arint-añgel óg imnár,
 ' ferg Dé rofig *f*orfart*ur*
 eterríg ocus phopul.'

6833 IOb baóg imgním cert,
 dondrig, dont-slóg basaín[s]erc,
 othír dothír *fr*íbrig *m*breth,
 ondríg díar*i*m rofáided.
            Ór'fáided Íob, bátrúag scél.

CXXI.

6837 F ergach fris Fíadu, féidm n-úag,
        aran-árim namórslúag,
 uair narbo leis asna*ch* cruth
 ambíathad na*ch* an-étiud.

6841 Bai ferg aili laDía ñdil,
 lathigerna donóebnim,
 diar'ort amfíid, mét gal,
 tue amnái iarnamarbad.

6845 Roraid Spirut Dé *fr*íGád
 aithesc glé, *cr*íchid, comlín:
 ' ráid *fr*íDa*uid*, nigó gaib,
 roga dó art*r*íbbrethaib.

6849 ' Secht *n*blíadna dó bochta búan,
 *ocu*s gorta conaimlúad,
 *no tr*ímis agair riacreich,
 *no gr*ís galair trib latheib².'
            [fo. 36 b. 2.]

6853 Roraid Gád *fr*í Da*ui*d tan,
 ciarbochrád riamenmanrad :
 ' toticfa dígal nochath
 triath'imrádud ñdiummasach.'

6857 Corogaid Duid iarsein
 asoerad *f*oranáimteib,
 dígal basmaith lais fodein
 tabrad *f*orru diaógréir.

6861 Dauid bahibdu rechta
 *fr*ícachtimnu tarmthechta,
 d'fís tríalla deochair dochath,
 Fíadu fr*is* fcochair, fergach.
            *F*erggach fr*is* Fíadu, fcidm n-úag.

CXXII.

6865 R osnort int-añgel cosnéid
        triachinaid diumsa Du*i*d,
 se*ch*tmoga mlli, mor scél,

dodíni mac n-Israhél,

6869 Dorigni Dauíd fogail
athirgi fothromdéraib,
cocétlodaib salm slechta,
in-étgodaib cilecda.

6873 Ri rodet dilgud derb, dein,
doDauíd diamórchintaib,
dodeccraib agnfm clithi
iarnahettlaib athirgi.

6877 Dodeochaid Gad glanbda gle,
comac n-amra n-Iesse,
con-erbairt fris, fath cenchlith,
'dena tegdais donChomdid.

6881 'Túargaib altóir doDia dil,
buidnib balcthoir donChomdid,
in-aria, cenlunni lí,
Ornaunndi Iabussi.'

6885 Dorinnscan Dauíd insein
doruirig nimi nóebgil,
nicheil frignim nglérda nglan
tempul sain ségda Solman.

6889 Mor mílli iarset roslas,
mor cét, mór ndíni ndronmas,
mor slúag rosmacht frisnúad sel,
nitrúag rosnort int-angel.
Rosnort int-angel cosnéid.

CXXIII.

6893 Dorodiúsaig Día amac
'naagid frifrituttacht,
mór d'ulc triabrathaib rogní
diaathair combad athri.

6897 Dor'inól slúag sleoda sneid,
in-agaid ndeoda nDauíd,
triabladblat feib rofirad
cotarmart aathrígad.

6901 Túargaib cosluagaib cosreith

combuadaib, combrithemnib[1],
nir'fírda dó dul donchath
iartecht corígna aathar.

6905 Abisolón, srethaib slúag,
rothinól cath claidebruad,
d'innarba Dauíd cotrén
nabeth forcrich n-Israhél.

6909 Glérdin rofersat incath
trenlir Dauíd comorrath:
riacruadgail nacórad crón
rotheich slog Abisolón.

6913 Ua[r]romebaid incath cerb
forAbisolón slegdergg,
among buidi, mín adath,
rogiul dogéscu darach.

6917 IOb trénfer derbtha treith
toisech míltnechta Dauíd,
donchath chródonn rogab greimm
atacomong dooenbeim.

6921 O shunn romarbad amac
dor'arbrad fothochomracht,
cotarmairt éc, bascél tróg,
dochumaid Abisolón.

6925 Asbert Iob, bascél treith,
fi[a]dintslóg mór, friDuid:
'ragab[2] bás baide fobrón
dochaine Abisolón.'

6929 IArum rogab aríge
Dauíd con-ilur míle,
uair dorochair leis icath
Abisolón slógbuadach.

6933 Dilliud forDuid dána
con-immud cechdrochdála,
Abisolón díandiumsaig
rianarian dorodiúsaig.
Dorodiúsaig Día [a]mac.

[1] The last two letters are obscure.   [2] MS. Ragabas.

CXXIV.

6937 Diatánic Dauïd andess
      darIordanan, nirb'imchres,
tárnactar 'nadáil cenlén
slóig Iuda, slóig Israhél.

6941 Rofer slóg Iuda coslán
fáilti friDauïd ńdermár,
bafálti fóil, nirbothrén,
failti sloig mac n-Israhél.

6945 Rofer Sephi, gléssib glór,
forséssib Abisolón,
          [fo. 37 a. 1.]
rotriall cath aili fogreim
mac Bachaire osléib Effraim.

6949 Sephi mac Bachairi braiss,
doclainn Israhél admaiss,
rothinól slóg, nirb'frisid,
d[o]chomhéirge friDuid.

6953 Romebaid fair, nifuair dín,
rian-Iób comuintir Duid,
corocht incathraig, cét mbla,
Abella Pedamacha.

6957 Corongiuil Iob ilar cath,
nirbochiuin cóir conarmrad,
condessid mardlúm dardreich
immondún docachóenleith.

6961 Bae banscal écnaid is'dún
iarfrecraib imcechglanrún,
d'acallaim Iób bái 'sinchath
doluid formúr nacathrach.

6965 Gorelic gairm, ba gním n-óg,
formac Sairb, nirbuerthróg,
donmúr fiadintslog immaig
condernai Iob d'acallaim.

6969 'A Iob it'foimsid frisíd,
achoimsid forslóg nDuíd,

nahimbeir luinni colén
formuimmi¹ mac n-Israhél.

6973 'Senfoccul buada, buan scél,
latuatha mac n-Israhel,
docachcheist chialchaid rotchná
iarfaig inPedamachá.'

6977 Roraid Iob, ilar dáil,
fiadintslog frisinmbanscáil :
'teilge cenn meic Bachairi 'mach,
nigébthar ell nacathrach.'

6981 Roradi inben iarsein
comblathi, cenimresain :
'ferr oenfer dontslog dodul
indá inmor domudugud.'

6985 Dorigned sain arIob
mac Sairb frisretha soerslóg,
cenn meic Bachairi immach
rolad darmúr nacathrach.

6989 Dorumalt Dauïd cenchess
ahorddan, ahairechass,
cofargaib friSolam slán
iarsin inflaithius forlán.

6993 Samma mac Geraid condith
iarńdebaid dó friDuid,
roslecht doDauïd cotrait
darIordanan diatánic.
          Diatánic Dauïd aness.

CXXV.

6997 Rogab Solam, srethaib slúag,
        rígi n-Israhél n-adrúad,
rí samlaid nifrïth sunn sel,
eter talmain isnóebnem.

7001 Con-écnu óg, cocruth glan,
targcai cechslóg séis Solman :
balór forggal oscachmaig
arorddan, arairmitein.

¹ MS. formuimme.

7005 Écna Solman, srethaib slóg,
osbith bladmar mardergór,
macsamla Solman, síth nglan,
nifrith dorigaíb talman.

7009 Dáarrig dec, digrais gair,
héd robátar icSolmain,
cach forachuaird, demin scél,
fordáthuaith dec Israhél.

7013 Frithalim tigi indrig
sloig sir Solman meic Dauid,
fritinol bíd ocus chiis
cachdfb icind cachoenmíss.

7017 Fess cech n-aidchi, cenchess cain,
tairbi tigi Solamain,
cenlubai lergg, leri lfi,
censelgc slebi nahuisci.

7021 Tricha miach cruithnecht osblái,
trifichit miach n-eornáe,
deichndaim fichet bó, nibréc,
ocus cet molt, ba morthrét.

7025 Arécnu, arordun oll,
frifrecru forgal fírdrong,
amru brígaib, brosnaib gal,
osrfgaib rogab Solam.
Rogab Solam, srethaib slúag.

CXXVI.

7029 IS leis rothurcbad olár
incumtach crichid comlán,
oscach clothmaig, cocruth glan,
tempul sruith sochraid Solman.

7033 Fácbaid Dauid, déde ndein,
diamarbad icSolamain :
Iob trén [   ] dlomad cath
ocus[S]ambe mac Gerad.

7037 Solam basúi saigtis máil
frífoglaim écnai imláin,
'coadrad, nidal cenbríg,

rohuc hed docach ardríg.

7041 Mac Dauid frítarba trén,
rfi macc n-amra n-Israhél,
[fo. 37 a. 2.]
cengói, cengeiss, cumtaig rath,
Solam isleis roturcbad.
ISleiss rothurcbad olár.

CXXVII.

7045 Oadrad indidail áin
dorat Día digail ndermáir,
forclainn Solman, sruth nasreith,
coroscartha frideichthreib.

7049 Síl Solman forróed, réim nglé,
rodastróeth rí rindnime,
cenforgal, cenmiad mathius,
cenordan, cenárdflathius.

7053 Mac Solman Robuam rofich
fordethreib conadligthib,
ocus hIrobuam roclos
fordeichtreib rogab flatheos.

7057 Solam básui snigtís druing
frífoglaimm n-ecnai n-eruill,
roscar fríbúaid isfriblaid,
ohuair adartha indidail.
Oadrad indidail áin.

CXXVIII.

7061 Rí dorat dígail, deilm n-úag,
forsinríg réil hIrobuam,
diancursaig infáith foleith,
diambái icadrad indídail.

7065 Domarbad indfátha áin
luid hIrobuam conagráin,
seccais alám, lathar ngrínn,
irmonclaideb ngarb ngérthinn.

7069 Diatormailt infáith inmbfad
dartimna nDé, baanrfad,

rí rofaed leo lán dogail,
iarsain cucaí diaargain.
7073 Ruri betha, bríg nadbréc,
rorude imgretha glangéc,
rochacht cachtí fogréin glain,
intí dorat indígail.
     Rí dorat dígail, deilm n-úag.

CXXIX.

7077 I Arn-écaib hIrobuam ráin
     dodeichtreib, deithbir golgair,
in-Israhél, foglór gal,
robái mór n-arracht n-ídal.
7081 Bái mór n-ergal ndegrach ndian,
bái mór doulc, doanríad,
etir déthreib, tolaib treb,
ocus deichtreib nan-imned.
7085 Bái dóib frítindríud mór cath
dian-indríud isdiatróethad,
cechsluaig 'mosech, fornig thaig,
dogeintib isd'echtrannaib.
7089 Bái, badeithbir, toirsi thrúag
fordeichtreib conamórslúag,
slúag nuall nan-idal cechthreib
imhIrobuam iarn-écaib.
     IArn-écaib hIrobuam ráin.

CXXX.

7093 R ogab rígi, réim n-achtach,
     Achab úallach imthaltach,
croda, conglandath, congail,
fríandamnad, fríatimmarcain.
7097 Fritimarcain cáich forecht
iarfinnaltaib fath fírchert,
fríadrad De, tolaib gál,
frímandrad n-ahgbaid n-ídál,
7101 Frihinnarba n-echtrann n-úag,

---

línib aclechtchlann comlúad,
frígním nglé nglériu cechcruth,
frireír nDé dohorddugud.
7105 IN-amsir Hele cenchol,
conglere, cenimíorddol,
fordeichtreib conagrad glé,
Achab ín rogab rígé.
     Rogab rígi, réim n-achtach.

CXXXI.

7109 R í dor'úargaib Héle fáith,
     glére crúanmaith cechcom-
     ráid,
lestar lán, cenáeb n-engaig,
inSpírta saér sechtdelbaig.
7113 Teorabliadna, buan inscél,
bái tart fortúaith n-Israhél,
nirelic deochair Día dil
broen fleochaid doib donoebnim.
7117 Ann dognid Héle amra
infirt n-aurdairce n-adamra,
oenmac nafedba foíeib
dothathbeogud ahécaib.
7121 Ort incóecait, bagnim glan,
dosacarddaib nan-ídal,
roloisc tene diblinaib
infeoil fíadnahardrigaib.
7125 Diabreithir baferr cechndáil
Héle condene noebnáir,
roloisc tene trom, tuaimnech
cét fer fortren, foruaibrech.
7129 Rohoirdnestar, arasceirce,
Héle, IIelesius airdeirce,
frígním cumtaig cóir cechgráid ¹,
combahé doib báprímfáith.
     [fo. 37 b. 1.]
7133 Dorurgabsat IIele fáith

¹ MS. frígním cech cumtaig cóir graid ; but a mark (.,) is under cech and graid.

slúaig aiṅgel nimi noebnáir,
fornem noebda niab nemed,
icarput dían dergthened.

7137 Tuistid talman, tolaib droṅg,
bladmar friſuismiud ferdroṅg :
isamru brígaib congaib
Rí osrígaib doruargaib.
    Rí doruargaib Héle faith.

CXXXII.

7141 R̲i ꞃuc Héle osceeꞩ rót
in-óenbaili coHenóc,
he dorat rath, ruithnib rían,
emnaide forHelessiam.

7145 Diar'luid Helessium cenlén
fectas dosruth Iordanén,
luid insruth forcúl, ceim cían,
laforngaire Helessiam.

7149 Diambennach, mod ṅgémlech ṅgle,
insruth nemnech nemide,
oṡhain cobráth, nibág brass,
conidhe insruth slán somblass.

7153 Dialuid set sáer, slan cenbrath,
Helesius lan donoebrath,
fobas martra rodasmacht
inmacrad romallachsat.

7157 Díarodail Día codían
derb labréthir Helesiam,
bagním tuicsi dontuaith dein,
sruaim uisci dothalmannaib.

7161 Ri frisindalat[1] intsluaig,
rii congradgart, conglanbuáid,
ri tarcai cechfein, fuaim ṅglé,
morí reil rofuc Hele.
    Rí ruc Hele oscechrót.

CXXXIII.

7165 D̲iambennaꞥ Helesius lor
mellach friꞓobair coemslog,
bec d'olai glannai bái is'treib
connárothallai il-lestraib.

7169 Oenmac mná, batoirm truagi,
bamarb dobide oenúaire,
atraracht abrath, beirt pían,
óshunn tanic Helesíam.

7173 Dorigni firt n-amra n-uag
Helesius fiad inmorsluag,
claimi Nemain doreir De
luid[2] agledail forGesse.

7177 Baſinbert Helessi lain
ocimthecht iartír Dathain,
friꞋuall n-aṅgel cenmailli
bainsluag dolándailli[3].

7181 INcorp roláad, luad ṅglé,
forlige lór Helessé,
atraracht cencheo, gním[4] cóir,
amal bidbeo fochetóir.

7185 O shunn cái Helessius arcel
eꞓrnoebu fornoebnem,
bafergach friu Dia donim
artharmthecht daratimnaib.

7189 Fedb rogáid cofobaid fíal
acobair forHelessiam,
indola glé, gleoir corath,
isdodeóin Dé rosbennach.
    Diambennach Helessius lór.

CXXXIV.

7193 R̲í doraraic doib mór slúag
fogradgrait echtrann n-
adrúad,
forro coṅgríbgail cherta

---

¹ Written over *doralat.*   ² Written over *luaid.*   ³ MS. dolandaille.   ⁴ MS. bagnim.

P   [IV. 3.]

dodígail atarinthechta.

7197 Ri rodatráll, tolaib droṅg¹,
fairne flan fortren, fortromm,
lín armaċh, censíl n-etla,
dodamnad am-morpheetha.

7201 Rí dosrat fogailib gail,
fodairib, fothromdíglaib,
foṡolaig cengrad, cengloir,
brónaig imbrait Babiloin.

7205 Secht mfli trénfer frṅóir
ructha imbrait ṁBabilóin,
oċusmíli, mét cachta,
doaes caċhahintliuchta.

7209 Deichmíli fer ferdais nual
iṡed rombai 'sinmórslúag,
cenmná, cenmacu folli,
cenaes ṅdán, ceniunachi.

7213 Rí tarceacht bith ṁbladmar ṁbras
rosmacht ceċn-adbar n-amnas,
rí congaib iarsiraib seircc²,
rí corígaib doraraic.
        Rí doraraic doib mór sluag.

CXXXV.

7217 R i tarlaic inlíc ochéin
        hicenn nadeilbi dontsleib,
isint-herdorinn óg cenrig
icscribunn coir caindligid.

7221 Rii roscar inríg roclos
fríarigi, friaardílatheos,
combái seċht [ṁ]bliadna foleith
amal nacethra ic[c]omgleith.
        [fo. 37. b. 2.]

7225 Ri roheirn dál domuin troig
corala ár inmórsloig,
diatuc leo cenmerbe ammaig,
cenn deOlferne 'sincathraig.

7229 Rí rofaed inn-aṅgel n-uag,
bagnim ṅdaṅgen frṁimluad,
feib imroraid, rigda scél,
dochobair mac n-Israḟél.

7233 Dia rohort frísaerbuáid sain,
fríóenhuair donanaimtcib,
noífichit mili, met cath,
ocus coeca arcet corad.

7237 Rí roreraig, rigda tráll,
iarn-edaib doEzechiam :
cóic bliadna déc, dochtaid dul,
doforcraid forasaegul.

7241 Ri ruc ingráin cuires cáṙh
diaróim ruithess corognath,
fri deich n-úara foracul,
fogne búada buan brígrun.

7245 Aṅdorigni morí raith
arsíl n-Adaim dobithmaith,
osbith builid, bág centreis,
islia tuirim is aisnéis.

7249 Formorgrain Med ocus Pers
Greic ocusRomain rigthess (sic),
forbriga betha comblait,
foraríga rí tharlaic.
        Rí tharlaic inlic ochein.

CXXXVI.

7253 R i roeirn³ doib dál tríarath,
        cidhed aman bahingnad,
dosíl Adaim, gradaib cruth,
cosmailius cosainigud.

7257 Doalmaib airbrib fonéim,
doénaib aidblib aéir,
dobfastaib bit cenblaid,
dohiascaib snait isrothaib.

7261 Dodechraib gotha nan-én
ocus acrotha comthrén,

---

¹ Written over *gionn.*   ² Perhaps *seircc.*   ³ Written over *Roroen.*

doberlaib cechmil bladmair,
dian-ergnaib, dian-iladbaib.

7265 Glé nihinunn seis nasmacht,
gne, nahintliucht, na admat,
naberla, naciall, nacruth,
nahergna *no* horddogud.

7269 Rí rodasgni, gnim glanna,
ildelba nan-anmanna,
ri congrad cenchredim cain,
morí ran roheirn dooib.
Ri roeirn doib dál tríarath.

CXXXVII.

7273 R i thuc doib ilar luba
triathalmain ahimthuga,
forberat uili immalle,
ciatecsamla itcosmaile.

7277 Sain ní diafognai cechluib
dosrósat Dia diadegthoil,
sasait, sergait, línait blait,
fcait, bethaigait, marbait.

7281 Ri rosfaillsig foriagail
fríataidbsin cechoenblfadain,
folígdath frídidnad suth,
fricrínad, frihurugud.

7285 Brechtrad cechdatha foli
clechtmaith dosrigni int-ardri,
dath amlaid fricetlud ṅglan
nibái foretgud Solman.

7289 Adamra indrig naruam rath,
nimtha luad aran-ilar,
atlfu luíbni fidbad fann
noruibni rinndglan retglann.

7293 Rí dosrergaib osbith balcc
fríserggad, fríinforbart,
niguath imbruc oscechtreib,
rí congrad dofuc dooib.
Rí tuc doib ilar luba.

CXXXVIII.

7297 R i roséer Abel centair
dogradmiad domuin der·
mair,
daroega, frísuilge scirc,
tríahuimle, tríaglanedpairt.

7301 Rí rosaer frítormach tríath
Noe nóebglan mac Lamiach,
ocus Abram fiadcachdruṅg
dearmgrad Caldeorum.

7305 Ri rosder Loth, lathar ṅdil,
dintslog, isadahingin,
diatargbad inplág badbda,
diatardad sár Sodomda.

7309 Ri rosder Isaac ochéin
dondidpairt isi[n]dardskéib,
diatuc int-aingel inmolt
diambai fonchlaidiub glénocht.

7313 Ri rosder Iacob doaitt
doláim Isau meicc Isaic,
diaṅdechaid fothuaith combuaid
dothig Labain meic Bathuail.

7317 Ri rosder fritreba tóir
Ioséph ossar [clainne] Iacóib,
[fo. 38 a. 1.]
dianfarslaic Dia trialáthar
dolámaib aderbráthar.

7321 Ri rosder Ioseph, fo fecht,
asincharchair in-Egept,
combahairri oscechclainn
orofúaslaic fís Forainn.

7325 Ri rosder Moisi, met rath,
dosruth Nfl cenabádad,
diar'ernil Dia, derbod raind,
forTermod ingin Forainn.

7329 Ri rosder Moise, mor sccl.
ocus popul n-Israhél,

doMuir Romuir, rígda smacht,
isdodiglaib nan-Egept[1].

7333 Ri *rosáer*, segda atóir,
dogín Balaim m*ei*c Beóir,
dialuid clann Isra*he*'l áin
doaittreib tíre Cannáin.

7337 Ri *rosder*, saerda [in]scel,
sluag noebda m*a*c n-Israhél,
diarosfuc, ruamna cenlén,
darsruth n-uarda n-Iordanen.

7341 Ri *rosder* Iessu mac Nún
diambai ictogail napr*í*mdún,
co*n*asluag dichra, dána,
dochathaib naCannana.

7345 Ri ran rodasá*e*r secho
Raab diráenaib hEricho,
diarlegsat, duiri athbach,
s*ech*t muir innapr*í*mchat*r*ach.

7349 Ri *rosáer* Oeth[2] ócda
dochlaidiub naCiclopda,
ocus Geodeon, gním ńdana,
doburba nambarbarda.

7353 Ri *rosder* Samson cenhír
dolámaib naFilistín,
diar'bris díarig roimsi rath
pr*í*mdo[i]rsi namorcat*r*ach.

7357 Ri *rosder* Susannam slain
diatucad isinmordáil,
donguforgull roches cath,
dian-erracht cach diaclochad.

7361 Ri *rosáer* Hele fáith
ocusEnoc án imthbláith,
fogr*í*andaib caidib cengeis
indiamraib blathib Parduis.

7365 Ri *rosáer* Dauid alchur
diambai aoenur is'dithrub,
diatuc incairig coglan

agailig indleoman.

7369 Ri *rosder* Dauid dána
dochathaib nacombága,
diatuc cenn Gólai, gním ńgúr,
combae f*or*bélaib Saúl.

7373 Ri *rosáer* Ezechiam slan
ciarb'focus adédendal,
diarohícad cosolmai
dongalur, dondinnlobrai.

7377 Ri *rosder* Daniel, deilm ńglan,
acuthí naleoman,
*ocus*Neman, rosóe lí,
asindindlobrai grandí.

7381 Ri *rosder* Michiam, mod ńhblaith,
dodium*us* uaibrech Achaib,
ocus Ionas fiadc*a*chclainn,
díntanic abrú bledmaill.

7385 Ri *rosder*, baleor dobuaid,
naNinuiandai fr*í*oenhuair,
dia rostarmchell, mor inmairg,
tob tened dic*a*choenaird.

7389 Ri *rosder* Toba, derb de,
diambai itroga nadaille,
isnatr*í*meic cosindrath
rodasaer is't[s]urnn tened.

7393 Ri *rosder* Petur c*ec*hcruth
bahecgal rianabádud,
dial-luid coCr*í*s*t*, cengói ńgle,
diambái f*or*dói nafairge.

7397 Ri *rosáer* Petar centair,
bahettal in-aurgabail,
dianf*or*slaic angel Dé dil
acosraib, acumrigib.

7401 Rí *rosder* Eoin bai tan
tr*í*anagnim ńgleóir ńglégian,
digae gona indnemi glais
ocus dindolai amnais.

7405 Rí slógdil rosaer cenlen
Maire mórdil Magdalen,
cenathelluch, deoda tlus,
d'atherruch in-immarbus.

7409 Rí saer Teclai ndfascaig ndil
onablastaib béldergaib,
isint-anfabrocht fortruth
bahadbalbocht dindfuatluch.

7413 Ri rosáer Pol, bláith aniab,
ocus noeb naslóg Siliem,
batar fochircolggaib cath
icrinchumgaib nacatrach.

7417 Romsaera Dia trebar trén
arDemun conadubnél,
[fo. 38 a. 2.]
feib rodasaer, slicht roscar,
cechnoeb remitrubarmar.

7421 Rí cengáeli caine imrúin,
ri conáibe oscechnoebdúil,
fogni cachminn, mocachmiad,
ri narind rosáer Abial.
     Rí rosáer Abial centáir.

CXXXIX.

7425 Rí roróen romaib cenmeth
cech ndoraid forcechoenleth,
uair bátar mogaid, mod nglan,
dorig nimi ocustalman.

7429 Ri dorat fothraig cechtúaith
congail, congruin, conglanbúaid,
conidhé aconn, acenn,
acathir Hierusalem.

7433 Rí dorat sobarthain sláin
forciniud n-amra n-Abráim,
mor ríg, mor faithi, mór mban,
génair oAbram armglan.

7437 Ri oscechrinn, ruathar ndil,

tuarcgab cachdind diadulib,
rosuidig frisid cechsreith
rí cendíth docachóenleith.

7441 Nicheil cachsúi segda slán,
manidcloe ergna n-imlán,
fogníat geill cechcoim n-inceil
donRíg réil roróen remib.
     Rí roróen romaib cenmeth.

CXL.

7445 Rí dosnúargaib óscech iath
Isaac, Iacób, Iosiaph[1],
Moisi *ocus*Iessu fófrith,
Samuel deoda ocus Dauid.

7449 Rí rochar Heli cechdia,
Helesium isIsaia,
Heremiam frifeba fiss,
Etzechel isDanielis.

7453 Hestra, Osse, Ohel án,
ocus Abdias imlán,
isMichiae, bafó fia,
Ambacuc is Fuffoniae.

7457 Agiae, Zachariae cencheist,
athair Iohain uasail Babtaist,
Misaelis fiadcechdrung
ocus Machabeorum.

7461 Rí d'anglib glanaib géraib,
ri d'arbrib fonemnélaib,
ri corígaib, rigda ail,
mó rigaib, rí dosfuargaib.
     Ri dosnúargaib óscachiath.

CXLI.

7465 Rí rosaer Sarra combúaid,
Rabecca ingin mBathuail,
nadfphiair, mor am-miad,
Lia lór ocusRachíal.

[1] MS. ioseph.

7469 Ri dosfuargaib oscechcrích
Ester, Conra isIudith,
mathri nafatha, mod rhbláith,
ocus indAnna banfáith.

7473 Ruiri richid, rí roscar
huili máthri nan-apstal,
nadfMaire, milib tríath,
máthair Iohain Elizafiath.

7477 Ri rodasaer oscechthreib
arcech n-olcc, arcech n-erbaid,
slúag nanoebuag immasech
lasluag namban n-athergech.

7481 ArhDia delbda, tolaib droṅg,
arFlaith fial, febda, foroll,
arClf, niclocn oscechblai,
Ri naroen rosaer Sarrai.
Rí rosaer Sarrai combúaid.

CXLII.

7485 Macc Zachair sainserce intslúaig
glainelce cenrhbathail rhbithbuaid,
mac Elizafeth, sid ṅglé,
remthectaid ríg noemnimé.

7489 IOhain Bab taisi, blaith ingein,
baremthechtaid Crist coemdil,
rosluind doMaire mormiad
diambai imbroind Elizafiad,

7493 Diatanic Maire, mor mfad,
dofis scel Elizafiad,
diaraid ria cenchaire cath
Maire máthair inChoimded.

7497 Hua Iobe cenathis cinn
dorinnscan bathis rhblaith bind,
gleoir indógraith óscechdáil
Iohain mórmaith mac Zacháir.
Mac Zacháir sainserce intslúaig.

CXLIII.

7501 Rí doraiga, ruathar ṅglé,
indflesc dochlainn Iesse,
indóg findlem, glan agné,
Maire ingen Ebraidé.

7505 INsa dosraiga ochéin
oaimsir athar Abéil,
baili buan cechberlai bind,
Maire úag ingen Iochim.
[fo. 38 b. 1.]

7509 Rí thanic donim nerta
diaroet chorp ṅdóinachta,
mó cech rhbríg ardeseirc ṅdil,
dothesargain sil Adaim.

7513 Rí dorósat bith rhbuidi,
conic traig ocus tuili,
robai nói mis, morda re,
imbrú naógda Ebraide.

7517 Ri thanic icolla crí,
hé donrosat donephní,
donfuaslaic dochum nimi
trí achoimpert nahingini.

7521 Huaislium rígaib rígda gein,
rí rogenair imBetheil,
dorarhgert cechfaith ochein
gigned iflaith Ochtauein.

7525 Diatánic Gabriel donim,
mor inglanmiad dondIngin,
mor inbrig De rodasta
doreir indríg dosraiga.
Ri doraiga, ruathar ṅglé.

CXLIV.

7529 Rí rogenair, ni bine,
domulluch nahIngine:
réil doralitni oscechrainn,
rian-Enair, in-ocht kallainn.

7533 Ri diar-rochet, cain caiṅgcn,
class aṅgel isarcha[i]ṅgel,
sid dodoenaib oscec*h*bruig,
indocbail Dé uasnemdaib.

7537 Rí roruithnig rétlaind ráin
riasnadruidib 'nachomdail,
diatucsatar leo lith lor
mirr ocu*s* tuis isdergór.

7541 Rí bái imBethil, buaid becht,
ruc reim techid in-Egept,
diambai inteduar oscec*h*maig,
diar'hort Heruad inmacc*r*aid.

7545 Rí tucad aness[1] iartain
oshunn rohort indarggain,
cor'alt iarsain, bagnim gle,
inNazáreth Galaile.

7549 Rí dessid, nitlaith atlf,
et*er*scribae isfarsaidi,
foraiarair, tr*i*amain tr*i*ath,
diambai Maire ocu*s*Iosiab.

7553 Rí roimchomairc, mor scel,
dosruithib mac n-Israh*é*l,
rí dorat mor cesta ṅgle
forsuidib rechta Moise.

7557 Rí romol Semeon bacoir,
diambái iconglanaltóir,
diatuargaib foradflaim,
ardruire nimi noebnáir.

7561 Rí dorat forngaire trén
forsruth n-amra n-Iordanén,
conarogluais, clú cengeis,
inhed rombas 'conbatheis.

7565 Rí tarrasair fiadintslog
moruiri fírmaith finnmór,
forsṅdessid inSpírut Noeb
laforggal Fiadat fírsaer.

7569 Mac Dé, Dia deoda cec*h*than,

baoen, batréoda derbglan,
nilié infor*u*allach fr*i*agair,
ri robúadach rogénair.
   Rí rogenair, ni bine.

CXLV.

7573 R i róaen, ʀothro[i]sc coglé,
   cethrachait lá ocu*r*aidche,
ardessmerecht docac*h*sruith,
indiamraib dorchaib dithruib.

7577 Ri tharlaic cuce, gné gaind,
nagorta foracholainn,
coroclóad Demun de
tr*i*asinn-aimsigud trede.

7581 Ri doraiga teglach ṅdil
diachumtuch et*er* dóinib,
dosil Abráim, árim ṅglain,
dáfer dec doapstalaib.

7585 Ri rochar Petar isPol,
Andreas uais isIacob,
Iohain, Pilípp, blaitb aṅg*us*,
Bartolom ocu*s*Tomus.

7589 Rí rochar Madian maith, mór,
isinglanfial Iacob,
Simon isTatha centass,
Matha, Marc ocus Lucas.

7593 Ri rochar dásessiur fer,
bahé atheglach toebgel,
ladeisciplu, noebda smacht,
ado soerda sechtmogat.

7597 Ri arroet bathis fosmacht
cenathis ardeismeracht,
rofigle cengaile gne
inrí dorigne inn-óene.
   Ri roáen, rothroisc coglé.

---

[1] Written over *anair*.

CXLVI.

7601 R i robennach, mellach búaid,
na secht lestru usci úair,
[fo. 38 b. 2.]
diamboe 'sinchoiblid gil glain,
dianderna infín inGalail.

7605 Rí imrulaid, rígda fecht,
combuidin móir 'nachoemtecht,
diar'hiicc inclam, comul nglé,
bae fortoeb naconairé.

7609 Rí ruthanic, tolaib droṅg,
incathraig Capharnaum,
diabrethir féin, feib rothúir,
rofccad mac inchetuir.

7613 Rí conattail il-luiṅg lóir,
in-ainbthine dein dermóir,
diar'choisc inṅgaeth corbothláith,
corabi inrianfeth robláith.

7617 Ri rofaed droṅg ṅdotchaid, ṅdúb,
'sindorcraid cenimforddúl,
diar'hícc fer fothedmaib tra
dogrethaib dremnaib demna.

7621 Rí rosas nacoicmili,
cenmotha slóg cechdine,
dochoicbargenaib, mod n-án,
ocus dondáocenbratan.

7625 Rí robennach, ferr cechgein,
nadáiasc, nacoicbargein,
cotarfuaraid léo foleith
dáchliab déc diafuidlechaib.

7629 Ni dinsid tiar na tair,
rí ín-hislib, rí in-arddaib,
adrell cechrig immosech,
ferr cechrig rí robennach.
Rí robennach, mellach búaid.

CXLVII.

7633 R i cos'tuctha dagalar
bodor ocuramlabar,
immuich arbélaib intslúaig
rodashicc isíndoenhuair.

7637 Ri conattaig, tuiccsi dáil,
deog d'uisque forsinṁbannscáil,
dian-ebairt frie centlais
bái coicer innacomgnais.

7641 Ri rohic, amra tola,
mnai truaig dindrobur fola,
diataraill alám focleith,
finna abrothirni innétaig.

7645 Rí rohicc mac nafedba
diantuc othoraib demna,
amra firt fiadroṅgaib dál,
diarohiccad inbacclám.

7649 Ri condranic forsinmaig
frideichnebur doclannaib,
nícian rolla fordala
comtar cocma comlana.

7653 Ri robennach secht ṁbargin
la bec d'iascc, nírbo daidbir,
facbait secht cloib d'fuidlib de
sloig nacetheoramfle¹.

7657 Ri rocháimchlai cruth cia cóir
intan luid islfab Taboir,
diatarfaid, gléalt cenhacht (?),
adéacht trianadoenacht.

7661 Tan bateist coicfer, gním n-og², Petar, Iohain islacob,
coṅgaissi ceilli, clú cass,
Moise ocutlele admass.

7665 Rí bethad buadaig, buan blad,
cli imgretha gluair ili gor : : :
nicerr fri'brig buidni bla

ferr ca*ch*ríg ri cos'tuctha.
Rí cos'tuctha dágalar.

CXLVIII.

7669 R í roirscart isroglan
tempul sóer segda : : :
tegdais dil deoda Dé bí,
bid teg n-amra n-aurnaigthi.

7673 Rí rothodiusaig ahuaig
Lazair balór dolánbuaid,
iarnaécaib, feib roclos,
in-adnacul cethri údenos.

7677 Mori réil, coméit glaine,
imrualaid muir ñGalaile,
cossaib tírmaib, deoda gáir,
fescur fiadnaaps*a*laib.

7681 Ri roshfcc fiadchuirib clann
forsintsét nadámac dall,
dianderna donchríaid chéir
*com*barosc roglan roréil.

7685 Ri rofuc immrim n-amra
indomnuch naglanphalma,
diatucad dó immasech
indassan isint-ochech.

7689 Rí frisin-erbairt inslúag
huili e*ter* tren oc*us* trúag ;
'dena arn-íc triabithu sir,
atb*en*nachda, ameic Da*uid* !'

7693 ArCoimdiu glé *cum*taig rath
t*ur*cbaid ce*ch*gne ce*ch*cumtach,
cain elí cendigna, cenchacht,
morí rígda rohirscart.
Ri rohirscart isroglan.

CXLIX.

[fo. 39 a. 1.]
7697 R i dorigne t*rí*acheill ñglain
humalloit diaaps*ta*laib
india dardain, foglóir gle,

riacaisc móir nahésserge.

7701 Ri rob*en*na*ch* tuara doib
imtrath nóna fochétóir,
dian-ebairt friuu t*rí*arath,
robui nech díb 'coaglebrath.

7705 Ri roraidi fr*íu* cogle
forgal febda firinne :
'nech uaib tic arth*us* donméiss
ishé ata fordrochséis.'

7709 IArsin dochuaid Iudas ass
con-ilur ihbriathar foglas,
commairni aríg, bagnim t*r*ait,
archuic uñgaib dec argait.

7713 Ri roraidi fr*íu* cocert
fr*í*sinslóg bái 'nachoemthecht :
'scaillfidir intret coglé
innocht immonn· oegaire.'

7717 IArsin asbe*ir* Petur bán
ocus aétan frilár :
'ní nomscarad fr*í*Cr*ist* cain
nifil innim notalmain.'

7721 Ri roraidi athesc n-uag
fr*í*Petur fiadinmorsluag :
'nomdiultfa fothrí t*rí*achleth
riasiu gaires incailech.'

7725 INri rodasalt sunn sel
fr*í*tinchosc, fr*í*forcetel,
roraid fr*íu* t*rí*acomrad cain :
'bid forcomdal iñGalaíl.'

7729 Cuaird nime imchlar betha bind,
suairc slan fr*í*sretha soérgr*í*hn,
gnim centathair taidbrit bi,
morí rachain dorigni.
Ri dorigni t*rí*acheil nglain.

CL.

7733 R i secht nimi, rí talman,
ardruiri nan-íladbar,

Q   [IV. 3.]

imrulaid etronn, fo fecht,
fristé tríbliadan trichat.

7737 Ri dochoid fecht forfolocht
bahé inri tairchert torocht,
diarochind Iudas inmbrat(h)
diambui ínglinn Iosofath.

7741 Ri rísfer failti osblai
Iudas tríaphoicc mbrathemdai,
rí cosrucad sluag 'nadail,
rí rucad in-aurgabail.

7745 Ri rúad rofucad hicacht
hitech coslúag nasacart,
diarodiult Petur cobras
nadrabe 'namuinteras.

7749 Rí rodamair cech ndigail
fophlagaib fiaderrigaib,
ri tarcbad fiadchuirib clann,
rí fors'tardad guforgall.

7753 Rí dochoid fricrann crucha
asathoil nir'athrucha :
ri noeb diatardad indneim,
rí goét 'nathoeb colagein.

7757 Ri dochoid iarsoeralt slecht
asadoenacht 'nadéacht :
rí rosáilset frian-úine,
rochainset nahilldúile.

7761 Tarblaing dorcha darcachmag :
mairb thalman asrachtatar ;
bathómnaig dúili Dé dil
diar'fodluig fíal intempuil.

7765 Rochichlaig cech duil, deilm nglan,
rochrithnaig nem istalam,
muir darcrícha rothriall techt,
críde cloch ciar roscáilset.

7769 Ri roches hicrraid chain
croich darcenn claínni Ádaim,
iarsin ruc creich, calma adrenn,
cotarat laim darhIffern.

7773 Ri rochuimrig Demun dub
diani[d]comainm Lucifur :
atat fochrithfeidm osain
sloig hIffirnn conan-amsaib.

7777 Ri dofuc brait hIffirn uair
apein, acrrthfeidm comtruaig,
rosuidig slánaib foadeis
forbruigib bánaib Parduis.

7781 Rí doeni, tolaib caíngen,
ri aíngel, ri archa[i]ñgel,
dessid iarsin, soerda clu,
osrigaib 'narigsuidiu.

7785 Mori rígíial forlassad,
isflaith firian forbhassach,
doróssat cechmbrig, mod ñgle,
ferr cechrig rí secht nime.
Rí secht nime, rí talman.

Conice inso corp saltrach narann + natri-
coicait duan. Ado hautem pert frífoisi(tin) 7
friathírgi, ocus adcich fri haisneis naheisseirgi,
conid daduain dec arthribcóictaib duan samlaid.

CLI.

[fo. 39 a. 2.]

7789 Isamaithrech, febda fecht,
aCoimdiu, domtharimthecht :
dilig dam cachcin romthe,
aCrist, ardotrocaire.

7793 Ardothitacht cain hicrí,
ardogein, amo noebri !
ardobathis inbuain hifus,
dilig dam cech n-immarbus.

7797 Ardochrochad colére,
omarbaib arth'eseirge,
tabair dam dilgud mothal,
aritFiadu firthrocar.

7801 Ardofresgabail soer sel[1]
cosinn-Athair *for*noebnem[2],
feib roradis *fri*m riatecht,
dilaig dam motharimthecht.

7805 Ardothitacht, déoda ingair,
domess *for*slog síl Adaim,
arnoeṅgr*a*d nimi cenchlith,
dílgi*ur* dam mochinaid.

7809 Arbuidin nafátha fir,
ardroṅg molbthach namartir,
dilig dam ca*ch*in romgab,
arfairinn nan-húasalathar.

7813 Archleir nan-aps*tal* cenchol,
arsluag nan-uag ṅdeiscipol,
arca*ch* noeb corath rigda,
dilig dam momígnima.

7817 Arce*ch* noebuaig osbíth bras,
arbantrocht nap*rí*mlaichas,
dilig dam ca*ch* cin fonim,
ar*M*aire n-amra n-Ingin.

7821 Armuint*ir* talman, torm ṅdil,
armunt*ir* nimi noebgil,
tabair dam dilgud basdech,
domchintaib uair[3] amaithrech.
ISamaithrech, febda fecht.

CLII.

7825 **N**imtha saegid *for*Dia ṅdron
con-ilur mod medar ṅglan,
*con*darcuiri arcr*í*chid ṅgel,
ruiri reb richid romchar.

7829 Relat *tr*iarintriuchta (?) ráid,
ács indintliuchta áin ém,
iarfinnalta *fr*isid sloig
inganta móir morig réil.

7833 Retha gaissi canar lib

cotibgaib cenbaisse blad,
dána cenecla nachneich,
slana iarsreith ecna corath.

7837 Coniarf*us* duib, duraib eim,
ni dorunaib moríg réil,
gleod ca*ch*cesta uair daruair,
leor buaid diafesta doleir.

7841 Denaid *fr*iartarba cenchrith,
amra rith relaid iarsreith,
nadibleisc linib run raith,
tur daith *for*ca*ch*ceist foleith.

7845 Cia 'cata, iarṅglé doléir,
dála De diareir rothúir,
ciamét naree, reim n-uag,
robui inri ruad riacachdúil.

7849 Cia dorat comairli coir
cenbríg ṁbroin dondrig hiruin,
nasiu nobeth bith ochein,
siu dogneth rí reil cachṅduil.

7853 Si[u]dognetis aiṅgil uais
artuais ce*ch*caiṅgil iarséis,
siu nobetis moini arbes
nagr*es* nadoine fondeis.

7857 Nariched natalam tir,
namuir mil met magar muad,
no na*ch*dúil glanglanna cél
nem nél *no* anmanna úag.

7861 Cia rochuimnig domrig rain
cengr*a*in cordascuibdig fein,
cech duil derb *fr*isoerbuaid slain
rosdelb *fr*íoenuair diaréir.

7865 Cia adbar adbal infess
diacess inbith bladmar brass,
incuman lib arca*ch*n-ai
ciabunad diambai inmass?

7869 Heisse rotheipi ce*ch* ṅduil

---

[1] Written over *for*nem.   [2] Written over ·chel + *coelum*.   [3] Written over ·isam.

iarruin rosleice [1] diaréir,
inrí doruasat cechcri,
int-uasabb rogni ingréin.
7873 Cia rolin dosilaib bith
dolubaib lígaib eenchleith,
cia rodelb fríathuil andath,
ciarath forcachluib foleith?
7877 Cia rosdechraig innacrí,
cia rosgni iarcechraig gleo,
cia cruthaig glanglanna clú
nadu nachn-anmanna beo?
7881 Bunad anman lib ingle
congaib gne glanbda col-lí,
ciacinn cenbaegul riangein,
saegul sein cechduini bí?
7885 Cia 'cata indarim úag
fil forsluag sil Adaim áin,
[fo. 39 b. 1.]
cia 'coata, cendánim duib,
árim nguir ganim cechtraig?
7889 Ónchetna duini robúi,
etir fer ismnái col-lí,
fordomun dérgidach Dé
gle cosndedinach atchí.
7893 Crícha aicgein airm itát,
aicbeil imrat, rígda inset,
cose nirosfoilsig mori
doneoch icrí rianaéc.
7897 Cid canat tonna, toirm trén,
cennachlén lonna frítóir,
congaibet gala, crech ngúr,
cachleth darmúr mara móir?
7901 Can tic tuili trethan tuairec
lethan cuairdd fobetha barcc,
cialeth fondomun rotháig
intan astrdig forcachtrachl?

7905 Cialín nashuag, srethaib droñg,
dosceil tonn muad mara mind,
ceti arbair trebait ann
dondleith tall dontalmain tinn?
7909 Fillit anglúni cognath
cechtrath cennachñdúiri dréil,
molad marcharait cohóg
canait cechslog dondríg réil.
7913 Cid roleth bith, brigach cuaird,
cid dogni suairc sirach set,
isindaidchi fríriad reb,
ocus gr̄an gel cidimthet?
7917 Ocus esca cid dodfeim
tan doceil nachñgesca ñglan,
cid dogni cithu gaeth cain,
cid nachgaim triabithu sam?
7921 Cialin naretlann adrann
mod inall fríarim oscech dind,
rethait rithrosc iarsetsain,
cidcotasgaib na sechtrind?
7925 Cia de ismo messar combuaid
infail uaib rofessad iarssr?
aer alad, ilar neil,
nó intalam tren trebach tír?
7929 Cia de islethiu domun dúr
no isdoimniu amúr, monur muad,
ciaso baili ata incrann
lethas barr daraer n-úar?[1]
7933 Cid 'mifoilñgi torann tren
cenlen lin abarann ihbúan,
argair cechn-ahél athrial
sair, siar, isinaher n-úar?
7937 Cia criathras usce n-an, n-uais,
iarluais forcach n-iathmass n-éis,
cia roalt crotha dogres
dorat bes forsrotha séis?

---

[1] Written over rosteippe.   [1] Written over núag.

7941 Cairm itat adbai nangaeth
baeth balnai imrát *fricach-*
ṁbruach?
neoil indaeoir, noithech bes,
cid doib dog*res* bid *forluad?*
7945 Cialin nangaeth carait nual?
ciabrig buan canait *frúmluad?*
ciadechair fail dararath?
ciadath ata *forcachgaeth?*
7949 Congili cinnas atat
na *secht* nimi nocbda cuaird?
cid dosgni fostaib cenbet?
ciamet fil 'nasostaib suairc?
7953 Cia 'coata tom*us* inchlair
richid rain *frifo*rus fír?
cia doroemadair ochein
diareir coemchathir indRig?
7957 Cade lín atheglaig lib
rosdedlaig Dia dil diathreib,
indfir rodelb betha brig
indrig robái rianagein?
7961 Tuirmid *tráariagla*, rét reil,
ciamét bliad*an* cob*rath* ṁbúan,
tuirid lib *tráb*escna bríg
ciahaes esca forsindhúan.
7965 Can dodechamar ille
forbith ché chetarchair gle,
infitir *forc*ialbann clú
ciadú cosatingam dé?
7969 Acht arṁDia, derb centair,
rondelb riandail domuin dúir,
'coarflaith cenguasacht, cenc*r*ich,
'coarrig donʀuasat cech̅dúil?
7973 Cia rogni cech̅ n-uili n-uag
lethan luad *frí*buidi ṁbríg,
acht monoebrí donim nél
arn-oenDia trén, ishé arṅdil.
7977 IS he doruasat cech̅ret

cenbet, arn-uasabb, nadbrec,
rí rosmacht *for*aessu ec
iarset rochacht gaessu Gr*éc.*
7981 Cometaid cenecla agáis
ecna cenbaes oibind bes,
doneoch dorucai mor*í*
bec dofucaid ni diag*ré*s.
7985 Tairinnid *forṁ*bréthir móir,
atibtroig treithfir fondríg,
[*fo.* 39 b. 2.]
ennga huimli duib lagáis,
nabid *for*báis nofribrig.
7989 Nabagaid ahecnu uag
nual cenecla c*ra*buid gúir,
lib niderb osbetha bríg
retha indríg rodelb cach̅dúil.
7993 Truag *forṁ*bith fodorchaib trel
*for*feb fothomthaib Dé dil,
ingnassaib garbdai cech̅cin
nidatglain *for*n-adbai hil.
7997 Hili huili dúili Dé,
dili druini dreim asmá,
iarnacáintuistin foleith,
coemthuicsin cach̅neich nimtha.
Nim*tha.*
8001 Ni hetr*a*igim rúna Dé,
gle nisteclaigim *fr*imla,
firthuicsi rig bethad bí,
anhed beo hicri nimtha. *Nimtha.*
8005 Ni naderna sen nasúi
nadrúi nisderbai bamá,
ciapsat guir *fr*icr*a*bud ṅglé
túir *for*dalaib Dé nimtha. *Nimtha.*
8009 ISme Oengus céle Dé,
coemdos gle clere fodchna,
diathuicthib deimnib De
tuicsin *forcach̅í* nimtha. *Nimtha.*
8013 Morí corunib, cain clú,

cach̄du diaduilib ata osbith,
balcc bladmar [ ] frı̄mre
ach̄t adrad frimre nimtha. Nim̄tha.

Deichdúan naheisseirge inso.

CLIII.

8017 B acoir doca*ch*cristaide ;
cianochiad cach̄thratha,
huamun domnaig trı̄staide
sech̄tmain rialathi m̄bratha.

8021 Biaid fogur fenedach
congairib grandaib garbaib,
isindomnuch dedenach
rian-eisseirge domarbaib.

8025 Ticfa nel derg tcinntide
atuáisciurd nime ninaig,
granna, gér, garb, geintide,
lethfaid dartalmain tinaig.

8029 Ticfa fleochud fuilide
asindnful dorcha dogor,
truag deochair diarcuiribne
linfaid inn-huili n̄domon.

8033 IMtrath terta tinscanat [1]
frossa fégfola fomnaig,
nitercca, niimscarat,
coti leth lathi indomnaig.

8037 Ticfat luaichthi lasracha,
ticfat toirne centola,
ticfat cruaidi casracha [2],
ticfat froslacha fola.

8041 O leuth lathi lanaide
cotrath nona nicletha,
fleochud fola falaide
fochetheora ardda inbetha.

8045 Tomadmann tuath talmanna,
cretha granna isglorae,
inmuir colin anmanna

[1] MS. tinscanait.

tet daramuru mora.

8049 Mairg cech̄n-oen 'nafrı̄thele
nach̄foichlidar cofooil,
uamun brátha bithféle
ciadogneimmis bacooir.
Bacóir doca*ch* crı̄staide.

CLIV.

8053 I sindlathiu tánaissi
dia-luain luaidfiter arbair,
nidatairdi aniussa
crı̄hnaigfid nem imthalmain.

8057 Tonna saile sétaigfit
frı̄snahairera ardda,
biasta bledmaill beccaichfit,
fochichret gaire garga.

8061 Guba granne golgaire,
cui cencheol, garg an̄gretha,
cenaine, cenforngaire,
fochethri ardda inbetha.

8065 Bethu bronach belgaide,
censid, censláine suba,
dron̄g togach condedgaire
iarh̄dith fortrágaib duba.

8069 Truaga dini domblassa,
bergga conbenfat bassa,
nisuan sidi somblassa,
lergga conlı̄nfat lassa.

8073 Ferad cach aneimele
friDia, din asda[i]thiu,
friar Coimdid con̄gelféle,
ararsoerad 'sindlaithiu.
ISsindlaithiu tánaise.

CLV.

8077 S intres laithiu lainderda
dia-mairt 'mu*r*tuairc amura
arCoimdiu cóir caindelbda

[2] MS. cosracha.

timmairgfid cuaird adula
    [fo. 40 a. 1.]

8081 Legf(ait) fothai fudomnai
    domuin dein, dál asderbu,
    crethfait clocha cruthamrai,
    *co*sceraitar *fri*andelbu.

8085 Dluma dergga teintide,
    niseol seim, nisuairc soraid [1],
    gura, cerpa, geinntide,
    fochichret cuaird indomuin.

8089 Turcgeba sruth sroibtened
    ahuillib talman tocbaig,
    cumgeba cruth croithfider
    *for*bruinnib betha broenaig.

8093 Bidoenbreo bíth br*a*inechda
    othathurcbail cofuined,
    linfaid cloencheo cairechda
    ce*ch*rind reil corian ruided.

8097 Ri cosaidbrib slanchaiṅgen,
    do*r*ósat gréne goho:
    con·arbrib aarcha[i]ṅgel,
    ronsoera 'sintresslóho !
    'Sintreslathiu lainnerda.

CLVI.

8101 'S inchethramad lithlathiu
    cetaine, cetaib omun,
    ticfe athach écaine,
    croithfaid inn·huili ṅdomun.

8105 Turcgeba inmuir mormoṅgach
    othalmain, tolaib tine,
    cumgeba agr*ith* glorglonnach,
    coroa niulu nime.

8109 Nuall nambledmall ṁbeccedach
    nambiasta ṁbélderg ṁbira*ch*,
    sluaig nasedlaṅg setfada*ch*
    forsintr*a*cht tírimm tinach.

8113 Dofuit sís arithisi
    trethan tromm, toromin n-adbal,
    *co*nnachfess afithissi
    cid teite fothuinn talman.

8117 Tic tathellach tathlúgud
    congnithaib fiadnaslogaib,
    atherruch *fri*aathnúgud
    combi 'nachrichaib coraib.

8121 Gaetha galacha gera,
    ginmara, cetaib ahél,
    combruet nafidbada,
    comberat leo 'sinn-ahér.

8125 IAlla ainble, engacha,
    imriadat cech n-iath n-allmar,
    diana, daingne, dedgarcha,
    diallait *for*biad intalman.

8129 Ticfait airde inganta,
    casrai cruaidi, cru gr*u*nna:
    síl n-Adaim a[t]timmarta,
    trúaga cechdu andala.

8133 Atbe*ra* insluag sirechta*ch*
    síl n-Adaim sernait srethu,
    an-athesc truag, d*i*nerta*ch* :
    ' ferr dún bas indabethu.'

8137 Bresma búana bruthacha,
    gr*u*tha grainne *co*ngairgge,
    sreba srúama sruthacha,
    consceraite*r* frifairge.

8141 Fillfidir nem, nassad glan,
    afudomnaib aadbair,
    cinnfidir agnas adbal
    comb[r]uifider *fri*talmain.

8145 Mac mor Maire Ingine
    ronsóera laprimmaithiu,
    arcac*h*n-olcc ṅ-óg n-indlide
    'sinchethramad lithlaithiu.
    'Sinchethramad lithlathiu.

[1] Written over *solam*.

CLVII.

8149 Coiced laithe lígaide
　　dia-dardain, tolaib tine,
ticfet toirne díglaidi
conscértar renna nime.

8153 Nicheil ca*ch*duil delgnaide
timmarta condattrúaga,
domun dur condedgaire
roscar fríabriga buana.

8157 Beti dorchai tr*i*amannai,
betit adhuatha adbail,
srebai solmai sfabardai
linfait ónim cotalmain.

8161 Toethsat ruibni rétlannai
sis asostaib asesta;
nisfoelsat atetbannai,
*for*muchthair grian isesca.

8165 Coe gr*a*nna *ocus* golgaire,
duba dian ocus toirse,
cenaine, cenfor*n*gaire,
censíd, censuba soillse.

8169 Sruama serba, seimlide,
fochasrachaib dosfemed,
muada merda meirblige,
isnalasrachaib tened.

8173 Dia deoda doroegasa
tarcai turu condaithe,
marca*ch*noeb romsoerasa
archuru inchoiced láithe. *Coiced.*

CLVIII.

[fo. 40 a. 1.]

8177 Sessed lathi lordata
　　dia-haine, tolaib tuile,
doberthar inmormart*r*a
ann *f*orsil Adaim huile.

8181 Nichélat indécnaide,

leir adfiadat iarsrethaib,
atbélat ec etlaide
cachmil beo roblais bethaid.

8185 Bidbrona*ch*, bidbrainechda,
cruachda focherdaib casrach :
nibaglorach gr*a*igechda
luarda colerggaib lasrach.

8189 Oslaicfitir coemdoirsi
richid ranmair cenbine,
domun *con*achoemsoillsi
*for*tuigthir arbair nime.

8193 Nanoeb isindnocbaiñgil
isindlassair lúaith lethain,
atsoer imca*ch*coemcha[i]ñgein
am*a*l iasc bis hitrethain.

8197 IArñdul acrí chaiñgnide
co*Crist* caid *f*ordoi dessel,
bithoentu achaiblide
cengoi madchi*n* rosessed.
　　Sess*ed* lathi lordata.

CLIX.

8201 Dia-sathairnn nasechtmaine
　　bíaid inbith focr*i*thur,
firfid gr*a*phainn gergaile,
am*a*l choire *f*orfichud.

8205 Fochicher achruadchasra
iarfeirg diagalaib glethib,
luadfit lergga luathlasra,
sinfit suas osnaslébib.

8209 Sergfait srotha serblomma
iarsrethaib siabrai sirfecht,
centuili, cenderbthonna,
cenrethaib riaglai rigrecht.

8213 Roinnfitir tr*i*athomthaigi
sithbe naslébi slemun,
cloifitir tr*i*achomchaire,
menmaigfitir codremun.

8217 Coclócfet nahaicneda
cechdúla, deilm asamru,
sóefeit nabiat attreba
et*er*beohu ocus marbdu.

8221 Ardrí richid rinnnime
Cr*ist* caid conic ca*ch*ñgr*a*phainn,
ronfaema ardinnbile
coronsaera día-sathairnn.
Día-sathairnn nasechtmaine.

CLX.

8225 I l-láithiu nalánchañgen
domnaig tadban diarñdoidñgib,
ticfait airbri archañgel
dochum talman líarCoimdid.

8229 *Congera* int-archa[i]ñgel
gairm gluair[1] óscriaid ce*ch*duine,
*for*sil n-Adaim n-ardaiñgen
con-héirset hili huile.

8233 ISsinchetna eisseirge
riacách foguth indaiñgil,
apstail conaseiselbe
coCr*ist* cenchrad diaca[i]ñgin.

8237 'Sindeisseirgi thanaisi
atressat fáthe inbetha :
foismedaig nisfailgaisi
dontress essérgi ingr*e*tha.

8241 'Sinchethramaid essergi
atrcisset martir thalman,
isincoiced eisseirgi
huilidettu noeb n-arbar.

8245 ISint[s]ess*ed* eisseirgi
heirgit othalmain ta[i]sced
aes óge, aes athirge,
nanoidin iarnarhbaisted.

8249 ISsintsec[t]maid eisseirgi
atraig ca*ch*oen coanmain,

atenid, atrommthuilib,
amuir, atir, atalmain.

8253 Tinolat droñg tóebadbal
dochum dála tr*ia*cr*i*thleidm,
muint*er* nimi noebarbar,
muint*er* thalman iss iffeirnn.

8257 IS fossud afledugud
liníb anduis andile,
asossud, asrethugud,
fiadgnuis réil rig *sech*t nime.

8261 Na *sech*t nime noebnara
fillfitir fodlaib fuiled,
gebaid tcne toebdana
otha thurcbail cofuined.

8265 Forhinnaib nalasrasin
seiss intsluáig innasrethaib,
osdindaib nacasrasin
*com*buaid fobrátha brethaib.

8269 Atre inrí robúadach
conidfoidreich doib huile,
*con*achroich deirg dodúalaig
fr*ia*aiss fiadgnúis ce*ch*duine.
[fo. 40 b. 1.]

8273 Seiss isuidiu amiadamla
Mac De Athar centimme,
innachuiriu gr*ia*namra,
adáapstal dec immc.

8277 Mac nahOge ebraide
dorósait slógu hisa[i]thiu,
din artróge delgnaide
diarñdfún isindlaithiu.
Il-láthiu nalánchaingen.

CLXI.

8281 INdomnuch nacomdála
iarn-eisseirge co[n]dremna[1],
nibaceim soer sograda,

---

[1] Written over *cruaid*.

[1] MS. dremuna, with dot over u.

R

tecait druiṅg duba demna.
8285 Tuir nan-arbar n-iffernna
cendil acarcraib comul,
fogarbdath acrithíedma
linfait inhuilí ṅdomun.
8289 Dofoethsat nahídala,
dee duib naṅgeinte cuilech :
nisfoelsat angnímrada
dobith fiadgnúis indRuirech.
8293 Ruibni ruada richessa,
tene derg troethas duisse,
duilgi trúaga trichessa,
con-ilur fergg friaṅgnárse.
8297 Congluaisfi fonn fudomna
domuin dein, dál condubai,
artúaisfi condodomnai,
cenbuaid, cenbrlg, cenbrugai.
8301 Coe granna ocus glammairecht
condith cenchoimsi ṅgretha,
cencennsa, censadailecht,
censíd frisoillsi sretha.
8305 Sreba siabra saraigter
snimaig forhinn nalasra,
cretha ciara granaigter
gnimaig forcinn nacasra.
8309 Guidem frisinmorchoimdid
incech huair arcomráda,
arsoerad diartrógdoidṅgib
indomnuch nacomdála.
       INdomnuch naconidála.

CLXII.

8313 I l-lathiu indluain lainnerda
       brátha frisṅdalat píana,
ferfait arbair aiṅgelda
catha frídemna díana.
8317 Troethfaidir droṅg dergnaide
triádremnu tolaib guba :

rian-aṅgliu centirbaide
mebais fordemnu duba.
8321 Conatóisiuch dolbaide
Lucifer léom asdúru.
in-Iffern ogolgaire
fochichrilar forcúlu.
8325 IArsin bertair fírbretha
fiadgnúis De forclainn Ádaim,
scertair iarnaṅgnímgreth(a),
decliraigfitir 'nandálaib.
8329 Dlomthar lat droṅg demnachda
ipfanaib úaraib Iffirn,
peccthaig censil ṅderbgarta,
fochiabraib cruadaib crithfeidm.
8333 Cechfirian foglangeltad
fordeiss Dé bí, buan bithfeidm ;
fodimiad cechanrechtach,
forlaim cli dochum n-Iffeirnn.
8337 INdformdig, ingúbrethaig,
inchosnamaig, inchuilig,
indruid, inderetecdaig,
ingeint, ingalaig guinig.
8341 INmeirlig, indadaltraig,
ingoaig gloraib guba,
in[t]santaig, indiumursaig,
indeithchich linib luga.
8345 INdferggaig, indetradlaig,
induinoirgnid condremnai,
aes ecnaig, aes athchossain,
aes indindlaig nosdedlai.
8349 IT he sin inprimpeccthaig
artrebat hIffernn húarach,
tiagait cenni d'ffrettlaib
laDemun ṅdremun trúagach.
8353 Dochum pene suthaine
icarcair guires grithu,
iatsom nipdat duthaine
icafulaṅg triabithu.

8357 Bethu brónach bithtoirsech
    ftu, dochtai iarsetaib,
    cuairt glórach, niclithchoimmsech,
    uacht, gorta, cráth fordetaib.

8361 Dia dil, tuistid dítnidi
    nandúla ndelbda ndegrach,
    ronsoera argliphiti
    [na]ndemna in-Iffurnn engach.

8365 INdnoib isindifrianaig
    doreir indAthar nemda,
    congerdar cendímiada[1]
    dochum flatha sechtedma.
        [fo. 40 b. 2.]

8369 Nassad side siráidde,
    amru cechnduis cenchithu,
    imcaissiu naTrinóite
    ognúis dognuis trâbithu.

8373 Bith isámaib sonmige
    iarmbas cendomgnas ndangen,

'nandalaib cendonmige
    dogres hicomgnais angel.

8377 Cenchrini, cengalara,
    censnfm, censaethar snfid,
    cenoccurus cotulta,
    cenaurchra broitt nabfid.

8381 Bith isoere sirsoillsi,
    classa caine, ceoil gelbda.
    innoebi censirthoirsi,
    cenhass, cenáes, cenerchra.

8385 Adroillemm, adaittrebam
    oentaid aingel cechtratha,
    liarCoimdid cocaitchennam
    iarmbuaid abrethaib brátha.

8389 Adfiadat indécnaide,
    doréir narfagla asmóo,
    imriadat cohéttlaide
    mili bliadna 'sindlóo.
        Il-lathiu indluain lainerda.

Finit, amen finit . ago D*ro gratias.* Feil Maire hifogomur indiu.

---

[1] MS. diamiada, with dot over first a.

INDEX VERBORUM.

As a rule nouns and adjectives are given only in the nom. sing., and verbs only in the
pres. indic. act. sg. 1. The bare numbers refer to the lines of the poem.

A.

achtach, 2881, 7093; from acht .i. corp,
? O'Cl.
adair, leg. agair?, 5955.
ad-aittrebaim, *I inhabit, possess*, 8385.
adbal-bocht, *vastly poor*, 7412.
ad-chocraim, *I combine, couple?*, 6045.
ad-fiadaim, *I declare*, s- fut. sg. 1; adfía-sa,
1785, pret. pass. sg. 3; adfét, 6823.
adlaic, *desire* (- adhailg, O'Cl.), acc. 3487;
pl. acc. -e, 4608.
adma, *wise, cunning*, 451, 4191. (adhma
.i. colach, O'Cl.)
ad-mass, admas, *excellent?*, 30, 5024, 7664;
sg. gen. m. 5050, 6950.
admat, *material*, 7266.
ad-rúad, *very red, very strong?*, 954, 2298,
4082, 4650, 5196, 5782, 6226, 6998, 7194.
ad-húar, *very cold*, 3966.
ad-úath, *terror*, 8158.
ae, 1303, *knowledge?* (ai no aol, O'Cl.).
1. áeb, sg. acc. 7111 = aibh no aoibh .i. cos-
mhailéas, *resemblance*, O'Cl.
2. áeb, *beauty* = óiph Z. 31, 63; sg. dat.
áib 4280; see an-aeb, lán-aeb, slan-aeb.
aél, ahél, 7935, 8122; haíal, 110, *a breeze*
= W. awel, Gr. ἄελλα.
ág, *battle*, 4688, 4814, 5589; cen ág, 2014,
5075; co n-ág, 5146.
agmen, *ten thousand millions*, 774, 780;
borrowed from the Latin.
áibnech, 5174, for oibnech, *sudden, quick*.
aicscid, *visible*, 330.

aidble bainn, *vastness of deed*, 4907; one of
the meaningless chevilles (*geiriau llanw*)
common in Celtic poetry.
aiducht, *bequest*, 2028.
aig, 6141, *keen?*, seems O'R.'s ' *aigh*, ge-
nerous, valiant,' cet tengad aig, Cogad
G. 50.
aig thaig, occurs with the preps. *con, fri*
3241, 6305, 6547, and *for* 2631, 3477,
6539, 7087.
áigarda, *pastoralis*, 5868; from ácgaire,
shepherd (áe, ói = ovis).
áigsin, acc. *fear*, 5960.
áigthech, *fearful*, 875.
ail, 4773; mó cech n-ail, 4451; amru cech
n-ail, 4513. Perhaps O'Clery's ail .i. arm,
weapon.
ailt, *house* (.i. teag, O'Cl.), 5158.
aimsigud, *temptation*, 7580.
ainbthech (an-fethech), *stormy*, 4681.
ainccess, 1126, 6023.
ain-étgud, *undressing?*, 5980.
ainge?, 6272.
aingelda, *angelic*, 8315.
ainne, *ánu*, 5432.
air-birech, *reproachful?*, 942.
airbre, *a host*, pl. dat. airbrib, 716 (airbhre
.i. sluagb, O'Cl.).
air-brigim, 271.
air-chron, *rebuking*, 826.
air-derg, *very red*, 898.
air-díbdad, *extinction*, 4372.
airdire dul, *conspicuous (the) going*, a cheville.

4735. So airdirc scél, 5121 ; airdirc rád, 5553.

airer, *a territory*; sg. dat. airiur, 2677 ; acc. pl. -a, 8058.

airerda, *pleasant*, 112 (airear .i. aoibhinn, O'Cl.)

airct, *space*, 2531.

airniul, 843.

air-phortach, air-fortach, ir-fortach, πρό-πυλον, *portico, vestibule* (?), 393, 406, 412 ; sg. gen. -aig, -aich, 392, 404 ; acc. -ach, 396 ; pl. n. -aig, -oich, 385, 389 ; gen. -ach, 398, 414.

airrí, *viceroy, governor*, 3464, 3565 ; gen. airríg, 3507 ; dat. 3542, 3550, 3564, 3610, 3728, 4034 ; acc. 3456, 3524 ; voc. airri, 3573, 3582, 3598.

airríge, *governorship*, 3372.

aislingthech, *dreamer*, 3112.

ait, 5455 ; do aitt, 7313 (the ordinary meaning, *place*, will not do here).

áith cen lén, *keen without hurt*, a cheville, 5249.

aithbi derrit, 1495.

aithmeis, 1022 ; acc. of aithmes, aithmheas .i. traghadh, *ebbing*, O'Dav. 55, O'Cl.

al, gen. pl. 42.

álaib, adj. *delightful*, 4927. Cf. Fél. Sep. 3.

alchur (leg. allchur?), 7365.

all, *great*, O'Cl. Compounds : all-glan, 1656 ; all-mar, 58, 2566, 6442, 8126.

allod, dat. pl. -aib, 6762 ; perhaps alladh .i. oirdhearcas, O'Cl.

alt, 4231, seems O'Davoren's alt .i. tech. Compounds cloth-alt, 463 : Conn-alt .i. teach Cuinn, O'Cl.

am, *when?*, am-rubart, 1869 ; am-rorfus, 1871.

aman, 7254.

ámarc, 6102 (amharc .i. locht, *fault*, O'Cl.).

ambreit, 5372, *barren, sterile*.

amlós, 1039, 3470.

ammail (nammail ?), 5558.

ammodair (?), 6761.

am-nert, *weakness*, 1750.

amrai rád, *wonderful speech*, 4233, a cheville. So amra tola, 7641.

an-aeb, *ugliness*, 18 ; hence the adj. an-aebda, Ir. Texte, p. 271.

anaimthis (?), 2278.

an-bil, *wicked*, 4718.

an-bhuais, voc. sg. 1742.

an-dind, 3334.

an-heóil, 3188 ; cf. a tír ancóil, *out of a hostile* (?) *land*, Cogad G. 54.

an-hettail, 950, *impure, impenitent* (?) ; cf. anetal, O'Don. Supp.

aníabrocht, 7411 – anfobracht, Corm. ; an-bhobhracht, O'Cl.

an-foros (an-for-íos ?), dat. 1634.

an-fost, 5702.

an-fosta, 1734.

añgbaid, *wicked*, 1512, 5484, 6138.

an-gluais, 118.

an-recht, *unright, evil*, 1660.

an-rechtach, *unrighteous*, 8335.

an-ríad, 878, 4462, 6232, 7070, 7082.

an-rían, 5394.

an-seól, 4882.

an-uimle, 1752 ; the abstract noun from an-humal, *unhumble*, 3206.

apad, *a warning*, 3284.

Aquair = *Aquarius*, 217, 233.

ar, 1482, for dar, *we are?*.

ár, rígi áir, 5421.

arann, for erunn, *pro nobis*, 4174.

ar-chíu, *I look at*, √cas ; ar-dos-cé, 4165 ; cf. ar-dot-chiat, LU. 120ᵃ; nim-aircecha-sa, LU. 74ᵇ; Rev. Celt. i. 46, ii. 490.

arco-fuin, 2081 : see Cormac Tr. p. 2.

ard, *high*, in compounds : -aitt, 178 ; -bile, 4267 ; -daingen, 8231 ; -flathius, 6502, 7052 ; -flatheos, 7222 ; -grain, 4255 ; -ruiri, 829, 1077 ; -slíab, 7310.

arg, 4757.

argra, 5459.

Ariet, *Aries*, 217, 237.

arim ṅglain, 7583.

arlassair, *allocutus est*, 3791, 4791; cf. ni arlasair Loegaire, LU. 114ᵃ.

arm, *weapon.* Compounds: -dos, 1030; -gal, 6342; -glan, 6486, 7436; -grad (leg. -rad?), 7304; -rad, 6958; -rath, 6315. Hence armacht, 6002.

arrodis (?), 4470.

ar-trebaim, *I inhabit*, 8350.

ar-túaisim, 2539, 8299: cf. Félire Ep. 374.

asaimdil (?), 1147.

as-oslaicim, *I open wide*, 4801.

assa, *whose is*, 4485.

atmaim, *I confess*; atamar, deponent pret. sg. 2, 1406.

atar-íail, *we are*, 3761. Cf. ar, supra, and co-ro-r, dar, infra.

*atbadim (*atbidim?), redupl. perf. sg. 3; atroebaid, 3997.

atcha, 4753.

atcoch, *I beseech*, pres. conj. pl. 3, ettgat, 710, perf. sg. 1; atethach, 817.

athach, 8103, *a blast*?; athach gaoithe .i. sidean gaoithe, O'Cl.

athbach, 473, 4683, 7347; sg. gen., athbaig, 5055; athfaig, 421, may mean *attack* (athbhach .i. ionnsaighidh, O'Cl.).

ath-chom-arc, 408; pl. n. -airc, 461, seems to mean *bulwark.* Cf. the words cited in Curtius, G. E. No. 7, and arc .i. dind, H. 2. 17. p. 131ᵇ.

ath-chossan, *contention*, 8347.

athelluch, 7407; perh. = aitheallach .i. ath-suidhiughadh, O'Cl.

athergech, *repentant*, 7480.

ath-rí, *an ex-king, a deposed king*, 6896.

ath-rígad, *to dethrone*, 6900.

athrucha, 7754, *he changed*; athrughadh, O'Cl.; s. v. cumsgughadh.

ath-sárgud, *to re-outrage*, 1546.

atib, *ye are*, 7986.

áttaig úaig (?), 5195.

aurdaig, 1087, 5237, 6757; irdaig, 4191.

aurgnaide, 4263.

aurraind, 4917 = urrainn, O'Don. Supp.

B.

bacán, *a hinge, peg*, 4295. O'Dav. s. v. brefe.

bacc-lám, *a lame-handed person*, 7648; di bac-laim, Laws i. 124. Hence O'R.'s bac-lámhach.

badb, comp. badb-rann, *battlefield*?, 5400.

badbda, *warlike*, 1904, 4763, 7307.

báeg, 5311.

báeth, *foolish, lustful.* Comp. -bét, 3450; -bríathar, 3186; -bríathrach, 4786.

báethigim, *I befool*, 1320, 1724.

báethrach, 1445.

bág, *fight*, in chevilles: b. cen gái, 2505; b. b. cen treis, 7247; b. amne, 6207.

bai, *good, profit* (W. budd), 6353.

baigthi treith, 2499.

bainn, 2559, 3291.

bal, 6485; b. immarbois, 1438; monuar b., 1425.

balc, *strong*, 2991. Compounds: -bethraid, 6291; -thor, 6882.

ballda, 1903, 4978.

balnae, *odorous*, 3813, 7942.

bonamail, *womanish*, 1226.

ban-búaid, 6118.

ban-fáith, *prophetess*, 7472.

bán-gleo (lit. a white fight), *a bloodless battle*, 3038.

banna, *active*?, 1195, 1226.

bánugud, 6255.

bar, infixed pers. pron. of pl. 2; na-bar-sílaid, 2611; ni-bar-torbae, 2625.

barann, 7934; .i. béim, a blow, O'Cl.

barc, fo betha b., 2819, 7902; os betha b., 3865.

bargena remĭúir, *panes propositionis, shew-bread*, 6172.

barr-glas, *greentopped*, 975, 1033.

básaim, *I kill*, ron-bás bath, 4059.

bassa, pl. gen. 6795.

bate, ro-das-bate, 5279.

bathail, 7486.

bé, 5974, 6015; .i. bean, *woman*, O'Cl.

béccaigim, 8059.

béccedach, 8109.

becht, *opinion, feeling, idea*, 2305, 3157, 3169, 4975, 7541.

béim forais, 6468 = céim forais, q. v. (béim, .i. céim βῆμα, *step*, O'Cl.); beim foris, Wb. 28ᵃ; béim forois, Sg. 138ᵃ. 7.

beirt, 2381, 7171; perhaps also glan abbeirt, 5371.

bél, *lip, mouth* (= χεῖλος); comp. -derg, 892, 7410, 8110; -trúag, 3890.

bélgaide, 8065.

beothach, *alive*, 28.

1. berg, adj. 897.

2. berg, pl. bergga, 8070.

bert, *a birth*, 1897.

bét, 3538 = béd .i. gníomh, *deed*, O'Cl.

bethaigim, *I quicken, feed*, 7280.

bethra, sg. gen., 2991.

bethrach, 977, *watery?* from beathra .i. uisge, O'Cl.

betbraid, 6291.

bíast = bēstia, in 3934 seems to mean *louse*.

bí = Lat. pix, sg. dat. bii, 2446.

bíim, *I wound*; nom-bífad, 5812; bhías .i. gonfas, O'Cl.; cp. bíth .i. guin, O'Cl. The pret. of *benim* is formed from the root of this verb.

bil, 1783, 2295, 6309; .i. maith, *good*, O'Cl. See an-bil.

bin, 3279, 5791.

bine, *crime*, 509, 630, 2936, 3786, 5877, 7529, 8190.

bith-, a prefix; -blaith, 984, 5814; -buchtae, 952; -chardess, 6048; -chommaid, 6708; -fognam, 5282; -diless, 2792; -docra, 3344; -feidm, 8334; -féle, 8051; -gres, 4912; -imputh, 200; -less, 3510;

-maith, 7246; -óentu, 8199; -phíanad 908; -raith, 3322; -rathe, 478; -rith, 168; -samrad, 976; -toirsech, 8357; -toirthech, 984; -úr, 478, 984.

bithe .i. bannda, *feminine*, O'Cl.; pl. dat. bíthib, 5814.

bitomain = bitumen, 2446.

blá, 3065, 3339, 3423; ós cach blái, *over every field*, 3435; ós bla, 6063.

blad, *fame*; acc. blaid, 7059. Compounds: -ailc, 6183; -bail, 415; -blat, 2326, 6899; -bras, 800, 1679, 6406; -mall, 3307.

bládmar, *famous*, 29, 315, 1466, 1903, 2669, 6243, 7006, 7138, 7213, 7263, 7866, 8015.

blaith, in chevilles; b. a denn, 11; b. iar ṁblai, 95; b. a seis, 541; b. a ṅgus, 7587; b. a niab, 7413; b. in gein, 7489. Compounds: -bind, 484; -ḟlesc, 3840.

blat, f. 4453, 5685; dat. 2271, 3243, 3655, 3755, 4143, 4901, 4957, 5251, 5685, 6211, 7251; acc. 747, 2455, 2655, 4815, 5287, 6367, 7279; gen. pl. 555, 5311.

bledmall, *a sea-monster*; sg. gen. 7384; pl. n. 8059; gen. 8109.

bloesc, *shell*, 165.

blóraid, 881.

bochta bríg, a cheville, 6733.

boirchech, 1033.

bolgach, bolcgach, *boils* ('ulcera et vesicae turgentes'), 3935.

borgach, 3787.

borr, *proud*, 4453; .i. ... móirinheanmach, O'Cl.

braen-búaid, braen-chath, 442.

brainechda, 8093, 8185; cp. braonach .i. brónach, *sad*, O'Cl.?

brathaigim (from mrathaigim), *I betray*, 1317.

brathemdae, *traitorous*, 7742.

brathlaṅg, 2690.

brathlaig (gen. sg. ?), 6207.

brathreib, dat. pl., 3139.

brécairecht, *lying*, 3484.

brece-harc, 2642.

brecht, *variety*, pl. dat., 56.

brechtrad, *variety*, 7285.

brecnata, *locusts*?, 3934.

bres, f. *noise*, acc., 5969 (breas, O'Cl.).

bresim, *outcry* (breisim .i. gáir, O'Cl.), pl. n., bresma, 8137.

brethach, *judicial*, sg. gen. m., 2532.

breud, *burning*, 879. Cf. breo, *flame*.

brígda, 5635.

bríg-rún, 7244.

broccach, *smelling like a badger*, 3458.

broe, 5469 : see bruim.

broenach, *rainy*, 977, 3221, 8092.

broenrad, 615.

brogach, *having bruige or lands*, 977.

broigthech, *profitable*?, 983.

bronn-gáeth, *wise-hearted*, 4566.

brosnaib gal, 7027.

brothirne, *fimbria*, 7644 (brothairne, O'Cl.).

brothlacb, 897, may be the same word as brothlach, *cooking-pit*.

bruc, sg. dat., 7295.

bruden, 931.

bruig, cen bassi b. 2309.

bruim (brúim?), *I break*; co m-bruet, 8123; bruifider, 8144. Perhaps co rod-broe, 5469, belongs to this verb.

brugai, acc., 8300.

bruinim, bruinnim? nobruindis, 4347.

bruissitis, 3968, for brissitis *frangebantur*?.

bruth, *fervor*, 879.

búaid, in chevilles: b. ṅglé, 39; b. néin (ṅdéin?), 1075; b. rúbil, 2295; b. ferb, 4341; b. becht, 7541.

buan, in chevilles: b. in scél, 7113; b. blad, 7665.

buide, 6055, 7513.

buidnib blá, 3423.

buili, 150.

builid, adj. 1893, 1903, 7247 (= builigh, 'handsome,' *Circ. of Ireland*, 146).

buiriud, *roaring*, 877.

C.

cachta, 5427, 5991.

cadla, *beautiful*, 626, 3351. Fél. Dec. 9.

cái, *ivit*, 7185; cogn. with Corn. ke *go*, and Gr. κίω.

caiblide, 8199, for coiblide.

caidib, dat. pl., 7363.

cáidius, cádius, *holiness*, 973.

caillte, 4215, for coillte, *violation*?, Laws, i. 58.

cáin, *fair*, in chevilles: c. a míad, 2489; c. in smacht, 2775; c. al-lí, 4895; c. caingen, 7533; c. clú, 8013; c. dind, 231. Compounds: -airliud, 1464; -be, 3700; -blá, 5691; -buide, 6055; -chlú, 5490; -chuaird, 1198; -delbdae, 457, 2977, 4354, 8079; -dliged, 7220; -ol, 973; -tír, 963; -tomus, 4234; -tuistiu, 7999.

caindelbra = *candelabrum*, 4342, 4367.

caingel (for caingen ?), 7854.

caingen ṅglé, 5463.

caiṅgnide, 8197.

cáinig, pl. n., 3753.

cairechda, 8095.

cáirech-thrét, *a flock of sheep*, gen. pl., 6348.

cais, *hatred*, acc. sg., 1015, 1019.

caitrebaim (?), rochaitreb, 6570.

calaib, dat. pl., 6167.

camair = Lat. camera, sg. dat., 6323.

canthus, 587, 711.

cass, adj., 4357, 5973, 7663.

caric = Lat. cārica, *dried figs*, 6310.

caterua, 10,000 × 1000, 768 ; from the Lat.

cath, *battle*. Compounds: -cláí, 4227; -eirred, 6512; -slat, 3258.

cathach, *warlike*, 5080.

cechraig, sg. dat., 7878.

céim forais, *path of knowledge*, 4391.

céir (Lat. cēra), *wax*, 4370 ; *a plaster*, 7683.

cel, *death*, 3685, 7185.

cél, *omen*, 3090; ON. heill, 5987, 7859;
.i. faisdine, *prophecy*, O'Cl.

cenmthat, 399; for cenmothát, *besides there are*, 3417, 3421.

cennaigecht, *merchandise*, 3506.

ceo, 7183.

ceól-grinn, 6670.

cerb, *keen*, 891, 6913 - cerp, 4767, 8087.

cerdacht, *a tinker's trade*, 4190.

cerdaib, pl. dat., 8186.

cernalach, 943.

cerr, 7667.

cert. Compounds: -chlass, 4586; -chúmma, 1972; -glaine, 268; -mullach, 5768; -rad, 5142.

cess, *sorrow*, 349, 1195, 2688, 3019, 3283, 3349, 3445, 3573, 5145, 6047, 7017; pl. acc. cessu, 5019. Ex *ced-tu. Cf. κῆδος?.

cessa, n. pl., 4300.

cessair, dat., 151.

1. cét, *first*; -adbar, στοιχείωμα, 22, 30; -chuinnscle, 6588; -muinter, 6260, 6568.

2. cét, *a hundred*; c. mbla, 6955; c. nglonn, 6513; cétaib omun, 8102.

céte, 2035, perh. O'Clery's céide .i. conair, *path*.

cetharchain, 980, seems a corruption of cethrochair, q.v.

cethern, *soldiers*, gen. -irn, 3538.

cethrochair, (= cethar + ochair), *quadrangular*, 4225.

cétlach, 2337, 4999.

cétlud, *beginning, unfulfilment*, 5979, 6871, 7287. Hence

cétludach, *unfulfilling*, 4872.

cétrud, 6205.

cétur ·· centurio, 7612.

cía (.i. fear, *man*, O'Cl.) - Osc. cêvs, Lat. civis; n. pl. ciai, 5888.

cíabair, *sadness*, 1439, 1775, 4775, 6099, 8332.

ciall. Compounds: cíalbann, 7967; -chaid, 6975; -maith, 4742.

cíallrad, 6282.

ciaragla (?), 2331.

ciasta, 891.

cilceda, *made of haircloth* (cilicium), 6872.

cimmid, *captive*, 3562.

cint: see ruathar.

cír-cholg, *a ridged sword?*, 7415.

cír-dub, *black-crested*, 78; ech círdub, LU. 106b.

cith, *fletus*, 1283, 1779; pl. acc. cithu, 683, 807, 6047, 7919, 8370.

claideb, *sword*. Compounds: -derg, 4982; -rúad, 5734, 5882, 6906.

claideb garmna, *a weaver's beam*, 5770.

*claigim, *I lament*, redupl. perf. ro-chichlaig = κίκλαγε, 7765.

claine, *leprosy*, 4641, 4644.

clannmór, *prolific*, 6802.

clár, *a plain*. Compounds: -bruig, 1794, 4664; -mag, 508.

clecht, 55, 93, 1923. Compounds: -chlann, 7102; -maith, 7286.

clechtach, 6017.

clemnas, *relationship by marriage*, 2420, 3781; 4844; 4958; from cliamain, q.v.

clen-chruind, 890.

clesamnach, *juggler*, 3420.

clethach, 2629.

clethe cinn, *crown of the head*, 5871.

clí, *housepost*, and, figuratively, *prince*, 831.

cliamain, *son-in-law*, 4553; 6100; pl. dat. clémnaib, 5340.

cliar na n-apstal, 7813.

clichet, *a collection?* (clichidh .i. tionoilidh, O'Cl.), 4238.

clichis, 277.

clisslud, *a leaping*, 5347, O'Dav. 64.

clith, .i. dluith no fir, *compact or true*, O'Cl. Compounds: -choimmsech, 8359; -chomnart, 5686.

clithemail, 5515.

clochad, *to stone*, 7360.

cloen. Compounds: -cheo, 8095; -ré, 3618.

cloithi bann, 5863.

con-glúaisim, *commovo*, 8297.

cór, *a chorus*, 4323.

corcar-glain, *purple glass*, 352, 4270.

co-ro-r, *ut nos*, 1619.

corptha, *corporeal*, 1115.

cosnamach, *contentious*, 8338.

cossar, 639.

cosraib, pl. dat., *fetters ?*, 7400.

cossaitech, *complaining*, 940.

cotach, *treaty*, 3041, 5937, 6737, 6750.

cráeslach, *maw*, 954, 5724.

craestuib ?, 947.

crechad, 4511.

credem-galar ?, 1508.

credim, acc., 7271.

cres, *narrow ?*, 3059 ; cress, 3529.

cretha, pl. n., 8307.

crethaim, *I tremble*, 8083,

crí, *body*, 311, 655, 675, 1080, 1109, 2019, 2059, 2383, 3927, 7517, 7793, 7871, 7877, 7896, 8004. Cf. κρέας.

criathraim, 41, 7937.

crichid, adj., 354, 579, 597, 705, 962, 1062, 1915, 3075, 3434, 4511, 4731, 4970, 5373, 5435, 6846, 7030. Compar. crichidiu, LU. 58ᵇ. In 3434 and 7827 it seems a subst.

cridsercach, 6016.

crimnach, 941, 3202, 3267.

crínad, *withering*, 7284.

crín-chumga, 7416.

crinhed, 705.

críntaig, 5987.

crislach, *womb* ; sg. dat. crisluch, 1638, where it means *the deep cavity of a river*.

crith-delm, 1767.

crith-feidm, 958, 1290, 7775, 7778, 8254, 8287, 8332.

crith-lam, *trembling-handed*, 1456.

crithnaigim, *I tremble*, 7766, 8056.

crithur, sg. dat. 8202, 8230.

cróda, in chevilles: c.lir, 75 ; c. gair, 4141 ; c. cacht, 4155.

cró-donn, *blood-brown*, 6919.

cross-figell, *cross-vigil*, 2062, 4080, 5094.

crúachda, 8186.

crúad, *hard*. Compounds: -chasra, 8205 ; -chórad, 5886 ; -gal, 6911.

crúan, 5686. Compounds: -derg, 4342 ; -maith, 7110.

ro-chrúas, *great hardness*, 6022.

cruthach, *shapely*, 572.

cruth-amra, *wonderfully formed*, 8083.

cúac (.i. cumhac no cumhang,O'Cl.),33,918.

cubuchol, sg. dat. = Lat. cubiculo, 2858.

cuclaige, f., *shaking, tottering, turning aside*, 6673 ; carpait hi cuclaigi, LU. 91ᵇ. Cf. ra-chuclaigetar a crideda, LL. 176ᵇ ; cuclighd Temra, cumascach Tailten, Rawl. B. 512, fo. 102ᵇ. 2.

cuchtai, 5327.

cuibdi cacht, 4591.

cuibdigim, *I adjust*, 87, 4713 ; p. part. p. cuibdigthe, 5430 ; inf. cuibdigud, 4547.

cuilech, *sinful*, 8290, 8338 ; from cuil .i. olc no toirmisgthe, O'Cl.

cuinleng, *conflict*, 1727.

cúl-lom, *bare poll*, pl. gen., 2378.

cuinnscle, *conflict*, sg. dat. -iu, 6584.

cuinia, cunia (Lat. cuneus), *a hundred thousand*, 764, 765.

cuire .i. buidhean, *a troop*, O'Cl., 8031, 8275.

cuirid, gen. sg. ?, 3434.

cuma, *grief*, dat., cumaid, 3602.

cumga, for cumce, 6306, 7416.

cummaim, *I make*, pret. pass. sg. 3, 5767.

cumtaig, 4757, 7043.

curtínad, *curtains*, gen. pl., 4890. 'Cortinae sunt aulaea,' Isidorus cited by Diez, s. v. *cortina*.

D.

da, 6135, .i. maith, *good*, O'Cl.

dacht, 2679, 3677, for docht, q. v.

dag, *good*. Compounds: -arm, 6186 ; -biad 1560 ; -cíall, 4110 ; -lóg, 5836.

deoda, *divine*, in chevilles: d. tlus, 539, 7407; d. nuall, 4415; d. gair, 7679; d. in gair, 7803.
deonaigim, *I accord, grant*, 1431.
dérach, *tearful*, 871.
derb, *sure*, in chevilles: d. tra, 111; d. de, 159, 7389; d. roclos, 3469; d. cen locht, 4245; d. cen lén, 5241, 6613; d. cen tair, 7969; d. colár, 4751; d. la cach, 4889; d. in rád, 5099. Compounds: -dein, 4738 = -den, 786; -demein, 1950; -dil, 1501, 4626; -dind, 990; -dith, 3154; -droṅg, 6371; -dúis, 1070; -fáth, 1046; -fís, 1958; -garg, 6654; -gart, 8331; -glan, 7570; -rand, 434; -rét, 2270; -thomus, 374; -thonn, 8211; -thurim, 932.
derbaim, *probo*, 26, 54.
derbdae, *sure, tried*, 35, 6787.
derbod raind, *confirmation of a stave*, 7317.
derfadach, 2080. Cogad G. 42.
derg, *red*. Compounds: -ár, 5100, 5648; -náma, 4036, 6368; -órdae, 476, 4360, 4368; -thene, 7136.
dérgidach, 7891.
dergnaide, 948, 8317.
der-múad, *very noble*, 4476.
dessa, 4385.
dess-dond, 2674.
dét-gal, 6375.
détlach, *bold*, 6379 (détla .i. dana, Fél. Prol. 242).
día dardáin, *Thursday*, 7699.
díal, 1559, for diall, *deviation*.
díallaim, *devio*, 8128, 3 sg. pret. dorheli (do-ro-ell), 2619; adrell.
díamra, 6715.
dían. Compounds: -arggain, 5588; -diumsach, 6935.
díartain, 885 = diardain, *anger, roughness*, O'Cl.
díascach, 7409.
dicerta?, 6593.
dicheoil, 2197.

dichial, 2075.
dichmaig, 6335, 6339, 6401.
dichra, *fervent*, 7343.
dichraidiu, 701.
diglaide, 8151, *vengeful?*.
dígrais, *excellent*, in chevilles: d. séis, 519; d. buaid, 1011; d. scél, 2665, 4623, 5039; d. gais, 3073, 4863, 7009; d. bes, 4911; d. in smacht, 2803.
digthim (?), 3203.
dilliud, 6933.
dílmain, *free*, 3945.
dimblaith, 6546.
dimbríg, 3514, 6786, *weakness, contempt*.
dimmain, 1137.
dinnraig, pl. n., 3549.
din, *protection*, in chevilles: d. ṅglé, 327, 4487; d. cért, 3011, 3581, 4855; d. cloth, 4915; d. cech síd, 6615.
dindchur, 335.
dind, dind-liss, 4413; dinn-bile, 8223.
dinduasad, 1844.
1. díne, *beginning* (.i. tosach, O'Cl.), 359, 5627.
2. díne, 990, 4027, 5447, 6890.
dí-nertach, *feeble, strengthless*, 8143. (dinerta, 2832, should prob. be dínertach.)
co-dínnim, *weakly*, 5035.
dinsaeth?, 67.
dínsid, 7629, *a despiser?*.
dírain, 6540, may be O'Clery's díorain, *a pouring or dropping*.
direcra, 2444, 5116, *incomparable, enormous*.
dirgnaim, 3262.
díscáiliud, 6050, *separation*. Hence
díscáiltech, 1912.
disceinmnech, 946; aiṅgil disceinmnecha (gl. apostataeque angeli), LII. 11^b.
diss (.i. dearóil, O'Cl.), 3347; cotdiss, 5953.
dítha, 1015, seems = dithu (leg. díthu), *injury*, O'Don. Supp.
dítnide, 8361, *protective*.
diuplaib, 544, may be a scribe's mistake

for *diuplaid*, dat. of *diuplad* O'Clery's *diubladh* .i. dídean 'shelter.'

ro-dlecht, 1301; pret. pass. sg. 3. of dligim.

dlomtha, 903 : cf. dlomhaisin, *destruction* ?.

dloṅgaim, 3555.

dluim, 2831 = dlúmh .i. iomad, *abundance*, O'Cl.

dlúim, 903, 3367, 6959, *cloud, darkness*, O'Cl.

dluthath, *caulking*, 2445.

docharda, 2901, *damaged*.

docht, 1256, 2003.

dochtaid dul, 7239.

dodig, 1894.

do-domnae, 8299.

do-dúalach, 8271.

dóc na fairge, *seabank*, 7396; doc dessel, 8198.

dóer, *base*. Compounds : -daingen, 1764 ; -mám, 1776.

dóeraim, dácraim, *I enslave*, 3599, 3665, 5289, 5293 ; ros-doernid, 5557, seems a mistake or license for ros-dóerai.

do-feimim, for do-emim, *protego, velo*, 253, 7917, 8170.

dogba, 4046.

doidṅge, f. 8226, *difficulty* ?; sg. acc. Ml. 37ᵃ. 10, Z². 1023, gl. 5.

doilge : see duilgi.

doimm, *poor*, 2649 (doim .i. daidhbhir, O'Cl.).

do-imm-thaircim, timmthaircim, do-s-r-im-thairc, 5406, 5430.

dóinech, *populous*, 990.

dolam, *slow*, 1253.

dolbaide, 8321, *feigned* and hence *false* ?.

dolbanrad, 3064.

dolma, *slowness*, 187.

do-menaim, *I remain*, do-ru-mensat, 3689.

domgnas, 8374.

do-midiur, 3rd sg. redupl. perf. ; dorocmaidir, 2709 = doroemadair, 7955, pass. pret. sg. 3 ; dorumat, 4243.

donad, 1227.

dond-leo, 3279.

donech (do-n-ech ?), 5564.

donessai, 3891.

dónmige, *adversity*, 8375 ; deriv. of dóinmech ; di sóinmechaib et dóinmechaib, Z². 863.

doraid, 7426 = doraidh .i. aimhréidh, *uneven*, O'Cl.

doráith, 3182, 6545.

dorchaid, 6397.

dorhell : see díallaim and Z². 873.

doromnat, 4639.

do-ro-tacht, 5200.

do-rua, *adveniet* ; do-t-rua, 6117.

doruaraid, *remansit*, 4985 ; tuaraid, 5071.

doss, 3467.

dramm, 2831 = dram .i. iomad, *abundance*, O'Cl.

drech, 939, 3479, .i. dealbh, O'Cl. ; ardreich, 1124. Compounds : -donn, 6610; -már, 866 ; -rothail (?), 4226.

dréil, 7910.

dremna, *madness*, 8282, 8346. The acc. pl. dremnu, 8318, seems to come from a subst. = O'Clery's dreamhan.

dremun, *mad, furious*, 1912, 5471, 7620, 8352 ; co-dremun, 8216.

drenn-galach, *battle-valiant*, 944.

dressachtach, 939, *wandering* ?; dreasachd .i. iomluaidhill, O'Cl.

drichnes, 883.

droch, *bad* (Skr. druh). Compounds : -ciall, 850; -dáil, 6934; -mac, 6138, 6148; -scis, 7708.

drochte, pl. n., 476, where *drochte dergórdai* is = *aurdrochtib dergóir*, LB. 109ᵃ.

drolaim (leg. drolain ?), *rings* ?, 4309 (drol .i. lúb, O'Cl.).

dron, *strong ; straight*, O'Cl. Compounds : -mas, 6890 ; -mind, 4506 ; -oll, 343.

drúad (?), 6777.

drubaim (drúbaim ?), *I stay, I remain* ?, 914 ; cf. a forrudrúb (gl. immoratus, Ml.

49ᵇ.), and drubh .i. tairisiomh no comh-
naidhe, O'Cl.

druimne, 4046.

druing, 35.

drumm (better druimm), *back, ridge.* Compounds: -derg, 5656; -lurgain, 2454,
2461; -ålat, f. sg. gen., 4272, 4892, dat.
4275, 4283, acc. 2454, 4277.

dú,*fit, proper* (.i. dual, O'Cl.).

duairc, *surly, stern,* 939, 4157.

dualach, *lawful,* 3, 2695.

duanach, *songful,* 339.

dúassach, *bountiful?,* 791, 5543. In 831
dúasach seems a subst.; cf. *laom*-duasach,
'very bountiful,' O'Don. Gr. 340, and
duass, *gift,* Corm. s.v. doss.

dub, *black, dark.* Compounds: -brecc,
2955; -dóire, 5286; -lúache, 904; -nél,
7418; -rocn, -raen, 5558, 6550; -rúad,
4046; -lhemen, 909.

duilgi, 883, 8295.

duinnig ?, 6543.

duin-oirgnid, *homicide,* 8346.

duirimthimmchellaim   (do-air-imm-do-
imm-t.), 346.

1. dúis, 1. séd, *treasure,* O'Cl., 1857, 3581,
4333, 4519, 8258, 8296, 8370.

2. dúis, *a champion?,* 3467.

duith, *base, infamous?* (opposite of suith,
Corm. s.v. duthchern?), pl. dat. 3235.
Hence apparently

duithe, acc. sg. -i, 2689.

dúr = Lat. durus (.i. cruaidh no doilidh,
O'Cl.), 3578; duraib eim, 7837, perhaps
belongs to this. Compounds: -chathach,
6115; -chridech, 4842.

dursan, 2424, for dirsan, *bad news!*

dúsaigim, dúsgaim, *I awake, rouse*; ro-n-
dúsaig, 6690.

E.

écaid, *narravit* (ex ath-gaid, √gad?), 3875,
s-fut. pass. pl. 3; con-éicsitar, 3771. Cf.

con-écid, con-ecestar, Ir. Texte, pp.
256, 319.

é-coitchenn, *uncommon,* 5517.

é-comnart, *unequal conflict,* 3806, 6552.

é-craite, *enmity* (W. anngharant), 3800.

é-cruthach, *shapeless,* 24, 148.

ed (= eadh .i. aimsior, *time,* O'Cl. ?), pl.
dat. edaib, 7238.

éis, 7938.

eisleis, eisslis, *neglect,* 5994, 6110, 6200,
6218, 6318, 6346 (eislis, O'Cl.).

eitchiu, 276; compar. of eitig, eidigh, .i.
gránca, O'R.

éittim, *vitio, I clothe,* 4817, 4840.

él, *criminal?,* 5477: cf. éliugud, *accusation.*

ell,*flock, multitude,* 1129, 2357, 3915, 6677,
6980.

ellach, *union,* 6334.

ro-ellacht, 3551.

emnaim, *I twin, I divide,* 2767; part. pass.
emnaide, 7144, where it means *doubled*;
cf. eamhnadb .i. dubladh, O'Cl.

ena, 4431.

1. engach, adj. *noisy?* (eanghach .i. glor-
ach no cainntech, O'Cl.), 72, 945, 2876,
4122, 4718, 5578, 6006, 8163, 8125, 8364.
Hence enchache (gl. scurrilitas), Z².765.

2. engach, *a babbler,* gen. engaig, 7111.

éo, 5752, *a tree?.*

éraim, *a firing,* 1071, 1468, 3497, 3667.

er-amra, *very wonderful,* 3586.

erbach, 4673.

er-baid, acc., 3430, *bane* (Curtius, No. 410);
erbada lathi brátha, *the banes of Dooms-
day,* Vis. Ad.

er-brón, *great sorrow,* 5741.

er-chol, *great crime,* 1874.

erctais, 4009, *they were filled,* erctais sluaig,
a cheville, 4009 = earcdaois na sluaigh .i.
do liondáis na sluaigh, O'Cl. ; earcadh .i.
lionadh, O'Cl. eretha buaid, 5513, perhaps belongs to this.

er-derg, *very red,* 922.

er-dornn, 7219, *great fist.*

eretecdach, *heretic,* 8339.

er-find, *very fair,* 1906.

er-garb, *very rough,* 2014.

er-glan, *very pure,* 1468 ; irglan, 5136.

érim (= éraim, supra), *a faring,* in chevilles ; é. n̄-gúr, 463, 469 ; e. n̄glé, 1267, 1831 ; é. n-úag, 1401, 2625, 5497 ; é. ñgrinn, 2253, 2567.

er-maith, *very good,* 2703.

er-marb, *very dead,* 4120.

ern-mass (= ernbas?), 4688, 5634.

ern-ól, 367.

er-oll, *very great,* 7058.

er-órdae, *very golden,* 532, 3432.

er-rí (= airrí, supra), *governor,* 3150, 7750.

ertach (= eardach .i. fésda no sollamain, O'Cl.), sg. dat. erdduch, 4600.

er-thróg, *very wretched,* 6966 = erthrúag, 1402.

erud, *fear,* 5914.

escra, *cup,* 3545, 3592.

espaid, *want, defect,* pl. dat. espadaib, 2456, where it seems to mean *apertures* or *windows.*

essel, 1328 = cisil .i. eiseolach no nemheolach, *ignorant,* O'Cl.

etar-lén, *great hurt,* 3762.

etere, eitteire, *hostage,* 3499, 3503.

etbait, *bird,* acc. 2520.

éthchech, éitlichech, *perjured,* 1612, 8344.

etla, *sadness, repentance,* sg. gen. 7199, pl. dat. ettlaib, 6876.

etradach, *lustful,* 8345.

étran, *interfering with?,* 2054.

étlaide, *sad,* 8183, 8391.

etraigim, 2684, 3178, 6018, 8001.

éttal, 5370, perhaps ettal, 7398.

exercitus, *ten thousand times ten thousand,* 765.

F.

faball, dat. 6040. Is this O'Cl.'s fabhall .i.

feacht no siubhal, or fadbull, *fuball,* adboll, aboll, *time, occasion,* O'Don. Supp.?

fachlái, 4228.

faebar-glonn, *edge-deed,* 6790.

fael, 4816, *wolf?.*

faicserad, *nearness,* 6124.

fáil = fael, q.v.?, 1670.

farsaidi, *Pharisees,* 7550.

fatal, 3563, *lingering, delaying.*

fath, 6879, .i. foghlaim, *instruction,* O'Cl. 7098. In 4315 fathaib seems a license for fothaib, pl. dat. of fotha, *foundation.*

feb, 1887, *good,* for feb, 7994?.

feba, 1962, 2027, 2075, 4438, 7451.

febda, *goodly,* 36, 696, 1074, 2557, 3147, 3779, 4288, 4856, 6377, 6790, 7482, 7706, 7789.

febsae (= feabhsa .i. eolas, *knowledge,* O'Cl.), 721.

fecht (= feacht .i. turas, *journey,* O'Cl.), 5947.

fechtach, 6015, leg. fechtnach?.

fechtaide, 2550.

fedbda, *widowed,* 4646.

fódim, 1507.

fíg-fola, gen., 8034.

feib, 417, 7675.

féidm n-úag, 6837.

felmáine, 5535.

féne, *champion,* 3992, 6015.

fénedach, 8021.

feochair glóir, 5443.

ferb (= Lat. verbum?), 4341.

fer-droñg, *a troop of men,* 6514.

fescorda, *vespertinus,* 4404.

feta, 4396.

feth (féth?), 2015, 2846, 4075, 4857.

fethet, 2646.

1. fia, 1221 = fiadh .i. biadh, *food,* O'Cl.

2. fia, 7455 = fiadh .i. tighearna, *lord,* O'Cl.

fiach, *debt?,* 2485, 2635.

fiad, 4788 = fiadh .i. fearann, *land,* O'Cl.

fiadrad, *deer,* 6281.

fian, f. sg. dat. féin, 6283 ; pl. acc. fiana, 6514.

fiantach, 915.

T   [IV. 3.]

fích, f. = Lat. ficus, sg. gen., 1360.

fíchomna, f. *fig-tree*, 1362 (omna, *oak*).

fidba, 5343.

fidrad, *wood*, 4224.

figlim, *vigilo*, 1079, 7599.

finbert, 7177.

find, *fair*. Compounds: -alta, 7098, 7831; -chass, 5974; -gel, 4638; -glan, 2962; -luad, 630; -mór, 7566; -muad, 636; -nár, 2030, 3700, 4950; -rúad, 3414; -topur, 500.

findlem, 7503.

fiñ-gabaim (?), fiñgebad, 5796; fiñgebad, 5820; (dingebsa, 5835 should perhaps be fiñgébsa).

fír, *true*. Compounds: -amnas, 1830, 1904, 5974; -breth, 8325; -chert, 7098; -chland, 1074; -chrúaid, 5586; chruind, 36; -drong, 7026; -druine, 2163; -dul, 1607; -eolas, 3474; -éttla, 8351; -find, 846; -fílaith, 1812, 6244; -fossad, 4384; fairbthe, 1938; -gaeth, 1318, 4590, 6030; -iarthar, 4256; -less, 322, 4438; -maith, 7566; -nóeb, 6062; -óentu, 6576; -roen, 5092; -sáer, 7568; -thind, 3216; -thóeb, 2468; -thrén, 2726; -thrócar, 7800; -thrúag, 1962; -thúachaill, 1670; -thúaid, 4440; (frisinn-eclais a firthúaid, *due north of the church*), -thuicse, 8003; -úachtar, 4332.

fíraid, 3355.

físsiu = Lat. visio, 3356.

fithis, 278.

flaith-rí, 2360.

foadoi (?), 643.

fobaid (- fobhaidh .i. luath no ésgaidh, *swift or nimble*, O'Cl.), 4195, 4555, 7189.

fochessaim ?, fo-t-ro-chess, 1746.

fo-chicher, 8205; fo-chichret, 8060, 8088; fo-chichretar, 8324; redupl. futures from focherdaim, *I cast*; so fóichursa (= fo-cl-chursa), TBF.

fochnáim (?), fo-d-chná, 8010.

fochrai, 4249 : cf. fochra claraid, *partition of boards* ?, Corm. s.v. Crannchaingel.

fodard, 3398, a license for fodord, *murmur*.

fodluigim, *I rend*, 7764.

foen-dul, 1887, for foendel, Laws, i. 212; fóindel (fo-ind-cl), *wandering, straying*.

foen-tracht, *a sloping strand* ?, 2602 (foen = faoin, O'R.).

fo-gaeth, *a sub-wind*, 48, 49.

foglas, 7710.

fo-grád, *sub-grade*, 4533; pl. foghrádha, O'Don. Supp.

folchligthe, 3557.

foidreich, 8270.

foil, *astute*, 3345. Hence foile, *astutia*, Z². 248. Cogn. with Lat. *in-volare*, Fr. *voler*. Cf. Corn. *fur* (gl. prudens); Br. *fur* 'sage'; borrowed from Lat. *fur*, 'homme de ruses.'

-foilce, 251.

foimsid, 6969.

foimsiu ?, 5623.

fóismed, 5322.

folach, f., *prop, support* ?, 4292, 4296.

folaimm, 3253.

folith, 6189.

follomnacht, *rule, governance*, 696, 6640.

folocht, 7737.

fomnach, 8034.

fomnad, 5281.

fónmissi ?, 5533.

fonn-luath, 2550.

fonn-rám, 1390.

fuoil : cofooil, *patiently* ? ; gu fóil, H. Soc. Dict.

for(n), *you*, infixed and suffixed pron.; do-for-fua, 5487 ; bid-for-coscraig, 4706.

for-aesa, 4330.

for-bassach, 7786.

for-clu, 1421.

for-dingim, *opprimo*, 3679 ; fo-s-r-or-diñg-setar (for for-s-ro-d.), 5297.

for-erainn, 2351.

for-étromm, *very light*, 4646.

for-failte, *great welcome*, 2951.

for-failtigim, 3715.

for-find, *very fair*, 258, 982, 1802.

for-fúacraim, *I proclaim*, 3729.

for-gal, 2678, 7026, 7051; forggal, 7003, 7568.

for-gellim, fo-t-r-oirgell, 3385; for for-t-ro-gell.

for-glicc, *very cunning*, 1235.

for-go, *choice*, 3708. (Cf. forgho séd .i. roghséd, O'Cl.)

for-iadaim, fodas nlada, leg. fodas riada?, 288; for for-das-roíada?.

for-lán, *very full*, 994.

formnaib snas, 5633.

for-muchaim, *I smother*, 8164.

forngaire, 8063, 8167.

forngairthid, *imperator*, 2367.

for-oll, *very great*, 1802, 7482.

forom nglé, 3091, 3845; f. cert, 3149; foromm cert, 3225; forum ngle, 2511.

forraib, pl. dat., 3919.

forrán, *assault*, 6710.

forróed (?), 7049.

for-rúad, *very red*, 2478.

forssaid, 3700.

for-sasaim, 617.

for-tromm, *very heavy*, 7198.

for-túath, *great tribe*, 3230.

for-tuigim, *I cover*, 8192.

for-úaibrech, *very haughty*, 3874, 7128.

for-úallach, *very proud*, 7571.

for-úamnach, *very timid*, 4396.

foscadach, f., *shade*, *shelter*, 1895 (fosgadh .i. sgáile, O'Cl.).

fos-scemel, *footstool*, 528, 544.

fossad, adj., *stable*, 1906; fossud, 986.

fotat, 3837; for fo-an-tát, *under whom stand?*

fot-dagain, *on thy account*, 1758, 1762, etc.

fothacht, 32.

fothair, 922.

fris-aicciur, *I hope*, *expect*, 4173.

frisamlai, 23, 4638; perhaps also 3821.

frisotharfa ?, 5853.

fris-(s)ellaim, 4299.

fris-toimsiur, 1901.

frith-éle, 8049.

frith-múr, *counterwall*, 413.

frituttacht, 6894, *opposition*, *contravention*.

froslacha, *showers?*, 8040.

fualrad, 206.

fuam, fuaim, in chevilles: f. tricc, 523; f. nglé, 1359; f. cert, 3311; f. fír, 6457; fuaim n-amra, 3309; nglé, 7163.

fuarír, *alas*, 1483; foríor, foraoir, O'Don. Supp.

fuidlech, *remains*, *leavings*, 7628.

fúatlach, *pallet*, *couch*, 7412; o fuatlaig (gl. a grauato), O'Mulc. Gl., H. 2. 16, col. 95 (fúat .i. clar no crann, O'Dav.).

fuiled, gen., 8262.

fuilgib, pl. dat., 4891, to folach?.

fuilide, *bloodred*, 8029 (fuilidhe, O'Cl.).

fuirigim, *I delay*; fo-rui-recht, 6041.

fuismiud, 7138.

fulach, 986.

fúrad, *preparation*, 5885.

furseóracht, *jugglery*, 6684.

G.

gabrai, dat., *horse*, 4781 (the nom. sg. is gobur, Corin.).

gabul-rind, *a pair of compasses*, 6664.

gáele, 7421 = gáile, q. v.

gáelim, 1341, 6167 = gaolaim .i. brisim, *I break*, O'Cl.

gáeth-gail, 5003.

gáethrige, *wisdom*, *cunning?*, 5978.

gáilaigim, 1723.

gailbech, *blustery*, 71; sg. gen. f., fogur gáeithe gere gailbige, H. 2. 17, p. 146ᵃ–146ᵇ.

gaile (leg. gáile), 3167, 3902, 5427, 6058, 6475, 6487, 7201, 7599.

gailig, sg. dat., *maw, belly?*, 7368.

gálne, 5919 = gaoine .i. maith, *good*, O'Cl.

gais galais, 6462.

gálse, 6027.

galach, *bold*, 8121, 8340.

galais, 6462.

galar medóin, 4158.

galma (.i. crúas, *bardihood*, O'Cl.), 5547.

garb, *rough*. Compounds: -chacht, 2227; -chess, 918; -dath, 8287; -gaeth, 4288; -gnímach, 5750; -greim, 6286; -grennach, 5784; -ionn, 3894; -ron (leg. -brón?), 4675; -sruth, 1678; thene, 902; -thenn, 6551, 6798.

garbdae, 1959, 3397, 5799, 7995.

garbdath, 8287.

garg-ruide, 1078.

gart, 3078, 6607; gart-glóir, 4527.

gartrad, 3606.

gcc congreim, 3085.

Geimin = Gemini, 218; Gemin, 241.

gcimlech, 5591; gemlech, 6325, 7149.

geint = gentes, 8340.

geintide, 8027; geinntide, 8087.

géir-chert, 3229.

géire, 6391, *sharpness.*

gelbdae, 3155, 3187, 4227, 4367, 8382.

gel, *fair*. Compounds: -féle, 8075; -gart, 2375; -glor, 5407; -gnúis, 4334, 4584; -grúad, 2750.

gelda, 5990.

gelt, 3441.

gemen, 190.

genbda, 5990.

ger-gaile, 8203.

gertha, 3470.

gór-thind, *sharp-strong*, 3438, 3628, 6076, 7068.

géssi, gen., 3615.

gestal, 4363 = geastal .i. gníomh, *deed*, O'Cl.

gial, *pledge*, 1935.

gialta, 2343.

ginmar, 8122.

ginól, 5899.

gláed, 6794.

gláedim, 6554.

gláim, acc., 5995.

gláma, 263, 3277; glaimma, 6383.

glammairecht, 8301 = glamaireachd, *constant babbling?*, O'R.

glamrad, *clamour?*, 920.

glan, *pure*. Compounds: -áeb, 5378; -aige, 5179; -áil, 5707, 6304; -aingel, 4604; -alt, 6038; -altóir, 4868, 7558; -bág, 5542; -blad, 659, 1203, 1799; -búaid, 2278, 2688, 4798, 5094, 5262, 7162, 7430; -chét, 5026; -chíall, 1582, 3306, 4106, 6127; -chobais, 4392; -chocráib, 3242; -dath, 7093; -díl, 1207; -dírge, 3371; -edparl, 7300; -elc, 6122, 7486; -fíal, 7590; -fír, 3523; -gaisse, 2830; -géc, 7074; -geltad, 8333; -geltaid, 3078; -gér, 6595; -glanna, 7859, 7879; -grád, 2913; -grían, 570; -léir, 3294, 3362; -lí, 2982; -mám, 2302; -míad, 3130, 7526; -phailm, 7686; -riad, 596; -rún, 1614, 6962; -thimna, 4612; -thogairt, 462; -thóisech, 4970; -tbor, 5138.

glanbda, 69, 2474, 5143, 6877, 7882.

glanna, 7167.

glann-chor, 5144.

glassa?, 6039.

glé, *clear*, in chevilles; g. cenimeth, 428. Compounds: -alt, 7659 (.i. glain-innsce, *clear speech*, O'Cl.); -brath, 7704; -chert, 3244, 3574; -druimm, 5560; -garb, 6462; -gelt, 3993; -glan, 3820, 4327, 7402; -graim, 1467; -nathir, 3856; -nocht, 7312 (pl. -nuicht, 1158); -ratb, 618; -thánac, 1695.

glea, 3999.

gléad, 2830.

gledail, 7176.

gléro, *abundance* (.i. iomad, O'Cl.), 6403.

gleith, *grazing*, 6299.

gleo-chuaird, 2651.

gruad, 6559.
guinech, *dealing wounds,* 3894, 8340.
gus, 1871, 7587; .i. gniomh, *deed,* O'Cl.

I.

iarfus, s-fut. sg. 1, of iarfaigim, *I ask,* 7837.
iarm-ua, *great-grandson, pronepos,* 3498, 3634, 5706; ind iarmui (gl. apnepotes), Ml. 119b.
iath (.i. fearann, *land,* O'Cl.), 7445. Compound: -mass, 7938.
íd, 6603; idh, *good, just,* O'R.: cf. *lōvs?.*
ifferna, 8285; a license for iffernach *infernal.*
il, *many,* 7996; where il seems a license for ili. Compounds: -adba, 7264; -delbach, 4212; -tairthech (a license for -toirthech), 4702.
ilar, *multitude,* in chevilles: i. mbla, 201; i. blad, 5465; i. mbrath, 875; i. crích, 6247; i. dáil, 6977; i. ndelb, 4361. Compound: ilar-cháin, 4314.
imbánugud?, 6255.
imbruc?, 7295.
imm-aithber, *mutual reproach,* 1479.
imm-amnas, *very harsh,* 1130, 3616.
immar, *as, like,* 581; later, mar, 2187.
immarbáes, 266.
immardol, 2410, for immfordol, q. v.
imm-árim, *a great number,* 4252.
immasech, *in turns,* 2743, 2899.
imm-athlam, *very rapid,* 896, 5354.
imm-chenn, *double-headed,* 1130.
imm-chloemchlod, *interchange,* 2397.
imm-chlóim, *I change,* 4697.
imm-chloithech, *changeful?,* 14.
imm-chobair, *to assist greatly,* 4556.
imm-chress, *very narrow,* 2646, 4264, 4414, 6938.
imm-chumung, *very narrow,* 342.
immdel?, 2881.
imm-dil, *very dear,* 4802.
imm-druine, *great skill?,* 566.
imm-eclach, *very timid,* 4830.

imm-esbaid, acc., *great deficiency,* 4966.
imm-forbiur, 3d sg., t-pret. imforba[i]rt, 3212.
imm-forddol (-dul), *great error,* 2458, 4234, 7106, 7618 (fordal, *error,* O'Cl.).
imm-format, *great envy,* 556, 3128.
imm-gann, *very bitter?,* 934, 2006, 3038, 6158 (gann .i. goirt, O'Cl.).
imm-gel, *very fair,* 2939.
imm-glan, *very pure,* 6520.
immirím, 4986.
imm-lán (immslán?), 7442, 7454.
imm-lén, *great weakness?,* 2138, 5570.
imm-nár, *very modest,* 3314, 4792, 5370, 6830.
imm-nertad, *great strengthening,* 5032.
imm-nochta, *great nakedness,* 6688.
immracht, sg. 3d, t-pret. of immágim?, 2641, 2825, 2847, 2913, 4210; imm-us-r'-acht, *drove it about?,* 5506; immact (gl. jecit), Lib. Arm., is the same word, minus the infixed ro.
immracul, 4106.
imm-ráim, *I row, or go, about,* perf. sg. 3; imra, 2647.
immrisnech, *contentious,* 3206; from im-bresan.
imm-ruachtain, 5883.
imm-séna, *great denial* (séna), 3772.
imm-slán, *very safe,* 2482, 2658, 5246.
imm-sruth, *a great stream,* 4160, where it seems to mean *diarrhœa.*
imm-thacht, 6503.
imm-tháirc, 4314.
imm-thaitach, 7094, a license for immtholtach, *very desirous.*
imm-thelgud, *defecation,* 5420, 6352.
imm-thesbaid, *great defect,* 4610.
imm-thláith, *very soft,* 4066, 5678, 7362.
imm-thimmchell, a i, *around him,* 5754, for n-i. *around you,* 3916.
imm-thoitach v. immthaltach.
imm-thrágud, *a great ebbing,* 2548.
imm-thrén, *very strong,* 5032, 6230.

leod, *mangling*, 880 (leodh .i. leadradh no gearradh, O'Cl.).

léom, *lion*, 8322.

lerg, *hillside*, 2870, 6298, 7019.   In 6779, 8072, 8188, 8207 the meaning is doubtful.

lerggach, 3279.

lére líi, 7019.

ler, in compounds: -glór, 366; -mór, 2722; -ól, 4443; -thol, 611.

lethan, *wide*, in chevilles: l. scél, 6215; l. smacht, 1295.

leth-rann, *half-part*, 2351.

leth-ulcha, *half-beard*, 6720.

letraim, *I tear*, *cut*, 6379, infinitive, letrad, 6376.

lia, *flood*, 1674 (.i. tuile, O'Cl.).

líacoir (líac-óir ?), 3370: cf. líag-dhealg, O'Cl.

lían-mag, 679.

lígaide, 380, 8149.

líg-dath, 7283.

líg-thorba, 1361.

lín, *number*, and dat. pl. línib, in chevilles: l. cert, 3373; l. a slóig, 3379; l. a tuir, 4471; línib sess, 1513; l. gal, 1543, 2949; l. luad, 2290; l. lathar, 2799; l. ell, 3915; l. drech, 3479; l. tuath, 3834; l. legart, 2834; l. gial, 2971, 2989, 3029, 5221; l. ollgraid, 4326; l. smacht, 6683; co línib scél, 5153.

lín-brat, *linen sheet*, 5972.

linn-muir, 2566 = muir-linn, 285, 287.

líth, *festival*, in chevilles: l. cengeis, 275; l. cenlén, 6657; l. cenmeth, 561; l. cenchol, 6327; l. cennach col, 2591; l. rochlos, 455; l. nglanna, 1201; l. ngarta, 5695; l. lán, 2783; l. lór, 2823; l. n-óg, 2853; l. fri báig, 4247.   Compound: líth-laithe, 8101, 8148.

liud, *accusation*, 4647; W. lliwed.

loburda, *weakened*, 2902.

loga, 998.   O'R.'s logha, *splendid*, from *lucnia ?*.

lóir, 2361.

loittim, *I hurt*, 3483.

lola (?), 2940.

lom-nachtach (for -nochtach), *quite naked*, 3214.

lonn, *angry*, (ógán lonn .i. ógán feargach, O'Cl., s.v. lonnógán).   In compounds: -bág, 5722; -bágach, 5726; -brass, 900, 3617; -bruth, 6795; -búaid, 6554.

lórdae, 225, 501, 4279, 5431.

lórdata, 8177.

lór-múad, 610.

lúad, *a speaking*, 7290, in chevilles: l. ndil, 369; n-éim, 1541; l. cert, 3143; l. ngrinn, 3437; l. ñgle, 3913, 7181.

luam, 6057.

luarda, 6791, 8188 (lúar .i. borb).

luath-lasair, *swift flame*, 8207.

lubrach, *diseased*, 2902, from lubhra .i. easlálnte, O'Cl.

luibne, *twigs*, 7291 = luibhne .i. meoir, *fingers*, O'Cl.

luth, 3031, 5913.

M.

mael, *tonsured*, and thence *priest*, 2256: but in 2975, *blunt*, *obtuse ?*.

magar, 7858, *small fish*, Corm. Tr. 120.

mag-réid, 308.

mainbthech, 4701, seems O'Clery's *mainbhtheach*; but the meaning (cealgach, *crafty*) which he assigns to this word does not suit in 4701.

mairre, 2733, leg. máir-ré ?.

mál, *prince* (maglos, W. mael), 1101, 3431, 4497, 5366, 6629.   In 865 it seems an adj., *noble* (mál .i. uasal, O'Cl.).

mandrad, *destruction*, 7100 = menradh .i. milleadh, O'Cl.

mares = myrias, μυριάς, *ten hundred thousand*, 766.

mathigim, 6663.

υ

2198; -glan, 4369; -gluair, 4074; -gorta, 3384; -grád, 6470; -grádach, 5738; -gráin, 5966, 7249; -iachtad, 916; -loiñges, 4748; -maith, 7500; -martra, 8179; -miad, 6414, 6482, 6672, 7490; -mind, 6806; -molad, 5922; -mong, 5362; -mongach, 8105; -olc, 1330, 1348; -pheccad, 7200; -phopul, 4104; -thrét, 7024; -thúath, 2780.

mudaigim, *destroy*, 1680, inf. mudugod, 6712, 6984.

muinbi, 2752.

muincinn, *a sea-strait*, 3987.

muirech, *lord*, O'R., 3925, 5263, 5583, 5926, 6629, (each réim imma muirech, L.L. 57^h).

muirlinn (= linnmuir, supra), 285, 287.

múra, 8078.

N.

nachar-, *not us*; nachar-lén, *do not hurt us*, 1726; cid nachar-cobrai, *why is it that thou dost not help us?*

náir, 1086, 4558, gen. náir, 1759, 4181, 5488, 6579.

narbar (= ná-rob-bar), *be ye not*, 4842.

nassad, 8369, in chevilles: n. ñdañgen, 811, 4175; n. ñdil, 2243, 2587: n. nglé, 467, 1095, 2537, 4932; n. ngrian, 2731; n. nglan, 8141; n. n-imlan, 2418. nassaid, 4315 is perhaps a metrical license.

necht, 573, *pure*.

néib, 419 = néim, 467, 7257.

nél, *cloud*, nuallaib n. a cheville, 5805.

nem-aicsid, *invisible*, 330.

neméle, *bemoaning*, 8073.

nemide, *poisonous*, 7150.

nem-nél, *heaven-cloud*, 7462.

nem-thech, *heavenly house*, 573, 2744, 2745.

nessaim, 534, pl. of nessam, *nearest*, 538, 540.

níab, 1819, 7135, 7413.

níahach, 112.

niam, *colour*, 4315.

nibar (= ni-b-bar), *be ye not*, 3641, nibur, 4871; nibfor, 4872; nifor(n), 1238.

ni-char-fail, *non nobis est*, 1560. For the ch, cf. ci-chib-foruireth, I. B. T.

nid-ar-n, *we are not*, 1609, 3626, cf. perhaps no-dar-bé-ne .i. biaidh linne, O'Cl.

nifor(n), see nibar.

ninach, 8026.

ni-r, *not us*, 2747; cf. for the pronoun nor-laoidheann .i. doni ar ngreasacht, O'Cl.

níth, 3615, 4085, 5967, 6041.

no for na, the article, acc. pl. 4304.

nocho-for-bia, *non vobis erit*, 4063.

noeb, *holy*. Compounds: -aingel, 8193; -arbar, 8255; -dind, 6026; -dúil, 7422; -find, 5488; -gel, 6886; -glan, 7302; -nár, 782, 2170, 3926; -nem, 128, 312, 6842, 7000, 7116, 7186, 7488, 7802; -rath, 7154; -rí, 7995; -riagul, 2339; -thánic, 2153; -thlacht, 1308; -úag, 4262, 5878.

nóisech, *famous*, compar. -u, 1145 (nóis .i. oirdbeirc, O'Cl.).

nóithech, *famous, conspicuous*, (.i. oirdheirc, O'Cl.), 13, 1463, 2291, 2758, 5140, 5173, 5589, 7943.

noithi máil, 2585, 6681.

nós, 1892.

núall, in chevilles: n. cencleith, 2617; n. cen lén, 6827; n. nad cress, 5189; nua-laib nél, 5805.

O.

óc, *young*. Compounds: -bó, *a young cow*, (acc. dual. dí ócbáe), 5426; -dam, 4112, 4120; -duine, 4589; -ech, 7688.

occurus, *hunger*, 8379.

ócda, 7349.

ochair, *edge*, 1746, 6578.

ochrach (leg. ocrach), *ravenous*, 848.

óegaire, *shepherd*, 7716.

r. ail, 7463; r. fecht, 7605; r. in sét,
7894.

ri, gen. ríg, *king.* Compounds: ríg-dáil,
6818; -doss, 796; -ñal, 568, 7785; -rann,
2650; -recht, 8212; -rún, 4134; -sossad,
550; -sruth, 504; -threb, 2647.

riges, 5190, for riches, *flame* ?.

rigthess (ríg-thess ?), 7250.

rind, rinn, *star.* Compounds: -balce, 123,
2671; -gel, 778, 4094; -glan, 7292;
-mas, 5636; -nem, 510, 7050, 8221, and
perhaps rind-rethait, 131.

rintriuchta (?), 1837.

rith-rosc, 7923.

ro for ra = fria, 1990, 2179, 2990: with
pron. rot, rut.

robar fola, *fluvus sanguinis*, 7642.

ro-balcc, *very strong.*

ro-bláith, 7616.

ro-búadach, *very victorious,* 7572, 8269.

ro-cháin, *very fair,* 4378.

ro-chrúas, *great valour,* 6022.

roddet, 1627.

ro-días, *a great pair,* 4470.

ro-dígrais, *very excellent,* 4378.

róc-mag, 616 (róe .i. magh, O'Cl.; rac .i.
fearann, ibid.).

roen. Compounds: -des, 1018; -mag, 510.

roenach, 4160.

ro-fín, *strong wine,* 6326.

ro-garg, *very fierce,* 6082.

ro-glan, *very pure,* 7684.

roginár, 627, 960.

ro-gnáth, 7242.

ro-réil, 7684.

rogud, 619 (gl. extensione), Ml. 37ᵈ.

ro-gúr, 5258.

roimsi, 7355, (roimhsi .i. peacadh, *sin,*
O'Cl.).

ro-maidm, *a great breach,* 6788.

romra, 3982, O'Clery's romhra .i. romhara.

ro-ro-char, *multum amavit,* 2816. Perhaps
rót-ro-baeth may be another example,

3119. So do-ro-r-chair, H. 2. 17, p. 165ᵃ,
unless this be a scribal mistake for do-
ro-chair.

ro-rúad, *very red,* 4160.

ro-sat (?), rosat glechert, 3574; rosat[t]
riuin (?), 3983.

ro-séim, *very slender,* 39.

rosso, 6123.

rót, 2287.

roithenach, *serene,* 3395.

roth, *wheel, orb* (?), 1077. Compound:
-mol, 199.

rúam, 6094, 7289.

rúamna, 7339.

rúanaid, *strong,* 6082.

rúan-dath, 205.

rúathar, rúathur. In chevilles: r. cint.
133; r. mbras, 4843, 6187; r. ñglé, 213,
3335, 4903, 5681, 6013; r. cert, 2659,
3795; r. n-án, 3411; r. ñdil, 3779, 7417;
r. ndein, 4765, 4937.

rub · Lat. rubus, 3815.

(ro)-rude, 7074.

ruided, 8096.

ruithess, 154, 7242.

ruithnib rían, 7143.

ruithnigim, *I cause to shine forth,* 7537.

ruth. In chevilles: lúath a ruth, 3107;
for-ruth, 3285, 4051, 7411; réim far
ruth, 6043.

S.

sacc, *sack,* 3548.

saccail, *to press into a sack,* 3547.

sacrad, f. *sacks,* 3036.

sacerdote = sacerdotium, 4488, 4494, 5156.

sadailecht, 8303.

saechtairthir, 979; perhaps for sechtair-thír.

saerda, *ennobled,* 7337.

Saigitair = Sagittarius, 220.

sain. In compounds: -chomnart, 5159;
-dil, 4224 (cf. sain-dílse, O'Don. Supp.);
-glice, 2861, 4093; -serc, 6834, 7485.

sainigthe, 4583, 5846.

sainigud, *differentiating, varying*, 7256.

sair siar, *hither and thither*, 7936.

sáir-dron, 802.

salm, *psalm.* Compound : -glan, 5822.

salmda, 6063.

samai (sammai ?), 6384, pl. dat. 8373.

samlaid, *altogether* ; note after 7796.

sam-súgud (?), 6095.

sanctáir = sanctuarium, 4256, 4258, 4317, 4320, 4522, 4602, 4618, 4900.

sathe, *swarm*, 6731.

scaichsiu, 2904, infin. of scuchim.

scél. In chevilles: s. do léir, 2719; s. cen chess, 3509 ; s. ngrinn, 3627.

scemel = scabellum, 546.

sciath, *wing*, 4316; du scíath (gl. alarum tuarum), Ml. 39ᵈ. 21 ; bua sciathaib (gl. pinnis suis), Ml. 39ᵈ. 23.

Scoirp = Scorpio, 219, 252.

scrus, 219.

seccle, 6337.

sechem, *shittim-wood*, 4224.

sechnad, 674.

sechrad (leg. sechnad?), 642.

𝕃 secht-delbach, *septiform*, 7112.

sedlang, 8111.

ségda, 1068, 3823, 4232, 4253, 5514, 6155, 6888, 7333, 7441 (scaghdha .i. ealadhanta, *learned*, O'Cl.).

segtait slóig, 459.

segunn, 6065.

seimlide, 8169.

seing, 5139.

seirgthe, 4287.

seirgthech, 1446, 2728, *withered, shrivelled ?*.

séis (= sensus ?), 651, 2393.

seiselbe, 8235.

seiss, 8266, 8273.

séiss (= séis .i. buidhen, *troop*, O'Cl.), pl. dat. séssib, 6946.

selach, *brewing*, 5355 ; sealaigh, O'Cl.

selbcha, n. pl.

selbda, 590.

sell, 2595, (perhaps seall .i. seal, *a space of time*, O'Cl.).

semnach, 2875.

séna, *denial*, 3881.

sencha, pl. n., 987.

seol, in chevilles : s. scim, 8086 ; s. snassi, 491.

serb, *bitter.* Compounds : -garg, 4758 ; -lomm (leg. lonn ?), 8209 ; -lonn, 6372.

sergaim, *I wither, dry up*, 7279, 8209 ; infin. serggad, 7294.

serig, *strong*, 4758, 5356, 5655 = sciric .i. láidir, O'Cl.

sesrachaib, pl. dat., 2455.

sesraib, pl. dat., *reservoirs, vats, barrels ?*, 43 ; so in H. 2. 17, p. 146ᵇ, na barca cona sesraib, cona claraib ; and pl. gen. LL. 169ᵃ, acc. dub-šesra di rotu rotaide monad. Cogn. with Lat. sit-ula ?.

sésta, pl. gen., 8162.

sétad, 651.

sétaigim, *I make way (sét)*, 8057.

sétfadach, 8111.

síabar, 907, *ghost ?*.

síabardac, 8159 = síaborthe, LU. 44ᵇ (?).

síabrae, 8210 ; síabra, 8305, n. pl.

sían-brat, 1772.

sid (síd?), 2611 ; sid nglé, 7487.

sídaigim, 5203.

sír, *long* ; iar síraib, 7215. Compounds : -áidde, 8369 ; -den(n), 5611 ; -díbad, 482 ; -drung, 2183 ; -ettla, 2086 ; -fecht, 8210 ; -iffern, 1772 ; -immthecht, 3748 ; -labra, 826 ; -sáethrach, 1446 ; -šassad, 4408 ; -šellad, 4164 ; -šoillse, 8381 ; -šolus, 362 ; -šotlaib (pl. dat.), 499 ; -šruth, 996 ; -thes, 154 ; -thoirse, 2112, 8383 ; -thuistin, 2818.

sírach, 6473, 7914.

sírechtach, 874, 8133 = W. hiraethog ?.

sirthech, 6372, *plundering ?* ; sírthe, *plundering parties*, O'Don. Supp.

sis, 6744.

síthbe, *rod*, 4284 ; síthbe na slébe ?, 8214.

sithech, 342.

sla, 4351.

slaide, 6097.

slamm, *floccus* ? slaimm in pl., used as acc., 5975 ; slamma snechta, *flakes of snow*, 524 : cf. slamanna, O'Cl., s. v. sloch sine.

slamm (?), 269, 5253.

slamm-derg, *red-clotted* ?, 4770.

slamm-rúad, 5356.

slán, *salvus*. In compounds : -ácb, 54 ; -chaingen, 8097 ; -dílgud, 1654 , -cim, 1006.

slánaib síd, 3275 (slán, *safety, repayment, indemnity*, O'Don. Supp.).

slasaim, 6889 (slas .i. slaighe no marbhadh, O'Cl.).

slassa, 4071.

slat-bríg, 5187 (slait 7 slatra .i. láidir, O'Cl.).

slattra, *strong*, 5365 ; adv. co-slattra, 5573.

slébbaire, *slovens* ?, 3483 (slaopair, H. Soc. Dict.).

slecht, 207, 4189, *cutting* ?. Hence slechtach, 2825.

sleg, *spear*. Compounds : -derg, 5338, 5790 ; -rúad, 6778.

sleoda, 6897.

slind (gae), 5761.

slis-fota, *longsided*, 5790.

sliucht, slicht, *track*, in chevilles : s. nglé, 2493, 3055, 3145, 4135, 4919, 5341, 6155-6479 ; s. sid, 5679 ; s. n-óg, 2859, 2893, 6605 ; s. roscar, 7419 ; s. cen chol, 5613 ; s. slán, 5203 ; s. n-án, 5213 ; s. co mbúaid, 3957, 4073.

slocht, *slaughter* (?), 5102.

slóg, *host*. Compounds : -búadach, 6932 ; -dil, 7406 ; -dún, 4550 ; -rath, 4498.

smachtaigim, 3637 ; Infin. smachtugud, 700.

snámach, 2513.

snas, 5633.

snéid, 1603, 3231, 3589, 4253, 6121, 6662 ; adv. co-snéid, 6425, 6865.

1. snfim, 3639, 8378.

2. snfim, snísit, 6514 = snisiot .i. dorighneadar cosnamh no cathughadh, O'Cl.

snímach, *sad*, 3747, 4930, 6474, 6529, 8306.

snó, 6759.

snúad, 5957, 6145, 6891.

sobáil, 2638.

sobarthain, 7433.

sód cen greis, 6649.

sodála, 60.

sodalbtha, 6155.

sodamna, 6118.

soenmind, 590.

soer, sóir, saer. In compounds : -áil, 6580 ; -alt, 7757 ; -bríg, 5543 ; -búaid, 7233, 7863 ; -dáil, 4498 ; -dron, 802 ; -grád, 3358, 3662, 4230 ; -grínn, 2863, 7730 ; -slog, 6986.

sóerda, saerda, 7337, 7783.

so-gabtha, 54 ; so-gabtais, 3251.

so-grád, 4182, 8283.

soidngib, pl. dat. *easy* ?, 4539 : cf. doidnge.

soimled, 4693.

soimse, 4366.

sofrse (better sáirse), *carpentry*, 4189.

solaig (sólaig ?), 7203.

so-menmnach, *cheerful*, 3518.

sonad, 823.

sonaide, 3382.

sonardib, pl. dat. 2778.

sónmige, *prosperity*, 8373 ; sg. dat. is-sóinmichi, Z². 863.

sonthach (perhaps = sonntach .i. luthgháiroach, O'Cl.), 4562, 4642.

so-síd, 6443.

so-smert, 6067.

so-thochta, 3237.

srábaib, pl. dat., 6780.

sreb, *stream*, 43, 5475, 8305 ; so sreb-derg, *redstreamed*, 6780.

7002, 7163, 8174. In 6679 the meaning
is obscure.

tarecacht, 7213.

tarfuaraid, 7627, *remansit.*

targtais, 6775, for do-regtais, redup. 2dy
pres. pl. 3 of torgim, *I come.*

ta-r-gelamtha, 2714 ; ta-r-glammair, 1637,
from teclammaim, tecmallaim, *I collect.*

targleo, 3015.

tarimthecht, *transgression,* 94, 574, 864,
1526, 1534, 1558. 6498.

tarmhic, 3259.

tarmmairt, tarmairt, 1688, 3260, 4717,
6444, 6923 ; tarmart, 4123, 4744, 6900 ;
tarmartad, 6735.

tárnactar, redupl. perf. pl. 3 of tair-icim,
6939.

tarrasar, *steti,* 1819 ; tarrasair, *stetit, mansit,*
1633, 2237, 5109, 5436 ; dep. perf. of
tairissim.

tarscur, 2294, for trascur, *overthrowing,*
inf. of trascraim.

tarsnu, *athwart,* 172.

tascaid, 3515 = taiscid, inf. of taiscim.

tass, 1829, 5107, 7591 ; tas .i. cumhnaidhi,
O'Cl.

tath, 2054, perhaps tath .i. taobh, *side,*
O'Cl.

tath-beogud, *to revivify,* 7120.

tathellach, 8117.

tath-lassair, 3792, *dry flame*? (tath .i. searg,
O'Cl.),

tathlûgud, 8117.

Tauir = Taurus, 217, 239.

tauttacht, *coming,* 4420 = tuttacht, q. v.

techel, *to flee,* 6219.

tech talman, 3196 = O.N. jarðhús, Landn. i,
ch. 5.

teclai, 6765.

teelaigim, 8002.

tecrais, 4439.

tedmnach, *diseased*?, 946.

teduar, 7543.

teipim, *I cut, separate,* 29, 7869 (teibeadh
.i. buain, O'Cl.).

teisc (for teist ?), 5846.

teist, *testimonium,* 3583.

telchinni, 4269.

tel-glas, *greenfaced,* 2670 (tel for tul).

terbaide, 8319, for terbaige ? : cf. a ter-
baig .i. a galar, Ir. Texte, 8:8.

terbaim, *I separate* ; ro-dos-terbaiset, 4653.

terchur, 4371.

tessaigthe, *torrid,* 159.

tét, 21 (téte .i. tuatha, O'Cl.). Compounds :
-adbul, 21 ; -bannai, 8163 ; -blai, 407.

tethrach, 978.

tho, *thy,* 1601, 6019 = to, 3824.

ti, 1317, for cl (?).

tí (for int-í ?), 5780.

tli, 4503, *design, intention.*

timm-gairim, 2477, 2717, 3045 ; do-r-im-
gair, 4950.   O'Clery's meaning (*I ask*)
does not suit.

timin-gaire, *an asking* (.i. iarraidh, O'Cl.),
2967.

timm-thaircim, do-s-r-imthairc, 5406, 5430.

timm-thosaim (?), do-r-imthas, 5973 ; do-
s-r-imthos, 6331.

timpán, *a stringed musical instrument, tim-
brel,* 4042, 6060.

tinach, 6261, 8028, 8112.

tinaim, *I melt away,* 3465 ; tin .i. leagadh,
O'Cl.

tindrad, 1047, 1297, 4223.

tindremm, tindrem, 5999, 6280 = tionnramh
.i. friathaileamh.

tine, 8106, 8150, *service,* O'Cl.

tinfissiu, 2108, *inhaling.*

tinninas, 6188.

titacht, *coming, advent,* 7793, 7805.

tiug-bás, 3614, 6726.

tiug-nár, *matins,* 810.

tláith, *weak, faint,* 2479, 7549, 7615 ; in
1571, *soft, tender.*

tlaith-chumtaig, 1103.

tláithe, 5351, *weakness.*

tlás, *weakness*, 1665, 3315; acc. tláis, 3613, 7639.

tlí .i. tlacht, *delight*, O'Cl., 1103, 3443, 5799, 5893, 6539, 7549.

tluachtar, 3539 = doruachtatar (?).

tlus, *pity, mildness*, 4039, 4551, 7407.

tnu (leg. tnú, *fire* ?), 3895.

to, *thy*, 3824: see tho.

tob tened, 7388.

to-chomrac, *conflict* (W. cyfranc), 1090, 1354.

tochomracht, *taedium*, 6922, Z³. 864.

tochta, 3072.

tóeb, *side.* Compounds. -adbal, 8253; -dána, 8263; -dein, 4434; -gel, 6366, 7594; -nocht, 1540; -thogud, 1051.

tóebach, 8090, *having sides.*

tóebtu, 6050, 6575, *being side by side.*

tóem ṅglé, 6083, a cheville, lit. *a clear jet.*

toga ṅglé, 5439, a cheville, lit. *a clear choice.*

togach, *chosen*, 339, 967, 978, 1096, 3241, 4291, 5665, 8067.

to-gáes, 1246, 2462, *fraud, circumvention.*

togud, 1052.

toichtbech, 4702.

toimdig, 1747.

1. tóir, *pursuit* (O'Don. Gr. 23), 3557.

2. tóir (.i. fóirithin, *succour*, O'Cl.), 3631, 3825, 4067, 4291, 6033.

toirchi, 6128.

toirm, in chevilles: t. ṅglan, 2033; t. trén, 7897.

toirt, sg. dat., 5971.

tola, *excess, multitude*, in chevilles: t. ṅglé, 2523, 2739, 5521, 6557; t. trén, 4575, 5519, 5617; cen tola, 8038. Pl. dat. tolaib tlacht, 15, 5747; t. tress, 85; t. smacht, 407, 4599; t. droṅg, 7137, 7197, 7481, 7609; t. tine, 8106, 8150; t. tuile, 8178; t. grinn, 2283; t. sreth,

2711; t. gair, 4387; t. gestal, 4363; t. treb, 7083, t. gal, 4467, 5034, 5821, 7099; t. dál, 4701; t. rún, 6647; t. rath, 6165; t. dliged, 6411; t. dind, 6805; t. caingen, 7781. Hence

tolach, *multitudinous*, 5077.

tolad, 1434; tolaid, 5727, should perhaps be tolaíb.

tolcaib, dat. pl., 6767.

tolg-dail, 4271, 6701.

tomthaib tríath, a cheville, *with threatenings of lords*, 4945; fo t. Dé, 7994, *under God's threats.*

tomthaigi, 8213.

1. tonn, *skin, surface* (.i. croiceann, O'Cl.), t. talman, 4124, 8116. Compounds: -gel, 6270; -glas, 978.

2. tonn, *wave.* Compound: -bán, 5232, 6162.

tóir, 4291.

tooir, 1101.

1. tor, *a lord*, 1703.

2. tor, *a multitude* (.i. imat, O'Dav.), 145, 5077, 6349, 6767, 7646; sg. gen. tuir, 145; dat. tur, 1165, 6831; pl. n. tuir, 8285; gen. tor, 6767 'mor tortrelmach', 4674, should be mór tor trelmach; acc. turu, 8174. Compound: trom-thor, 5614.

tór, 2457, *fatigue?.*

toracht, 6078.

torainn. In chevilles: t. ṅglé, 129, 2197; t. ṅdil, 1589.

torgbad dáil, 5103.

torgbáil, 4272.

torm, 6771, 7821.

torocht, 7738.

torom, torum. In chevilles: t. ṅglé, 1937, 3883, 3909, 4007, 4091.

toromm, 4153, 4761, 4839, 5415, 5895; t. n-adbal, 8144; t. n-án, 189.

torraim, *has watched over*?, (cf. torruma), 6828.

1. tracht, *trace ?*, 2855.

2. tracht, *strength*, 5295.

3. tracht, *strand*, 7904.

traig, acc., 4375.

1. tráig, *ebb*, 2538, 7904; fo-tráig, 3465.

2. tráig, *strand*, 3702, 5250.

trait, 3767, 7711 - traid .i. luath no opann, *swift* or *sudden*, O'Cl. Hence

traite, 6769.

1. trebthach, *farmer*; but in 3741, *shepherd ?*.

2. trebthach, adj., 4702, *cultivated ?*.

trechess, 227.

treithe, 2855; gan treithe .i. gan ainéolas, *without ignorance*, O'Cl.

treith-fer, 7986, *an ignorant man* (treith .i. ainéolach, O'Cl.).

trell, trel, 2291, 4593, 6697, 7993.

trelmach, 4674, 4759, *having harness* (trelam).

trem-úr, 2546, *very recent.*

trén. In compounds: -athbach, 4683; -brat, 189; -chóraid, 2404; -áláag, 2626.

tréoda, *trinal*, 7570.

treóir, 1169, 1899, *vigour, power.* Of the same or a like meaning is

treórud, 1043.

tres, sg. acc. tris, 3315.

tres-rann, *a third part*, 3784.

tretel, 2131.

tre-thaibledach, 2448, the tristega (τρίστεγα) of the Vulgate, Gen. vi. 16.

1. trethan, *foot* (treathan .i. troigh, O'Cl.), 3644, 4200.

2. trethan, *sea*, 2233, sg. dat., 353; pl. n. (noeb) -trethna, 494; dat. trethnaib, 6697; acc. trethnu, 5254. The gen. sg. trethan, 7901, and the dat. sg. trethain, 8196, seem to belong to an n-stem.

triallach, 111.

triamain, *weary*, 7551.

triamnnai, 8157.

triamnach, *weary*, 5619.

trice, 1926, *frequent ?*, 5325, *urgent ?*.

trichem, 353.

trichessa, 8295.

trichtaige, *a space of thirty years*, 1096; in-áis trichtaigi, LU. 34^b.

trist, *curse*; cen trist, 1047, 2239.

tristaide, 8019.

tuidme, *binding together*, 4278.

tuidmidib, pl. dat., 4291.

tuinech (- Lat. tunica), pl. n. tuinchi, 6719.

tuire, 3838.

tuiridein (leg. tuirigein ?), *bouse-pillar*, 4520 (tuirighin tuir fhuilnges tech, Forus Foc. LL. 395^a).

túis (= Lat. tus), *incense, frankincense*, 7540.

tuisc, acc. sg., 247.

tunscanad (?), 6232.

túr, *searching*, 4133, 6344. The compound trom-thúr, 906, 5266, seems to belong to a different word.

turadaíb, pl. dat., 4690.

turba (from the Lat.), 10,000 × 100,000, 772.

tuscurnud, *fiction, falsehood*, 3324.

tuttacht, *coming*, 2330, 4415 = tauttacht, q.v.

U.

úa,i, *perfect.* In compounds: -commus, 3172; -ríar, 4128. Hence

úagdae, 3634.

úaibrech, *proud, haughty*, 7382.

úaichlech, 945, *full of pride* (uaichle .i. uallcha, O'Cl.).

úais (.i. uasal, O'Cl.), 117, 4280, 6021, 7586, 7937. The nom. pl. m. uais, 7853, seems from an adj. *uas.

úamnach, *terrible*, 875.

úarach, *chilly*, 942, 8350.

úarda, *chilled*, 7340.

úas-abb, 7872, 7978; cf. abb (- abbas), 831.

úasal-techtaire, 692.

úas, prep. with suffixed pers. pronouns:
    sg. 2, uasot, 1142 ; pl. 3, uasdaib, 565.
uilidettu, *wholeness*, 8244.
úine, *time, season*, acc. pl., 7759.

uiscide, *watery*, 40.
uran (?), 4803.
úr-feóil, *fresh meat*, 4628.
úrugud, *growing green*, 7284.

CORRIGENDA.

Line
990 *read* derbdind.
1004 *read* Fufratén.
1004, 1006 *after* 'Tibris' *insert* (*sic*).
1395 *read* lethan smacht.
1478 *read* in-huacht gortai.
1541, 4417, 5263 *read* n-eim.

Line
1904 *read* badbda.
2397 omit the first comma.
2419 *after* 'Noe' insert a comma
4674 *read* tor trelmach.
6787 *after* 'trén' *and* 'raind' insert a comma.